Interweaving Innocence

Interweaving Innocence
A Rhetorical Analysis of Luke's Passion Narrative
(Luke 22:66—23:49)

Heather M. Gorman

◆PICKWICK *Publications* • Eugene, Oregon

INTERWEAVING INNOCENCE
A Rhetorical Analysis of Luke's Passion Narrative (Luke 22:66—23:49)

Copyright © 2015 Heather M. Gorman. All rights reserved. Except for brief quotations in critical publications or reviews, no part of this book may be reproduced in any manner without prior written permission from the publisher. Write: Permissions. Wipf and Stock Publishers, 199 W. 8th Ave., Suite 3, Eugene, OR 97401.

Pickwick Publications
An Imprint of Wipf and Stock Publishers
199 W. 8th Ave., Suite 3
Eugene, OR 97401

www.wipfandstock.com

ISBN 13: 978-1-4982-2473-4

Cataloguing-in-Publication Data

Gorman, Heather M.

Interweaving innocence : a rhetorical analysis of Luke's passion narrative (Luke 22:66—23:49) / Heather M. Gorman.

x + 198 p. ; 23 cm. Includes bibliographical references.

ISBN 13: 978-1-4982-2473-4

1. Bible. N.T. Luke XXII, 66-XXIII, 49—Criticism, interpretation, etc. 2. Bible. N.T. Luke XXII, 66-XXIII, 49—Socio-rhetorical criticism. I. Title.

BS2595.2 G62 2015

Manufactured in the U.S.A. 10/29/2015

For Jamey—my love, my support, and my best friend

Contents

List of Tables | viii

Acknowledgments | ix

1 Introduction | 1

2 Tools for a Rhetorical Analysis | 29

3 Scene 1: Pre-Trial Hearing (22:66–71) and the Formal Trial (23:1–25) | 74

4 Scene 2: Transition to the Cross (23:26–32) and the Informal Trial (23:33–49) | 117

5 Synthesis and Conclusion | 161

Bibliography | 183

Index | 195

Tables

Table 1   Contents of the *progymnasmata* organized by author | 41
Table 2   Order of events in the passion narratives of Mark and Luke | 80
Table 3   Parallel charges against Jesus and Paul | 94
Table 4   Luke's reorganization of Mark 15:1–5 | 96
Table 5   Markan material in Luke 23:6–16 | 103
Table 6   Luke 23:39 and *Gospel of Thomas* 79 | 127
Table 7   Responses to Jesus on the cross in Luke and Mark | 134

Acknowledgments

It is humbling to think of all the people who have contributed to my educational journey, which reached its formal culmination in my doctoral dissertation. The study that follows is a revision of that work. My Bible professors at Cincinnati Christianity University introduced me to the academic study of the Bible and were among the first to encourage me to minister to the church through teaching. It was a joy to study under them, as it is now a joy to call them friends and colleagues. This work is somewhat of a tribute to Drs. Kenneth Cukrowski and James Thompson, two of my beloved professors at Abilene Christian University, who kindled in me a love for both the Gospel of Luke and ancient rhetoric—two of my research interests that came together in this project.

I am especially grateful to the New Testament professors in the Graduate Department of Religion at Baylor University who guided me academically and professionally as I finished my formal education. They set high expectations for their students and equipped us to meet those expectations. I hope this work is a reflection of the excellence expected of Baylor's New Testament doctoral students. I offer my foremost thanks to my *doktorvater* Mikeal Parsons who has been a mentor to me in every sense of the word. I cannot overestimate the value of his willingness to help me develop this project, his expertise in Luke-Acts and ancient rhetoric, and his commitment to helping me finish this project as I began my first full-time teaching position. Kelly Iverson provided invaluable guidance throughout my writing process. This study is better because of his insights into the Gospel of Mark and his insistence on careful writing. Bruce Longenecker and Lidija Novakovic served as final readers for this project, which is fitting in light of the feedback and encouragement they willingly provided for me during my time at Baylor. Finally, Martin

Medhurst guided me through the larger field of rhetorical criticism and graciously served as an outside reader.

I was truly blessed with wonderful colleagues at Baylor—Nick, Brian, David, Peter, Lindsey, Mike, and Justin, to name only a few. Their encouragement academically, professionally, and spiritually made me a better scholar, teacher, and person. It was a joy to share this leg of my academic journey with them. My family supported my education from the very beginning through their prayers, visits, and ceaseless encouragement. Their commitment to the Lord inspires my work. Words cannot adequately express my gratitude toward my husband, Jamey, who supported me on good days and bad with his patience, faith, constancy, eternal optimism, and love. Without the countless sacrifices he made in his own education and work, I would not have been able to finish this project. Finally, in between this dissertation's completion and publication, we welcomed our sweet Anna Marie into the world. She reminds me daily of what is most important in life and brings me more joy than I could have ever imagined.

1
Introduction

The Problem

LUKE'S PASSION NARRATIVE IS distinct from those of Matthew, Mark, and John in several ways: it includes content that the others do not, it strongly emphasizes Jesus' innocence, and it has parallels with the trials and deaths of main characters in Acts. These differences, along with other facets of Luke's passion narrative, have resulted in Luke's passion narrative being one of the most studied sections of Luke's Gospel.

Despite this attention, at least three issues remain unsettled with regard to the interpretation of Luke's passion narrative. First, scholars debate what sources Luke used in composing his narrative: did he use only Mark, additional written sources, oral traditions, or some combination of these three? Second, scholars debate the best translation of δίκαιος in the centurion's confession in 23:47, along with how this relates to Luke's larger characterization of Jesus. Third, scholars debate the function of the parallels between Jesus in Luke and Paul and Stephen in Acts. How do these parallels contribute to Luke's larger purpose? I begin this study by exploring how scholars have approached these interpretive issues along with their various solutions. Since these approaches have left the conversation in somewhat of a stalemate, I then propose to approach these interpretive issues in Luke's passion narrative anew with the aid of rhetorical criticism.

Interpretive Issues in Luke's Passion Narrative: The State of the Question

The Sources of Luke's Passion Narrative

The presence of several unique features in Luke's passion narrative and an order somewhat distinct from Mark's have led to a mass of speculation on the sources behind Luke's passion narrative. While the question over the sources of Luke's passion narrative cannot be divorced from the larger question of the sources of Luke's Gospel,[1] Luke's account of Jesus' death has its own set of problems that has led the source-critical discussion in its own direction. For example, while much of the discussion of the sources of Luke's Gospel outside of the passion narrative revolves around the potential use of Q, Q is rarely a part of the conversation about Luke's passion narrative because there are few minor agreements between Matthew and Luke against Mark in their passion narratives.[2] Without Q as a possible source for the passion narrative, scholars are forced to explain the origin of non-Markan material in other ways. The observation that Luke does not follow Mark's order as closely in his passion narrative as he does elsewhere in his Gospel[3] also sends scholars in search of a way to explain Luke's order.

---

1. For a summary of the source issues of Luke's Gospel, see Tyson, "Source Criticism," 24–39. Tyson describes the four primary solutions to the Synoptic Problem as they relate to Luke (the Two-Document Hypothesis, the Farrer Hypothesis, the Griesbach Hypothesis, and the Lindsey Hypothesis). I treat my own view of the Synoptic Problem in the methodology section of this chapter.

2. Kloppenborg, *Formation of Q*, 85–87. Kloppenborg rejects the notion that Q had a passion narrative. Though some scholars have proposed that Luke derived some of his special passion material from Q, Kloppenborg points out that "such proposals do not, however, succeed in proving the existence of a passion *narrative* since in all cases they concern *sayings* which do not even deal directly with the passion" (85, emphasis original). For proponents of Luke's use of Q in his passion narrative, see Hirsch, *Frühgeschichte des Evangeliums*; Bundy, *Jesus and the First Three Gospels*; Burkitt, *Gospel History and Its Transmission*.

On the other hand, the few agreements between Matthew and Luke against Mark in the passion narrative put the nail in the coffin of Q for Farrer Hypothesis proponent Michael Goulder: "As long as we had a firm definition—Q had no Passion story—it looks as if we had a hypothesis excluding certain possibilities: Luke did not know Matthew, so there could be no significant [minor agreements] in the Passion story." Since there are agreements in the passion stories between Luke and Matthew, Luke must have used Matthew, he posits. See Goulder, *Luke: A New Paradigm*, 10.

3. Jeremias, *Eucharistic Words*, 97–99; Schramm, *Der Markus-Stoff bei Lukas*, 50; Soards, *Passion according to Luke*, 13; Schweizer, *Good News*, 354.

Harrington's history of research on the Markan material in Luke 22:54—23:25—a grand total of 1,003 pages that interacts with over 1,500 authors—demonstrates that the sources behind Luke's passion narrative have not lacked scholarly attention.[4] Nonetheless, despite the volumes and pages devoted to the topic, scholarship remains divided over what sources Luke did or did not use in constructing his passion narrative, in part because of differing approaches and assumptions.[5]

The source theories regarding Luke's passion narrative fall into two categories, broadly speaking: (1) those who argue that Luke's only written source[6] was Mark, and (2) those who argue that Luke used a written source or sources other than Mark. When I speak of a "written source in addition to Mark" in this study, I am referring to a non-canonical written source, not to Matthew or John.[7] We will explore each of these groups in turn.

Mark as Luke's Only Written Source

A prominent stream of scholarship posits that Luke did not use any written sources besides Mark when constructing his passion narrative.[8] These scholars attribute the special Lukan material to either Luke's own creative hand or to his incorporation of irrecoverable oral traditions, but generally emphasize the former. Notable advocates of this theory include

---

4. Harrington, *Lukan Passion Narrative*. For a more manageable survey, see Bovon, "Lukan Story," 88–92.

5. In his influential monograph on Luke's passion narrative, Taylor describes four methods used in approaching the sources behind Luke's passion narrative: "(1) the numerical or statistical method, (2) the literary or stylistic study, (3) the form-critical approach, and (4) the use of historical criticism." Taylor, *Passion Narrative*, 31–37.

6. Here I follow Brown in distinguishing between a source and tradition. By a source I mean "a sequential (most likely written) account of the whole passion or a good portion of it," and by a tradition I mean "isolated items of information or brief episodes of various derivation, many of which would have circulated orally." Some scholars attempt to reconstruct sources, but rarely do they attempt such for traditions. See Brown, *Death of the Messiah*, 66.

7. On Matthew and John as potential sources for Luke's passion narrative, see the methodology section below. Furthermore, because the literature on the topic is so extensive, I am focusing primarily on the most prominent scholars in the last fifty years. For a more comprehensive survey from 1891–1997, see Harrington, *Lukan Passion Narrative*.

8. For a survey of redaction critics who dispense with a special source from 1960 through 1997, see ibid., 566–676.

Raymond Brown and Frank Matera.[9] Brown allows for Luke's incorporation (whether consciously or not) of non-written traditions not utilized by Mark;[10] Matera made room for non-written traditions in some of his earlier works, but his later works emphasize Luke's sole use of Mark.[11] Despite this distinction between the two scholars, the heart of their analyses (and those of others who hold this view) rests on Luke's creative editing of Mark's passion narrative toward his own theological interests.

Two primary observations lead scholars like Matera and Brown to conclude that Luke did not use a written source in addition to Mark: (1) themes and theological interests in Luke's passion narrative that are prominent elsewhere in Luke and Acts, and (2) Luke's stylistic and compositional tendencies.[12] I will address both of these in turn.

First, scholars who dispense with a written source behind Luke's passion narrative notice the theological continuity between Luke's passion narrative and the rest of his work, which suggests to them that Luke

---

9. So also Soards, *Passion according to Luke*, who only treats chapter 22, but argues that Luke did not have a continuous written passion source besides Mark. Cf. Untergassmair, *Kreuzweg und Kreuzigung Jesu*, 1.

10. Brown says, "On a general level, to imagine that Matt and Luke worked only with writings (Mark, Q, perhaps the special material), much in the manner a modern scholar works with copies of Mark, Matt, and Luke, staggers the imagination. Can one seriously believe that Matt and Luke knew nothing of the passion before they read Mark, and what they already knew was not blended (perhaps unconsciously) with what they read?" See Brown, *Death of the Messiah*, 45. He later comments that Luke combined oral traditions with Mark to produce his narrative, but did not use either Matthew or John. See ibid., 92.

11. In his 1985 article on the sources of Luke's passion narrative, for example, Matera says, "I am arguing that Luke did not have another continuous [passion narrative] in addition to Mark. It is clear that at times he may have drawn from individual traditions not known to Mark. But when he does so, he integrates them into Mark's narrative." See Matera, "Death of Jesus," 472, n. 11. Cf. Matera, *Passion Narratives*, 155, 170. However, from 1989 onward, he became more adamant that Mark was Luke's only source. He says, "[i]n each instance these differences can be explained in terms of Luke's redactional activity and ... there is no need to appeal to other traditions, or to another version of the passion narrative in addition to Mark's." See Matera, "Luke 22,66–71," 48. He makes a similar statement in "Luke 23,1–25," 550.

12. Also determinative for Brown are the different constructions hypothesized by those who posit an additional written source. Some attribute only the material that has no Markan parallel to the source (though not all of this material is relegated to a source). Others attribute Markan parallels to the source if the parallels appear in some sort of changed form. These different working methods result in vastly different constructions of Luke's supposed source, which diminishes their likelihood, Brown thinks. Brown, *Death of the Messiah*, 66–67.

is composing his own material rather than incorporating source material. Their assumption is that if one can make sense of a change from Mark's passion narrative to Luke's in light of Luke's wider narrative and theology, then it suggests that Luke was not drawing on a source other than Mark.[13] For example, these scholars view the second criminal's positive response in Luke as "the culmination of the Lukan pattern of acceptance or rejection that has characterized the response of people to the earthly ministry of Jesus."[14] Since it aligns so well with one of Luke's larger theological goals and could feasibly have its origin in Mark, these scholars see it as Luke's creative adaptation of Mark, possibly under the influence of oral tradition.[15]

Second, these scholars note stylistic and compositional tendencies (e.g., removing doublets) that suggest Luke's passion narrative could have come from his use of Mark alone. Brown notes, for instance, the contrast between the infancy narrative, which is a complete non-Markan block written in Semitized Greek, and Luke's passion narrative, which contains interwoven Markan material and has a style not particularly dissimilar to Mark.[16] He even suggests, "[i]f one only had Luke's [passion narrative] without a copy of Mark, I doubt that one could successfully isolate two distinct sources behind it."[17] Matera also points to the evidence of Marion Soards, who shows that in other instances where Luke differs significantly from Mark it is not necessary to posit another source.[18] Soards reminds us, "That Luke often follows Mark closely should not create a maxim that he always must do so, as if Luke wrote in a rigidly uniform manner."[19]

---

13. Matera, "Death of Jesus," 484. See "Refutation 6" in chapter 4 for an example of Matera relating Luke's changes of Mark's centurion's words to his Christology.

14. Soards, *Passion according to Luke*, 111.

15. See "Refutation 4" in chapter 4 for a fuller discussion.

16. Both Brown and Matera, like the other schools surveyed in this study, acknowledge that Luke draws on Mark more freely in his passion narrative than he did in the rest of his Gospel. See Matera, *Passion Narratives*, 153; Brown, *Death of the Messiah*, 67.

17. Brown, *Death of the Messiah*, 265–66 (quotation from 266).

18. For example, the level of verbal agreement between Luke and Mark is lower in the transfiguration (Luke 9:28–37//Mark 9:2–8) than in the passion narrative. He points this out to expose "a fallacious assumption . . . that the Passion Narrative is qualitatively different from the rest of Luke's Gospel." See Soards, *Passion according to Luke*, 122.

19. Ibid., 123; Matera, *Passion Narratives*, 154.

In sum, those who posit that Luke had no written source(s) in addition to Mark for his passion narrative base their hypothesis primarily on the theological continuity between Luke's passion narrative and the rest of his Gospel and Acts and on Luke's stylistic and compositional tendencies. They work under the assumption that Luke was a creative and capable author, not just a cut-and-paste editor.

A Non-Canonical Written Source in Addition to Mark [20]

The discussion of a source behind Luke's passion narrative is complex. The terminology for the source(s) varies widely, as does the extent and nature of the source.[21] For some, Luke drew upon L—a source that he used for the rest of his Gospel (Bovon, Fitzmyer; possibly Schweizer).[22]

---

20. A variation on the theory that Luke used Mark is that Luke used a different version or versions of Mark than that which survives in the canon. Fuchs, *Sprachliche Untersuchungen zu Matthäus und Lukas*, for example, argues that Luke used a revised edition of Mark. Cf. Trocmé, *Passion as Liturgy*, 27–37. More recently, Tolppanen, "Source Critical Reassessment," has argued that Luke derived his triple tradition material not from canonical Mark but from either a single non-canonical Markan source/tradition or two non-canonical Markan sources/traditions. While his analysis is of Luke's whole Gospel, Luke's passion narrative is one of three key pieces of support for his thesis that "Luke did not use canonical Mark as his source" (295). Using statistical analysis in a vein similar to Taylor, he points out that (1) "the general verbatim agreement level between Luke and Mark notably diminishes in their Passion-Resurrection sections compared to their non-Passion sections. While verbatim agreement in the non-Passion section is 37.5 percent, it is only 22.8 percent in the Passion-Resurrection section"; (2) "The Lukan order of material differs from the Markan order four times more often in the Lukan Passion-Resurrection Narrative than in the Lukan non-Passion narrative"; and (3) "The number of non-Markan passages in the Lukan Passion-Resurrection section is much higher than in its non-Passion section in relation to the length of these sections" (297–98). He finds it inexplicable that Luke would "change his copy-editing technique so remarkably when he moved from his non-Passion section to his Passion-Resurrection section," so he posits that Luke used a different source: either a single non-canonical Markan source/tradition or two non-canonical Markan sources/traditions, which "had the same origin [as canonical Mark] but different development histories, developing in partly different directions probably due to the interaction of orality and literacy" (iii). Though this theory varies from Taylor's significantly, I am not treating it separately because it works with similar assumptions (i.e., that Luke uses Mark the same way throughout his entire Gospel; that divergences suggest a different source) and some similar methods (i.e., statistical) as Taylor.

21. For a survey of what verses various scholars classify as "special Lukan material," see Soards, *Passion according to Luke*, 15–16. He summarizes: "[L]ittle of Luke is not thought by someone to be special Lukan material" (16).

22. See Bovon, *Luke 1*, 6–8. For a more thorough discussion of his source theory as

Others think Luke drew upon Proto-Luke,[23] a work that resulted from Luke's combination of Q and L, which he later expanded when writing his Gospel (Jeremias, Taylor, Grundmann).[24] And still others do not comment on the source's connection with "special material" earlier in Luke (Green, Marshall).[25] Some think Luke inserted Markan material

---

it relates to the passion narrative, see Bovon, "The Lukan Story of the Passion," 92–102. In the latter he explains that Luke's special material ("L") fits within the gospel genre and was literarily superior to Mark. He proposes that L was to Luke what Mark was to Matthew (102). Both Schweizer and Fitzmyer are skeptical of describing L in too much detail. Fitzmyer says that L is "not necessarily written" (64). He later describes it as a "'source' in a broad sense, either oral or written, but which is not to be put on a par with 'Mk' or 'Q'" (83). And later still he refers to L as "a designation for source(s) of information about the Jesus-story in the early Christian community Luke would have tapped in various ways" (85). Schweizer argues for a written source (351), but will not say with certainty whether that is L in the passion narrative (354). He only notes, "Purely oral tradition cannot explain these observations" (346). See Fitzmyer, *Gospel according to Luke*; Schweizer, *Good News according to Luke*.

23. Terminology for and the extent of what Taylor calls Proto-Luke varies among scholars. Taylor describes the nuances of the various scholars' theories in *Passion Narrative*, 3–11, 17–23.

24. Taylor builds on the monumental work of Streeter, who argued that Luke produced Proto-Luke when he combined Q and L (Luke's special source) around 60 CE. Luke then inserted Markan material into the framework of Proto-Luke to produce his Gospel a few decades later. See Streeter, *Four Gospels*, 199–222. For more on why Streeter thought Luke used the framework of Proto-Luke instead of Mark, see 208–12. Similarly, Taylor argues that "the substance of Lk. xxii–xxiv was put together independently of Mark, and that it existed as a document before the evangelist had seen Mark. At a later time he expanded the Passion narrative by inserting extracts from Mark." Taylor, *Passion Narrative*, 125. For a list of the Markan insertions, see ibid., 119.

Jeremias' description of the source is much less detailed than Taylor's. From 22:14 onward, Luke's narrative "is no longer built upon a Markan basis, but comes from *Urlukas*." Grundmann thinks that Luke's special tradition (SLk) "may have been joined to Q," but he follows Grant in describing SLk as "nothing more than a little loose, but fairly homogeneous collection of material that Luke had collected from various locations." See Jeremias, *Eucharistic Words*, 99; Grundmann, *Das Evangelium*, 17; Grant, *Growth of the Gospels*, 62.

25. E.g., Green, who describes it as "a second, unified narrative *like Mark's*" (104, emphasis original). It "has numerous points of contact with the Johannine passion narrative" and "was part of a developing narrative" (i.e., it was not a collection of isolated fragments) (103). Marshall comments that "the existence of a connected 'L' source . . . has not been confirmed by [his] investigations" (31), but that "there can be little doubt of [the presence of] non-Markan source material" (785). At times he refers to this as "a separate tradition" and at others "his special source" (847). See Green, *Death of Jesus*; Marshall, *Gospel of Luke*.

into the framework of the source (Taylor, Jeremias),[26] while others think Luke alternated between large blocks of Mark and large blocks of the special source (Bovon).[27] We could spend chapters elucidating the details of these various theories, but of most concern here is not the details of the source (its name, its date, or even its extent), but rather how these scholars conclude that such a source existed and the assumptions lying behind that conclusion.

Often times studies arguing for the use of a special source are based on a numerical or statistical method with special emphasis on word counts.[28] Not all source-positing scholars agree on what should be attributed to Luke's hand and what should be attributed to Luke's non-Markan source, however.[29] For example, Taylor, relying on the distinctive word lists from Stanton and Rehkopf, argues that Luke composed 23:6–16 himself rather than relying on a source because these verses contain so many of Luke's own words and phrases.[30] Easton, on the other hand, thinks that Luke derived the pericope from L.[31] John Donahue's observation of such attempts to divide the text by sources is apt here: "the suggested divisions of the text of the Passion Narrative . . . encourage a fragmentation of the text which rivals attempts early in this century to divide the Pentateuchal

26. Taylor, *Passion Narrative*, 125; Jeremias, *Eucharistic Words*, 99, n. 1.

27. Bovon, *Luke 3*, 241.

28. Taylor does not specifically intimate his criteria for locating source material, but Matson summarizes his approach well: "Taylor uses a number of criteria to distinguish between Lukan material and the various sources: statistical patterns of 'Markan' words, Lukan style, Lukan theology, and the order of events. No single criterion is decisive, but a combination of criteria can be strongly suggestive. In order to find that a verse was based on Mark instead of an alternate source, *the* key factor is usually the existence of a mathematical preponderance of Markan words in the verse; usually this would require more than 50 percent of the verse being very close to Mark's language." Matson, *In Dialogue*, 243.

In addition to Taylor's *Passion Narrative of St. Luke*, see also his "The Value of the Proto-Luke Hypothesis," 476–77; *Behind the Third Gospel*; "Rehkopf's List of Words and Phrases Illustrative of Pre-Lukan Speech Usage," 59–62. Cf. Trocmé, *Passion as Liturgy*, 27–37. While word counts do play into his analysis, see Green's critique of statistical analyses as a means of determining sources: Green, *Death of Jesus*, 18.

29. For a summary of different scholars' positions on what parts of Mark Luke used for his passion narrative, see the chart in Neirynck, "La matière marcienne dans l'évangile de Luc," 196–97.

30. Taylor, *Passion Narrative*, 87. Cf. Stanton, *Gospels as Historical Documents*; Rehkopf, *Die lukanische Sonderquelle*.

31. Easton, *Gospel according to St. Luke*, 343. For more scholars' assessments of whether this pericope is Lukan or pre-Lukan, see "Refutation 2" in chapter 3.

narrative into a multitude of J's, E's, and P's."[32] Also determinative for some who posit a special source behind Luke's passion narrative are the connections between Luke's and John's passion narratives. Instead of positing literary dependence between the two books, these scholars argue instead that the writers relied on a common narrative.[33]

While not always the case, a key assumption unites many scholars who posit a special source behind Luke's passion narrative: content and order that differ from Mark are best explained by Luke's reliance on another source, rather than on his own traditions, creativity, or theological aims.[34] Thus, those who posit a special source for Luke's passion narrative often approach the text asking if words or phrases in Luke can be attributed to Luke's editorializing or to Mark.[35] If they cannot, they attribute them to another source. Verbatim agreement is key to determining if another source was involved. This method (and subsequent results) has been critiqued for its subjectivity, despite its adherents' confidence in its

---

32. Donahue, "Introduction," 15; cited in Green, *Death of Jesus*, 12–13.

33. See, e.g., Taylor, *Passion Narrative*, 37; Marshall, *Gospel of Luke*, 853; Schweizer, *Good News*, 355; Green, *Death of Jesus*, 103; Bovon, *Luke 1*, 7. See below for more on the relationship between Luke and John.

34. For example, when analyzing the differences between the centurion's confession in Mark and Luke (discussed more fully under "Refutation 6" in chapter 4), Taylor concludes that Luke must have been relying on a separate source since "it is very improbable that δίκαιος in the centurion's confession (v. 47) is a modification of υἱός θεοῦ in Mk. xv. 39." See Taylor, *Passion Narrative*, 96. Cf. a similar mentality by Jeremias (discussed more fully in "The Big Picture" in chapter 3) and Schramm on the differing orders between Luke and Mark. See Jeremias, *Eucharistic Words*, 99; Schramm, *Der Markus-Stoff bei Lukas*, 50–51. For a critique of this assumption, see Soards, *Passion according to Luke*, 18.

35. One of the more systematic explanations of how to determine if something is pre-Lukan or Lukan is in Rehkopf, *Die Lukanische Sonderquelle*, 87. Rehkopf dubs something pre-Lukan if "1) in Lk selten oder nie von Lukas selbständig gebraucht wird. 2) im MkSt sonst weitgehend oder immer von Lukas ersetzt wird. 3) einem Synonym oder einer ähnlichen lukanischen Vorzugswendung gegenübersteht. 4) im Nicht-MkSt ein relativ häufiges Vorkommen aufweist. 5) in der Apostelgeschichte in Reden oder Wir-Stücken selten oder nie zu finden ist." Cf. Jeremias' six-point list in Jeremias, *Die Sprache des Lukasevangeliums*, 8.

objectivity.³⁶ Often times this position results in a picture of Luke as more of an editor than an author.³⁷

The Translation of δίκαιος

A second issue that has left scholars at an impasse in the interpretation of Luke's passion narrative is the translation of δίκαιος in the centurion's proclamation in 23:47. Though the proclamation only differs from Mark by a few words, the substitution of δίκαιος for Mark's υἱὸς θεοῦ is significant (Mark 15:39). Scholars fall into three camps on this issue: those advocating for a translation of "righteous" or "just"; (2) those advocating for a translation of "innocent"; and (3) those advocating for a dual or overlapping meaning between the terms.³⁸ The first translation emphasizes the messianic implications of δίκαιος by drawing connections with the Suffering Servant. The second impacts whether Jesus' death should be viewed as a martyr's death and whether Luke's larger work should be understood as having a political apologetic motive. The last attempts to be inclusive of both of these interpretations or sees Luke constructing different meanings for different readers.

---

36. Word counts and statistical analyses can give the impression of objectivity, but the differing results amongst scholars (often the result of different words lists, etc.) suggests that this method is far from objective. Nonetheless, Taylor's comments reveal his optimism about the objectivity of statistical analysis: "It is not claimed that numerical considerations taken by themselves are enough to prove that a special Lukan source is drawn upon in Lk. xxii. 14—xxiv. 11, but it is suggested that the statistics point definitely in this direction, and that the hypothesis becomes almost a certainty if it is further supported by literary and stylistic criticism." Taylor, *Passion Narrative*, 33–34. Easton makes a similar comment about the value of linguistic analysis: "A considerable subjective element is bound to exist in any list [of Luke's vocabulary] of this sort; for instance, it is difficult to determine whether some passages in Lk are really based on Mk or not (particularly in chs 22–23). *But the bulk of the evidence is unambiguous, and in work of this sort only bulk counts.*" See Easton, *Gospel according to St. Luke*, xxv (emphasis added). For a critique of this approach, see Matson, *In Dialogue*, 246–47.

37. Easton's comments are suggestive: "The analysis made thus far of Lk's sources is a guide to his methods as an editor; it is rather idle to speak of a 'plan' of the Gospel, for its construction was determined very largely by the order of the sources." Easton, *Gospel according to St. Luke*, xxx.

38. For an evaluation of the merits of these various stances, see Brown, *Death of the Messiah*, 1160–67. See chapter 5 for my evaluation of these stances in light of my rhetorical analysis.

Notable scholars in the first camp include Schweizer, Karris, Nolland, and Doble.[39] These scholars intimate at least three reasons for translating δίκαιος as "righteous" or "just" in 23:47.[40] First, δίκαιος and its cognates elsewhere in Luke and Acts are never restricted to the meaning of "innocent." The two nearest in context—δικαίως in 23:41 and δίκαιος in 23:50—mean "justly" and "righteous." Second, Luke's description of the centurion's words as praise or glorification (δοξάζω) suggests a "theological thrust"[41] to the verse, which a juridical interpretation like "innocent" does not capture. Third, the recitation of Ps 31—a psalm of the righteous suffering one—aligns Jesus with the righteous one and Son of God,[42] which Luke develops in Acts though people's proclamation of Jesus as ὁ δίκαιος, a title usually translated as "the righteous one" (Acts 3:14; 7:52; 22:14).

Notable scholars in the second camp include Kilpatrick, Talbert, Schmidt, and Cassidy.[43] These scholars typically intimate three reasons for translating δίκαιος as "innocent." First, this translation accords with the larger theme of Jesus' innocence in Luke's passion narrative. The explicit testimonies of Pilate, Herod, and the second criminal regarding Jesus' guiltlessness argue for a similar interpretation in 23:47. Second, a proclamation of "righteous" (in the Ps 31 sense advocated by those in the first camp) would not be fitting speech for a Roman centurion. Kilpatrick muses, "If, however, it is argued that δίκαιος here has the suggestion of 'the righteous one', apart from the question whether the adjective alone can imply so much, it is equally difficult to understand why such an ambiguous expression, obscure to any but a religious Jew, should be put into the mouth of a heathen centurion."[44] Finally, this interpretation aligns with

---

39. Schweizer, *Good News according to Luke*, 362; Karris, "Luke 23:47," 65–74; Nolland, *Luke 18:35—24:53*, 1155, 1159; Doble, *Paradox of Salvation*, 25–183.

40. I follow Karris most closely here, but the other scholars provide similar reasons, though not necessarily all of them. Karris states explicitly, "I will argue that *dikaios* does not mean innocent, but means righteous" (65). This stands in contrast to his position from the prior year where he cautioned against "get[ting] trapped in an either-or-dead-end discussion" and instead said that *dikaios* "means both 'innocent' and 'righteous' in 23:47." For this earlier position see Karris, *Luke*, 110.

41. Karris, "Luke 23:47," 66.

42. Ruppert, *Jesus als der leidende Gerechte?*

43. Kilpatrick, "Theme of the Lucan Passion Story," 34–36; Cassidy, *Jesus, Politics, and Society*, 72; Talbert, "Martyrdom in Luke-Acts," 99; Schmidt, "Luke's 'Innocent' Jesus," 117–18.

44. Kilpatrick, "Theme of the Lucan Passion Story," 34. While Kilpatrick's article is

what they see as Luke's purpose in Luke (and Acts)—to show that Jesus (and his followers) were not politically subversive.⁴⁵ If even the centurion who oversaw Jesus' death deems this leader of the movement innocent, Christianity must not be a threat to Rome. Furthermore, since Luke and Acts have parallel purposes to some extent, the emphasis on Paul's innocence in Acts further mitigates for a translation as "innocent" in Luke.

Often, though not always, the interpretation of δίκαιος as innocent is related to the view that Luke casts Jesus' death in line with the ancient noble death and martyr traditions.⁴⁶ The thesis that Luke presents Jesus as a martyr goes back to Dibelius, but has been further developed by scholars like Ruppert, Talbert, Carroll, Kloppenborg, Collins, Sterling, and Scaer, who find parallels between Luke's account of Jesus death and the deaths of Socrates and the Jewish martyrs.⁴⁷ Because so many other elements of Luke's passion narrative align with the noble death/martyrdom tradition (e.g., the depiction of the Last Supper as Jesus' last words to his disciples, the presence of friends throughout the narrative, the manner of Jesus' death—noble, without fear, regret, grief, or crying⁴⁸), these scholars often interpret the centurion's confession as "innocent" to accord with the emphasis on innocence that noble death/martyrdom accounts often included.⁴⁹

Finally, the third camp, probably the largest of the three, seeks to avoid the extremes of the other two, which exclude one interpretation in favor of the other. Advocates include Büchele, Beck, Fitzmyer, Matera, Green, Brown, Bock, Marguerat, Neagoe, and Easter.⁵⁰ Some emphasize

---

dated, many recent commentators rely on Kilpatrick's article as a basis. On Kilpatrick and the emergence of the "innocence" translation, see Doble, *Paradox of Salvation*, 70–75.

45. See below for more on the political apologetic motif in Luke and Acts.

46. The opposite of this is true, as well. Karris, for instance, a strong advocate of the "righteous" translation, denies that Luke presents Jesus' death as a martyrdom. See Karris, "Luke 23:47," 68–70. Other opponents to the martyrdom view include Untergassmair, *Kreuzweg und Kreuzigung Jesu*, 162–63; Matera, *Passion Narratives*, 68–70.

47. Dibelius, *From Tradition to Gospel*, 201; Talbert, *Reading Luke*, 212–25; Talbert, "Martyrdom in Luke-Acts"; Carroll, "Luke's Crucifixion Scene," 118–19; Kloppenborg, "*Exitus Clari Viri*," 106–20; Collins, "From Noble Death," 481–503; Sterling, "*Mors Philosophi*," 383–402; Scaer, *Lukan Passion*.

48. For more details on the connections between Jesus' death and the noble death/martyrdom traditions, see especially Kloppenborg, "*Exitus Clari Viri*," 108; Talbert, *Reading Luke*, 212–25.

49. On innocence as a theme in the noble death/martyrdom traditions, see Sterling, "*Mors Philosophi*," 398–99; Kloppenborg, "*Exitus Clari Viri*," 113.

50. Büchele, *Der Tod Jesu*, 54, n. 233; Beck, "*Imitatio Christi*," 42–43; Fitzmyer,

one translation without denying a secondary place for the other. Easter, for example, argues that the primary connotation is christological and thus ought to be translated as "righteous," but he acknowledges that this notion does carry the connotation of innocence.[51] Others argue that Luke intended δίκαιος to carry a double meaning. For example, Marguerat thinks that δίκαιος would have connoted innocence for non-Jewish readers and righteousness for Jewish readers, while Fitzmyer's view of the stages of composition of Luke's Gospel leads him to conclude that δίκαιος had one meaning ("innocent") on the lips of the historical centurion (i.e., during "stage 1" of the composition of the Gospel) and another meaning ("righteous") for the readers of Luke's Gospel (i.e., "stage 3").[52] These both-and approaches stem from a recognition that "just," "righteous," and "innocent" are related ideas and allow room for Luke to have intended a double meaning of sorts, even if emphasizing one over the other.

Luke's Passion Narrative, Parallels, and the Purpose of Luke-Acts

The third interpretive issue under consideration here is the function of the parallels between Jesus in Luke and Stephen and Paul in Acts and how these parallels relate to Luke's larger purpose. Attempts to explain the function of the parallels can be placed into three sometimes overlapping categories: apologetic motivation, pastoral motivation, and theological motivation. I will summarize each of these motivations then explore them in further detail below.

The apologetic motivation—which takes various forms—is probably the most common proposal. One variation of this proposal is the political apologetic, said to prove that Christianity was not threatening to the Roman Empire (Cadbury, Conzelmann, Kloppenborg, Heusler). Another variation suggests the apology is on behalf of Rome—an attempt to show Christians or potential Christians that Rome was not a threat to them (Walaskay). Still another variation is the apology for Jesus or, more commonly, Paul (Mattill). The sufferings of these protagonists needed defense,

---

Gospel according to Luke, 1515; Matera, "Death of Jesus," 479; Green, *Death of Jesus*, 99; Brown, *Death of the Messiah*, 1163; Bock, *Luke*, 377; Marguerat, *First Christian Historian*, 69–70; Neagoe, *Trial of the Gospel*, 102–3; Easter, "'Certainly This Man Was Righteous,'" 35–51.

51. Easter, "'Certainly This Man Was Righteous.'"

52. See Marguerat, *First Christian Historian*, 69–70; Fitzmyer, *Gospel according to Luke*, 1520.

so Luke aligned their stories to present Jesus' death as a noble one and Paul's sufferings as following those of Jesus, the model. The pastoral motivation also takes differing forms, ranging from the concern to set up Jesus and the parallel characters in Acts as a model for Luke's readers (Mattill, Carroll, Neyrey, Grundmann) to the concern to show continuity between Jesus and the church (Radl and Talbert). Finally, a theological motivation for the parallels sees a requirement for Peter, Stephen, and Paul to suffer like prophets in the same way that Jesus did (Moessner). I will explore each of these proposals in more depth, highlighting when possible the proposals that focus on Luke's passion narrative and its parallels.

The political apologetic understanding was popular among both English and German interpreters in the twentieth century.[53] Cadbury views Luke's two works as "Luke's defense of Christianity from charges brought against it as breaking Roman law."[54] The stories of Jesus and Paul needed explanation if they did not want to appear suspect, so Luke constructed the hearings of Jesus and Paul in a similar fashion, blaming the Jewish leaders and exonerating the Romans. Conzelmann argues similarly, "It cannot be disputed that Luke's apologetic aims are political."[55] These apologetic aims, he explains, are most evident in Jesus' passion and in Paul's missionary journeys. In Luke's passion narrative, "the political supremacy of Rome is the sole point at issue. The whole account presented in Acts confirms this finding."[56] Luke aims to show that being a Christian is no threat to Roman law,[57] and Jesus' passion and Paul's trials demonstrate that reality, particularly through their multiple declarations of innocence.

Many scholars today still espouse this view. Kloppenborg, for instance, affirms that Luke's presentation of Jesus attempted to remove suspicion that Christianity was politically subversive.[58] Heusler, too, sees

---

53. For a brief history of research prior to Cadbury on the function of this presentation of Jesus and Paul, see Moessner, "'The Christ Must Suffer,'" 221; Rowe, *World Upside Down*, 53. Walaskay traces this proposal as far back as Heumann in 1721. See Walaskay, *"And So We Came to Rome"*, ix.

54. Cadbury, *Making of Luke-Acts*, 308.

55. Conzelmann, *Theology of St. Luke*, 137.

56. Ibid., 139.

57. Haenchen comes to the same conclusion on Luke's purpose but, because he writes on Acts, focuses primarily on Paul. See Haenchen, *Acts of the Apostles*, 102.

58. Kloppenborg, "*Exitus Clari Viri*," 107, n. 9. He does not restrict the purpose of Luke's characterization of Jesus to this interest, however. He also argues that Luke depicts Jesus' death in the line of other illustrious persons whom his audience would recognize.

the parallel depictions of Jesus and Paul as an attempt to convince Rome that Jesus, Paul, and Christianity did not threaten the state. Toward this end, Rome's governors repeatedly affirm the innocence of the characters in both Luke and Acts. She even describes this apologetic purpose as "widely agreed upon" amongst NT exegetes.[59] Rowe also recently assessed, "Without question, the dominant trend in NT scholarship has been to read Acts as a document that argues for the political possibility of harmonious coeval existence between Rome and the early Christian movement."[60]

Though this view holds the day, it has not gone without critique and counter proposals. Gaston, for instance, also sees the parallels as an attempt to defend the church, but instead of the government being the address of the apology, Gaston argues that it is the synagogue. The picture of Roman injustice, the sharp contrast between Pilate's declarations and the Jews' demands, and the setting of the charges against Paul in the context of a debate with the synagogue all point to "an agonizing relationship of [Luke's] community with an outside group"—the synagogue.[61] Another critique comes from Walaskay, who argues the exact opposite of the dominant thesis. Instead of the parallels demonstrating that Christianity was not threatening Rome, Walaskay argues that the parallels show that Rome was not threatening to Christianity—Luke writes "an *apologia pro imperio* to his church."[62] That Roman leaders found Jesus and Paul innocent multiple times shows the government acting congenially to Christians.

Another variation is that of Mattill, who still sees the parallels serving an apologetic purpose but instead of the apology being for Christianity or for Rome he sees it being "an irresistible apology for Paul."[63]

---

59. Heusler, *Kapitalprozesse im lukanischen Doppelwerk*, 259–60 (translation mine).

60. Rowe, *World Upside Down*, 53. Recent surveys documenting this trend include Horn, "Die Haltung des Lukas zum römischen Staat"; Neagoe, *Trial of the Gospel*, 9–12; Walton, "State They Were In," 1–41.

61. Gaston, "Anti-Judaism," 151–52.

62. Walaskay, *"And So We Came to Rome"*, 64 (emphasis original). For other critiques of the thesis that Luke was defending the church to the Romans (though these are not related to the parallels between Luke and Acts), see Cassidy, *Jesus, Politics, and Society*, 128–30; Barrett, *Luke the Historian*, 63; Maddox, *Purpose of Luke-Acts*, 20–21, 90–97.

63. Mattill, "Jesus-Paul Parallels," 37. Mattill does not limit his study of the parallels to the passion/trial narratives, but he does devote significant attention to this portion of the stories.

Paul's sufferings needed explanation, so Luke aligned them with Jesus. Luke 6:40 ("A disciple is not above the teacher, but everyone who is fully trained will be like his teacher"[64]) points to this notion,[65] especially since, in Luke, Jesus says this to a broad circle of disciples (6:20), which in later interpretation could include Paul.[66] Mattill also appeals to 1 Cor 11:1 ("Be imitators of me, just as I am of Christ") as confirmation of his exegesis of Luke 6:40: Paul does not call the Corinthians "to imitate Christ directly but rather the concrete copy which they have in Paul."[67] Ultimately, then, the purpose of the Jesus-Paul parallels is to show "how Paul is perfected by his experiences, especially suffering, to be like his Model and Master, and thus himself be a model for his churches."[68]

We now move away from the apologetic motive to an interpretation similar to that of Mattill's (i.e., with emphasis on Jesus as model) but without the apologetic emphasis. This interpretation—which understands Jesus as the model for Luke's readers—also has a strong scholarly backing. Carroll understands Jesus as the "model martyr," followed in Acts by Stephen and Paul (though not completely in the case of the latter, since Luke does not narrate Paul's death in Acts).[69] With the potential of persecution and martyrdom for Luke's community (Luke 21:12-19), "Christians will find in Jesus' death (imitated by Stephen) a model for their own."[70] To the Luke 21 reference that Carroll highlights[71] Neyrey also adds Luke 12:8-12, another of Jesus' predictions of the trials and persecution that his followers will face. But these passages are more than mere prophesies fulfilled in Acts, Neyrey explains: with the parallels that Luke constructs between Jesus and characters in Acts, "Jesus himself is the archetype and model of the Church's experience.... He is the prime

---

64. All translations of the Bible are my own.

65. Mattill, "Jesus-Paul Parallels," 40–41. He thinks this verse anticipates the sufferings not just of Paul, but also of Stephen, James, and Peter.

66. Ibid., 43. Cp. Matthew's Jesus who speaks a similar saying to the Twelve (10:5, 24).

67. Ibid., 44–45. He also points to similar statements in 1 Thess 1:3–8; 2 Thess 3:6–9; Phil 3:17; 1 Cor 4:16; 11:1; Gal 4:12.

68. Ibid., 46.

69. Carroll, "Luke's Crucifixion Scene," 118–20.

70. Ibid., 119–20.

71. Neyrey details the ways Luke redacts Mark 13:7–9 (Luke 21:12–15) to accommodate his own perspective, which paves the way for the parallels between Luke and Acts. See Neyrey, *Passion according to Luke*, 85–88.

witness and his moral example is intended to be followed."[72] Grundmann, too, explains the parallelism in terms of the relationship between Jesus and the church—Jesus' time has "beispielhafte Bedeutung" for the time of the church, because the church's life is determined by Jesus' example. The mission of the church includes the whole person, and thus may include death, as Jesus, Stephen, James, and Paul exemplified.[73]

Two of the most detailed studies on the parallels across Luke and Acts both appeared in 1975: Walter Radl's *Paulus und Jesus im lukanischen Doppelwerk: Untersuchungen zu Parallelmotiven im Lukasevangelium und in der Apostelgeschichte* and Charles Talbert's, *Literary Patterns, Theological Themes and the Genre of Luke-Acts*. Both of these works intimate extensive parallels between Luke and Acts.[74] Though their works are different in many ways, both Radl and Talbert interpret the parallels as pointing to continuity between Jesus and the church,[75] a need prompted by the delay of the Parousia, according to Radl.[76] Radl's thesis is informed by Plutarch's *Parallel Lives*,[77] which presents the Roman Empire as a continuation of Hellenism. A similar use of synkrisis by Luke suggests to Radl that though there is a temporal distinction between the ages of salvation history in Luke (i.e., that of Jesus and that of the church), the parallels between them (particularly those of struggle and suffering)

---

72. Ibid., 88. Neyrey also briefly mentions the apologetic role that Jesus' prophecies in Luke 12:8–12 and 21:12–15 serve. Because the many trials and proceedings against Jesus and his followers were "potentially scandalizing," Jesus' prophecies about them demonstrate his authority and control over the events in the lives of his disciples. Elsewhere he adds that Luke's emphasis on the innocence of his protagonists functions as a "strong political apology . . . for Jesus and the early Church, especially in light of the Roman-Jewish war so recently concluded" (83). Thus, while Neyrey sees Luke's primary goal as setting up a model for his readers to follow, he also sees a secondary apologetic purpose.

73. Grundmann, *Das Evangelium nach Lukas*, 4. Others adopting this interpretation include Brown, *Death of the Messiah*, 1068–69; Matera, *Passion Narratives*, 205.

74. They do not limit their study to the passion narrative and its parallels as I have. To the extent possible I will focus on their assessment of the passion narrative parallels, but their conclusions are based on their assessment of the parallels within and across the whole books.

75. Radl, *Paulus und Jesus*, 374; Talbert, *Literary Patterns*, 97.

76. Radl, *Paulus und Jesus*, 374.

77. For his discussion of *Parallel Lives*, synkrisis, and their relation to Luke and Acts, see ibid., 253–54.

means that there is no shift from one age of salvation history to another but rather similarity and solidarity between them.[78]

Talbert, too, relies extensively on the ancient literary tradition for help in interpreting the parallels.[79] After analyzing the principle of succession in the philosophical tradition (especially Diogenes Laertius' *Lives of Eminent Philosophers*), he argues that Luke employs the *imitatio magistri* motif in his construction of the Jesus-Stephen parallels. "Luke wants to ground the disciples' acts in the deeds of Jesus. . . . In Luke-Acts such parallelism is frequently used by the author to emphasize unity. . . . Luke describes the death of Jesus as a martyrdom in order to give a basis for Christian suffering-martyrdom."[80] Unfortunately for this study, Talbert does not reflect specifically on the significance of the parallels between Jesus' trial and passion and the trials of Paul, besides to say that Luke shapes the trial sequence in Luke after that of Paul.[81] Talbert is more concerned with the correspondences between Luke 9 and Luke 22–23,[82] which asserts "a continuity between the one who works miracles and preaches in Galilee and the one who suffers and dies in Jerusalem."[83] While the *imitatio magistri* motif is somewhat similar to Mattill's thesis, Talbert differs from Mattill in that he views the parallels as part of Luke's larger concern to legitimate Christian teaching, tradition, and leadership succession in a time plagued by heresy and schism (cp. Mattill's emphasis on the potential suffering and persecution of early Christians, which engages more thoroughly the texts treated in this study).

If the above proposals can be categorized as apologetic and pastoral explanations, the final proposal can be described as a theological explanation. David Moessner, who, like the other writers, does not focus exclusively on the parallels of the trials and deaths, argues that Luke binds Peter, Stephen, and Paul to Jesus because the former "must suffer rejection like their Messiah, because that is the very manner in which the fulfillment of the messianic history takes place within the promised plan

---

78. Ibid., 395.

79. A bulk of his effort is directed toward showing that balance was a key principle in ancient literature. See Talbert, *Literary Patterns*, 67–70 (on classical literature), 71–75 (on Jewish literature), and 75–77 (on early Christian literature).

80. Ibid., 96–97.

81. Ibid., 22. This comment follows Talbert's intimation of the parallels on 17–18.

82. Ibid., 26–27.

83. Ibid., 120.

of God."[84] Peter, Stephen, and Paul are bound to the same fate as Jesus, as the cycle of Israel's history is one of continued disobedience and rejection of the prophets God sends to it.[85]

Observations

That these issues remain unresolved (or at an impasse) suggests the need for a fresh approach to Luke's passion narrative. As the above survey has shown, the most common approaches to Luke's passion narrative have been source, redaction, and narrative criticism. Notably absent from these approaches is rhetorical criticism, despite its proven value for interpretation of other areas of the Third Gospel, as discussed below. In light of this observation, I now turn to an explanation of the approach of this study—a compositional-rhetorical approach—and why I think it has the potential to help us adjudicate between the various positions outlined above.[86]

Rhetorical Criticism of Luke's Passion Narrative: A Proposal

Methodology

The prominence of rhetorical studies of the NT,[87] and of Luke's Gospel in particular,[88] makes the absence of a full-scale rhetorical analysis of Luke's passion narrative somewhat surprising. Although some scholars have analyzed various rhetorical aspects of the passion narrative as part of a

---

84. Moessner, "Christ Must Suffer," 224.

85. Ibid., 225–27.

86. Once this analysis is complete, I evaluate the strengths and weakness of these various proposals in light of my findings.

87. See, e.g., Watson and Hauser, *Rhetorical Criticism*.

88. See, e.g., Kurz, "Hellenistic Rhetoric," 171–95; Kennedy, *New Testament Interpretation*; Morgenthaler, *Lukas und Quintilian*; Hughes, "Parable," 29–41; Parsons, "Luke and the *Progymnasmata*," 43–63; Parsons, *Luke: Storyteller*; Brookins, "Luke's Use of Mark," 70–89.

larger study[89] or as one section of a commentary,[90] a full-scale rhetorical analysis of Luke's passion narrative is lacking due to the dominance of other methods like source, redaction, and narrative criticism. Here I argue not that rhetorical criticism should replace these other methods but rather that it should be used in conjunction with them.

The primary method of this study is "compositional-rhetorical criticism." This entails looking at the changes that Luke made to Mark (hence "compositional criticism"[91]) and analyzing Luke's passion narrative with

89. For example, Martin argues that the topic lists in the *progymnasmata* provided a "compositional template" for ancient biographies, including Luke. He only briefly discusses Luke's passion narrative under the topic "manner of death." Elsewhere, Tolppanen studies several Greco-Roman and Jewish authors (e.g., Josephus, Philo, Valerius Maximus, Tacitus, Livy, various OT passages, Diodorus Siculus, 1QapGen, and Psudeo-Philo) and argues that ancient authors were consistent in paraphrasing their sources (i.e., they either copied them almost word for word or paraphrased them extensively). Because he thinks Luke handles Mark inconsistently (i.e., Luke resembles Mark more outside of the Passion-Resurrection narratives than inside them) he argues that "Luke derived his triple tradition material not from canonical Mark but from either a single Non-Canonical Markan Source/Tradition (NCMS/T) or two NCMS/Ts, which Luke used consistently." Luke's editorial work in his passion narrative is only one facet of Tolppanen's larger source-critical study. Finally, Reich touches on several rhetorical figures in Luke's passion narrative, but this is only a small part of the rhetoric of the passion narrative and of Reich's study. See Martin, "Progymnasmatic Topic Lists," 18–41; Tolppanen, "A Source Critical Reassessment of the Gospel of Luke," ii–iii, 1–3, 10–14, 123–44, 295–300 (quotation from iii); Reich, *Figuring Jesus*.

90. Despite its title, Meynet's rhetorical analysis of Luke is quite different from what I undertake here. Meynet describes his approach as similar to structural linguistics in its three goals: (1) to isolate the units of the text at different levels of organizations; (2) to describe the relationships between those units; and (3) to express the meaning of the text as it is revealed though its composition. This approach results in one of the two volumes of his commentary being a map of the various relations between units of Luke. See Meynet, *L'Évangile selon Saint Luc*, 11.

Also, though not a commentary, Morgenthaler devotes one section of his study on Luke and Quintilian to Luke's "rhetorizing" ("Rhetorisierung") of Markan material, but does not discuss the passion narrative in that section, save for in a brief section on statistics (232) comparing Luke's words to Mark's (229–57). In a later section on Luke's special material the passion narrative only appears twice. First, he mentions the two criminals on the cross as an example of antithesis that Luke took from his source and, second, he refers to 23:31 as a metaphor that (when combined with other figures in Luke) shows Luke's concern for adorning his narrative (281–309). See Morgenthaler, *Lukas und Quintilian*, 229–57.

91. I adopt the term "composition criticism" from Haenchen, who suggests the term "Kompositionsgeschichte" in place of the more commonly used "Redaktionsgeschichte" because the former suggests that Luke did not just combine or edit his sources, but also composed some of final product. See Haenchen, *Der Weg Jesu*, 24.

an eye toward ancient rhetorical technique, particularly as described in the rhetorical handbooks and *progymnasmata* (hence "rhetorical criticism"). Rhetorical criticism views the New Testament documents as "complex, interrelated wholes, and recognizes the argumentative nature of these texts."[92] Compositional criticism needs little justification due to its widespread use in biblical studies today, but rhetorical criticism—comparatively newer on the scene—requires some justification.

Though not without critique,[93] rhetorical criticism has become a common way of analyzing the New Testament in recent years and has

---

Soards, who treats Luke as an author and not just an editor, adopts this term as well. See Soards, "Tradition, Composition, and Theology," 224. Though composition criticism is a common way of analyzing Luke's passion narrative, when coupled with rhetorical criticism it has the potential to yield new results.

92. Watson and Hauser, *Rhetorical Criticism*, 110.

93. Described in ibid., 111–12. Mitchell describes these critiques and provides able responses to them. See Mitchell, "Rhetorical Handbooks," 350–52.

More recently, Padilla has critiqued those approaches that suggest Luke's familiarity with the *progymnasmata* by pointing to Luke's lack of intertextuality with Greek prose authors (with whom students would become familiar in tertiary levels of education) and his lack of speech pairing (i.e., rebuttals or defenses). He concludes, "It is possible that Luke received primary and probably some measure of secondary education in the literate context, but, when it came time for higher education, he did not follow the literate track but followed the scientific or technical track" (436). See Padilla, "Hellenistic παιδεία," 416–37. First, Padilla's argument from the absence of intertextuality with Greek prose authors and speech pairing neglects one of the primary functions of the rhetorical education—namely, that students were taught principles that they could adapt to their own rhetorical ends. A student's familiarity with a technique or exercise did not necessitate its use in their works. Second, and more importantly, despite Padilla's concession that the educational boundaries were in flux during the time of Luke's writing (and thus that "Roman education, roughly during the period in which Acts was written, was in a stage of transition, with the *progymnasmata* increasingly becoming the domain of the secondary level of literate education" [419]), he nonetheless proceeds throughout his study as if the *progymnasmata* were at the tertiary educational level instead of the secondary level. See my refutation of this idea in chapter 2 and my argument below that many features of Luke and Acts weigh in favor of Luke's familiarity with a level of education comparable to that represented in the *progymnasmata*.

Even if one were not willing to grant Luke a secondary level of education, however, one still ought to grant that an understanding of the basic principles of persuasion in the ancient world can help us understand Luke's Gospel (and, indeed, the rest of the NT). Regardless of Luke's educational résumé, he was trying to persuade his audiences (Luke 1:1–4; Acts 1:1–3), so he would have attempted to communicate in ways that his audience would have understood and found persuasive. On that basis alone, the ancient rhetorical tradition helps us understand Luke's work by helping us understand how ancient people conceived of arguments, narration, and composition, even if they

provided fresh insights into the interpretive issues of several New Testament books, Luke included. Recent studies on rhetorical figures, chreia, fable, narrative, paraphrase, and prosopopoeia in Luke have yielded promising results for understanding Luke in light of the ancient rhetorical tradition and suggest that a similar study of Luke's passion narrative will be profitable.

Though the results of those studies can speak for themselves, I will nonetheless offer a brief justification of why the *progymnasmata* and other rhetorical treatises of the ancient world ought to aid our understanding of Luke. The *progymnasmata*, or preliminary exercises, were a common component of intermediate education; they were a series of exercises that gradually increased in difficulty that a student of rhetoric, poetry, or history would practice as preparation for speech composition or historiography.[94] One first-century *progymnasmata* author, Theon, describes the exercises as "the foundation of every kind of discourse" (*Prog.* 70 [Kennedy, 13]).[95] Students practiced various exercises that taught them to process information, identify important features of the text, and compose their own prose. In short, the exercises provided students with argumentative techniques, patterns on which to build their own compositions, and material to adapt to their own literary needs.[96] Because they were widespread (both geographically and chronologically) and because they reflect the curriculum of early stages of education, the *progymnasmata* are a fertile place to learn how ancient writers were thinking about constructing persuasive arguments. Ruth Webb explains, "Precisely because they [the *progymnasmata*] are elementary, they reveal the lowest common denominator of that training and reveal the basic conceptions of language, categories of composition, and modes of thought which informed both the production and reception of rhetorical and other texts."[97]

The rhetorical handbooks represent a more advanced stage of rhetoric studied in preparation for civic life. At this stage students studied speech making: invention, arrangement, style, memory, and delivery. Despite the fact that the rhetorical handbooks represent a level of training

---

lacked formal training.

94. For a more detailed discussion of the *progymnasmata* and rhetorical handbooks, see chapter 2.

95. On the notation system and translations of the *progymnasmata* cited in this study, see chapter 2.

96. Webb, "*Progymnasmata* as Practice," 290–91.

97. Ibid., 292.

beyond that which Luke likely received (few advanced to this level of education), they can still be used to inform our understanding of the rhetorical techniques under consideration here because of the overlap between the *progymnasmata* and the rhetorical handbooks on many of the exercises. Furthermore, these handbooks, though advanced, nonetheless demonstrate how ancient composers conceived of their works and how audiences might receive them. Finally, the ancient rhetorical tradition (and the handbooks in particular) proves especially apt for this study since its focus is on the passion narrative. Many of the rhetorical theorists' comments are aimed specifically at those preparing for court (e.g., Quintilian, *Inst.* 5.13.44). Luke, of course, was not writing an oration to be delivered in court,[98] but the theorists' comments are nonetheless particularly apt for this analysis since Jesus' trials and the theme of testimony are key parts of Luke's passion narrative. Since Luke is telling a narrative about a trial,[99] it would be quite natural for him to employ themes, topics, and arguments from the forensic sphere.[100] He does just that with his employment of the topics of refutation and confirmation.

Furthermore, the quality of Luke's Greek, his ability to write the longest surviving canonical gospel, his ability to succeed that account with a second volume, and his capacity to work with sources (Luke 1:1–4) suggest that Luke may have been familiar with educational content similar to that represented in the extant *progymnasmata*.[101] I am not suggesting that

---

98. Here we do well to remember that the application of rhetorical techniques was not a rigid science, nor was it limited by genre (see, e.g., Quintilian, *Inst.* 2.13). Quintilian explains that the rules of rhetoric can function as an aid to speaking "if they indicate the main road, and not just some one narrow track such that anyone who thinks it a sin to stray will need to walk as slowly as a tightrope walker" (2.13.16 [Russell, LCL]). The overlap between the various *progymnasmata* exercises (discussed in chapter 2) testifies to this flexibility as well. See also Gibson, "Learning Greek History," 103–29. Gibson discusses how the *progymnasmata* prepared students not just for oratory but for those writing poetry, history, and other genres. Further, Cribiore points out that "writing occupied a fundamental place in rhetorical education," which counters the notion that rhetorical training was not for writers. See Cribiore, *Gymnastics of the Mind*, 232.

99. On the sheer volume of Luke and Acts devoted to forensic trials, see Neyrey, *Passion according to Luke*, 84–85; Hogan, "Forensic Speeches."

100. That Luke narrates Jesus' trial does not necessarily imply an apologetic motivation for the passion narrative.

101. Luke's literary expertise has long been acknowledged. See, e.g., Streeter, *Four Gospels*, 548; Cadbury, *Making of Luke-Acts*, 4; Goulder, *Luke*, 115; Johnson, *Gospel of Luke*, 12–13; Parsons, *Luke: Storyteller*, 32; Jeffrey, *Luke*, 2–3.

Luke knew the specific *progymnasmata* or handbooks discussed here. Rather, I propose that the content contained in these *progymnasmata* is representative of the education Luke may have received, evinced by his capacity to write such sustained narratives as Luke and Acts. These exercises were a part of the rhetorical culture in which Luke lived; thus, even without direct access to these resources, he was likely familiar with the techniques contained therein.

Thus, the *progymnasmata* and the rhetorical handbooks are a fertile place for modern interpreters to learn what ancient writers—in this case, Luke—thought about composing narratives and constructing persuasive arguments; by looking at the exercises an ancient student would practice and at the ways a student would use and categorize such exercises, a modern interpreter is better able to understand an author's conception of her or his work and the ways an audience might hear it. The rhetorical techniques of refutation and confirmation, rhetorical figures, synkrisis, narration, and paraphrase are especially helpful in shedding light on the issues surrounding Luke's passion narrative.

Finally, before turning to the argument and framework of this study, it is necessary to intimate my view of the Synoptic Problem since a component of this study relates to Luke's use of sources. Along with the majority of scholars, I believe that Luke used Mark as his primary source for the entire Gospel. Luke supplements Mark with other traditions (cf. Luke 1:1–4), probably both oral and written.

Scholars have recently shown a renewed interest in the Farrer Hypothesis, a source-critical solution to the Synoptic Problem that dispenses with Q and instead argues that Luke used both Mark and Matthew. Luke's use of Matthew, for which Farrer Hypothesis proponents argue,[102] would explain the few agreements between Matthew and Luke against Mark in the passion narrative.[103] For example, two of the most significant Matthew-Luke agreements—the description of Peter weeping at the end of the mocking scene (Matt 14:65; Luke 22:62) and the question from the mockers (Matt 14:72; Luke 22:64)—may reflect Luke's knowledge of

---

102. See Farrer's famous articulation of the theory that bears his name in Farrer, "On Dispensing with Q," 55–88. More recently, however, see Goulder, *Luke: A New Paradigm*. Goodacre, now one of the more famous proponents of the Farrer Hypothesis, describes Goulder as "the leading exponent of the view, the scholar who has done more than any other to work out the argument in detail. . . . [A]t present his is the only substantial commentary on Luke's Gospel working with the thesis that Luke used both Mark and Matthew." See Goodacre, *Goulder and the Gospels*, 22.

103. See Bovon, *Luke 3*, 227, for a list and explanation of these minor agreements.

Matthew. Alternatively, they may also reflect phrases that had become popular in oral tradition.[104]

The primary portions of Luke that prompt the source critical debate over his passion narrative, however, are not those portions where Matthew and Luke agree against Mark. Those portions where Matthew and Luke do agree against Mark merit study informed by the ancient rhetorical tradition, but Luke's potential use of Matthew does not resolve most of the issues that drive the source critical discussion of Luke's passion narrative. That is, the material that solicits such divided responses amongst the scholarly community are not those portions where Matthew and Luke agree against Mark, but rather those portions where Luke and Mark differ markedly.[105] Thus, because scholarly attention has focused on Luke's potential use of a non-canonical written source, and since Luke's potential use of Matthew does not significantly impact that discussion, I will not explore the relationship between Matthew and Luke in this study.

104. Besides Goulder's proposal that Luke used Matthew, other proposals to explain their agreements against Mark include contamination of Luke's text by statements well-known from Matthew or another source common to both Luke and Matthew. On the former, see Bovon, *Luke 3*, 227. On the latter, see Nolland, *Luke 18:35—24:53*, 1098–99. Fitzmyer attributes both of these instances to "L," but does not explain how that relates to the overlap with Matthew. If one does not accept the Farrer Hypothesis, Soards' assessment of Luke 22:63–65 seems the best explanation of the Matthew-Luke agreements in the passion narrative: "The differences between the basic narratives of Luke and Matthew are striking. Except for this line [Matt 26:68/ Luke 22:64], which is not found in Mark's story, Matthew closely follows Mark's order and action; but Luke differs from Mark's story in both narrative order and detail. The differences between Luke and Matthew make it unlikely that independently they used a common written source. It is even more unlikely that independently Luke and Matthew composed and added exactly the same five-word question . . . to the account of the mockery of Jesus. Thus, one best understands this striking agreement by inferring that Luke and Matthew knew the same non-Markan tradition; and, the dissimilarities between the accounts of Luke and Matthew make it unlikely this tradition was written. Therefore, it seems justified to conclude that Luke and Matthew had access to the same oral tradition in Greek." See Soards, "Literary Analysis," 89.

105. When Farrer Hypothesis proponents attempt to explain those other portions (where no apparent connection exists) as Luke's use of Matthew, it discredits their case. Goodacre challenges Goulder when Goulder posits that Luke derived the Herod pericope from Matthew. Goodacre refers to this as one of Goulder's "least plausible" solutions. The remainder of Goodacre's assessment is worth noting, as it reveals some of Goulder's underlying assumptions: "Goulder can be seen to be looking most eagerly for some justification of Luke's having created L stories. In the case of Herod, Goulder makes this explicit: before he introduces his theory he says that Luke 'cannot simply have manufactured a hearing before Herod from nothing' (758)." See Goodacre, *Goulder and the Gospels*, 254–55.

A fuller treatment of the source issue of Luke's passion narrative (i.e., not just entertaining the possibility of a special non-canonical passion source) would need to explore Luke's potential use of Matthew, but such a treatment is beyond the scope of this study. This lack of treatment and my conclusions on the source issue should not be understood as either confirming or denying the validity of the Farrer Hypothesis. Rather, I hope my analysis will provide a basis for further explorations of the Farrer Hypothesis, both inside and outside of the passion narrative.

Finally, because of space constraints I will not address the relationship between the passion narratives of Luke and John in this study.[106] The similarities between the two passion narratives have resulted in a host of theories to explain the relationship between the two: Luke used John,[107] John used Luke,[108] the two used a common source,[109] or the two used common traditions.[110] I find the final option most convincing because of the nature of the similarities between the two, which are more in terms of thought content and order of the narratives than word agreement.[111] This understanding of the relationship between Luke and John supports my larger thesis here that Luke's passion narrative is explicable without recourse to a written source besides Mark.[112]

---

106. For a history of research on this topic, see Matson, *In Dialogue*, 21–90. Because Matson has so carefully intimated the various theories and their adherents, I only point to a few of the adherents below.

107. Ibid., 444. He concludes, "[I]t is very reasonable to read Luke as having used John in addition to Mark." Elsewhere he notes that he is open to the possibility of this being an earlier version of John (264).

108. E.g., Neirynck, *Jean et les synoptiques*. Cf. Matson, *In Dialogue*, 58–71.

109. E.g., Boismard, *Synopse des quatre Évangiles*, 40. Cf. Matson, *In Dialogue*, 63–67.

110. E.g., Brown, *Death of the Messiah*, 91.

111. Matson, *In Dialogue*, 91–163, describes the points of contact between the two as (1) Close linguistic or striking substantive similarities; (2) Common order; (3) Common geographical references; (4) Common individual facts or allusions; (5) Common omissions; (6) Common named characters; and (7) Common themes or theology.

112. It also cautions against theories like Matera's (described above) which allow for minimal, if any, influence of oral tradition.

Argument and Framework

This compositional-rhetorical analysis of Luke's passion narrative entails reading Luke 22:66—23:49 with ancient compositional and persuasive strategies in mind, as described in the ancient rhetorical tradition. Such an analysis contributes to the interpretive questions described above in three ways. First, regarding the source issue, it provides new explanations for the reasons Luke's order differs from Mark and for the potential origin of special Lukan material through an understanding of ancient paraphrase and narration. Second, it highlights Luke's key theme of innocence by showing that Luke structures his passion narrative as a debate about Jesus' innocence through the use of the common topics associated with refutation and confirmation. The presence of these topics—topics that were commonly used in court settings—and their use as a key structural device in the narrative suggests that one of Luke's primary concerns is to portray Jesus as *politically* innocent. The placement of rhetorical figures throughout his narrative supports this concern. While not denying that δίκαιος carries spiritual or christological connotations, this study challenges those works that downplay or deny the political connotations of Jesus' innocence. Third, based on ancient examples of synkrisis, this analysis suggests that part of the purpose of Luke's characterization of Jesus in the passion narrative (especially when set in parallel to Paul and Stephen in Acts) was to set up Jesus as a model for his followers in case they would face similar persecution or death.

My analysis proceeds in three phases. First, in chapter 2 I describe the tools for the rhetorical analysis of Luke's passion narrative. This includes an introduction to ancient education, a review of the various sources (the treatises on the *progymnasmata*, collections of exercises, and rhetorical handbooks) and their contents, and an analysis of the exercises relevant to this study: refutation and confirmation, rhetorical figures, synkrisis, narration, and paraphrase. Chapter 2 provides the necessary foundation and background for the remainder of the analysis.

Chapters 3 and 4, the heart of the study, are the compositional-rhetorical analysis of Luke's passion narrative. These chapters bring to bear the findings of chapter 2 onto Luke's passion narrative. I follow Luke's argument from Luke 22:66—23:49, noting how Luke's structure, argument, style, and use of sources conform to or diverge from the techniques described in chapter 2. Chapter 3 analyzes the trial proper (Luke 22:66—23:25), which includes Jesus' appearance before the Jewish council, the accusations against him, and his trials before Pilate and Herod. Chapter 4 analyzes Luke 23:26–49, which, though not a proper trial, can still be viewed as an informal trial. Here Jesus is "tried" by the soldiers, the criminals, God, and the centurion.

Chapter 5 highlights the specific techniques at work in Luke's passion narrative. Whereas the preceding two chapters followed Luke's text and discussed the techniques where appropriate, chapter 5 treats each of the techniques in turn (refutation and confirmation, rhetorical figures, synkrisis, narration, and paraphrase) and summarizes their role in Luke's passion narrative. After this summary, I bring my findings to bear on the three interpretive issues described above: (1) the sources Luke used in composing his passion narrative; (2) the translation of δίκαιος in 23:47; and (3) the function of the parallels between Jesus in Luke and Paul and Stephen in Acts.

2

Tools for a Rhetorical Analysis

Introduction

THIS CHAPTER IS A description of the tools necessary for a rhetorical analysis of Luke's passion narrative and is composed of three major parts. The first part introduces ancient education and serves to situate the sources of this study—the *progymnasmata* and the rhetorical handbooks—in their larger socio-historical context. The second part reviews the various sources used here—the treatises on the *progymnasmata*, collections of exercises, and rhetorical handbooks. This section includes discussions of the sources' dates, origins, authors, and contents. The third part, the heart of the chapter, analyzes what these various sources say about the exercises or techniques that will aid our study of Luke's passion narrative: refutation and confirmation, rhetorical figures, synkrisis, narration, and paraphrase.

Ancient Education: A Brief Synopsis

Education in the ancient Roman world is best described as a three-stage process, though the walls between the stages were at least semi-permeable.[1] Students would begin in the primary or elementary stage,

---

1. Here I rely on Morgan, *Literate Education*; Cribiore, *Gymnastics of the Mind*; Marrou, *History of Education in Antiquity* (originally published as *Histoire de l'Education dans l'antiquité*). It is worth noting that Morgan builds upon one of Cribiore's previous studies: *Writing, Teachers, and Students in Graeco-Roman Egypt*. I have chosen Marrou as the primary representative of the "traditional view" because of how influential his work was and because Morgan and Cribiore often set their work in contrast to his. In contrast to the traditional view, their work suggests "more fluid learning situations" in which "the boundaries between levels were not completely impermeable" (Cribiore, *Gymnastics of the Mind*, 2).

where they would learn the alphabet, basic reading skills, syllables and words, recitation, how to write their name, and counting. The content of primary education was relatively stable, though the order in which students learned the material varied.[2] After mastering these skills, students who continued their education—admittedly, a small number—would then advance to the intermediate or secondary stage, where they would study the poets and classical writers.[3] Here students learned the rules of

---

While both Cribiore and Morgan see their studies as critiques of the traditional understanding of education advanced by scholars like Marrou et al, these newer works do not necessarily render null the findings of the earlier works. In fact, Cribiore found the "traditional" three-stage view valuable enough to use in her study, despite her evidence that ancient education was more flexible than three strict stages. She says the three-stage model "is still realistic enough to represent properly the characteristics and functions of the various levels and the tension among the different aims and audiences that each targeted. Even if the boundaries between levels were not completely impermeable, the educational contents of each appear well defined as the levels progress in difficulty." Ibid. Alternatively, Morgan proposes a model with "core" and "periphery" material. The core "includes what most people learned, what they learned first, and in the case of reading, what they went on practising longest" (*Literate Education*, 71). The periphery included "everything outside the 'core', but it would be in no way homogeneous" (72). In her model, grammar (stage two of the traditional model) and rhetoric (stage three of the traditional model) "are peripheral in that few people appear to have learned them and they are virtually all in the most accomplished schoolhands we possess" (72).

One of the key differences between the studies of Morgan and Cribiore and that of Marrou is that the former rely much more heavily on the evidence from papyri, ostraca, tablets, parchment, and private letters in Egypt than did Marrou (indeed, this evidence is the basis of their studies). Marrou interacts with the papyri, but much more sporadically. Marrou builds most of his study on the works of elite authors like Plutarch, Quintilian, and Dionysius Thrax. Morgan and Cribiore consult the elite sources, but they do so to see whether and when the elite literary texts and the sub-elite papyri "coincide, and when practices in literary texts and papyri, and in the rather different social groups from which they derive, diverge" (ibid., 6). Ultimately Morgan finds convergence in some places and divergence in others. The studies of Cribiore and Morgan are especially valuable to this study because they bring to light examples of actual practices of teachers and students. In other words, the papyri do not simply talk about education or educational exercises—they *are* the exercises.

2. Cribiore, *Gymnastics of the Mind*, 161–69.

3. It seems that, outside of fables and gnomic sayings, the bulk of the study at this stage was of the poets. See ibid., 202. Admittedly, there is a considerable difference in the attrition rates between boys and girls in ancient education. While there is some evidence of females' advancing to higher stages (particularly elite females), the higher stages were occupied primarily by males. Cribiore comments, "Even though access to education was smoother for girls of the upper class, it is likely that not many of them went beyond the primary level" (ibid., 75). On women in ancient education, see ibid., 74–101; Morgan, *Literate Education*, 48–49.

punctuation and how to identify the parts of a sentence, they studied etymology and letter-writing, and they "began drafting simple and short texts such as elementary summaries and paraphrases of what they had read."[4] Finally, a small portion of the students would advance to the final stage, where they would study speech composition, at times with the aid of rhetorical handbooks. At this stage, a student would "transition from passive recipient of education to active user of it."[5]

The studies of Teresa Morgan and Raffaella Cribiore provide a necessary reminder that the function of the teacher and the organization, structure, and content of the education varied depending on the circumstances. For instance, grammarians—teachers traditionally thought to have only provided secondary instruction—sometimes provided primary instruction as well.[6] While educational theorists like Quintilian differentiated between types of teachers, the titles used for teachers were often "exchangeable."[7] Furthermore, schools did not always divide students into separate classes based on their abilities, but would sometimes have students of different levels in class together.[8]

Of key interest to this study is the place of the *progymnasmata* or "preliminary exercises" and the rhetorical handbooks in ancient education.[9] The *progymnasmata* were series of exercises that gradually increased in difficulty that a student of rhetoric, poetry, or history

---

4. Cribiore, *Gymnastics of the Mind*, 191–215 (quotation from 215).

5. Morgan, *Literate Education*, 198.

6. Cribiore, *Gymnastics of the Mind*, 38. While Marrou implies standardization of the teachers (i.e., the grammatist [γραμματιστής] at the primary level, the grammarian [γραμματικός or φιλόλογος] at the secondary level, and the rhetor [σοφιστής or ῥήτωρ] at the tertiary level, even he admits that this "theoretical distinction between them did not always work out in practice." Marrou, *History of Education*, 223. Booth even suggests that "elementary learning was not always regarded and did not always exist as a distinct stage of education in first-century Rome." See Booth, "Elementary and Secondary Education in the Roman Empire," 4.

The inconsistency among the ancients in what terms they used for the various teachers makes our attempts to distinguish what teachers taught what subjects that much more complicated. See, e.g., Suetonius, *Gramm.* 4, on the different terms for teachers that were prominent among the Greeks and Romans. This inconsistency may also reflect the fluidity between roles and levels within education.

7. See Morgan, *Literate Education*, 28. Cf. Cribiore, *Gymnastics of the Mind*, 50–56.

8. Ibid., 41–44.

9. See the section entitled "*Progymnasmata*" below for more on the contents of the *progymnasmata*.

would practice as preparation for speech composition or ancient historiography.[10] Theon, author of a first-century *progymnasmata*, viewed the exercises as "the foundation of every kind of discourse" (*Prog.* 70 [Kennedy, 13]),[11] not just the foundation of oratory. When practicing these preliminary exercises, students learned how to process information, how to identify important features of texts, and, for the first time, how to compose their own prose.[12] They developed facility in invention, expression, the ability to follow paradigms, and the ability to structure speeches.[13] The value of the exercises was that they "furnished speakers with a store of techniques of presentation and argumentation, with flexible patterns on which to model their own compositions, and a set of common narra-

---

10. On the *progymnasmata* as preparation for historiography, see Gibson, "Learning Greek History in the Ancient Classroom," 103–5.

George Kennedy describes these preliminary exercises as "a sequence of assignments in reading, writing, and speaking which gradually increase in difficulty and in maturity of thought from simple story-telling to argumentation, combined with study of literary models." See Kennedy, *Progymnasmata*, x. For more information on the *progymnasmata*, see Webb, "*Progymnasmata* as Practice," 289–316; Stamps, "Rhetoric," 956; Cribiore, *Gymnastics of the Mind*, 221–30.

11. English translations of the *progymnasmata* are from Kennedy, *Progymnasmata*. The Greek text of Theon consulted and cited is the most recent critical edition: Patillon and Bolognesi, *Aelius Théon: Progymnasmata*. Their edition contains both the Greek and Armenian text of Theon with a French translation. Prior to their edition, Butts published a critical edition of the Greek text of Theon, which was the first to be based on all of the extant Greek manuscripts of Theon and a study of the Armenian manuscripts. When it was completed in 1987, his was the first translation of Theon's *Progymnasmata* into a modern language. Prior to Butts, the most recent critical edition was Spengel's, which is now over 150 years old. Kennedy's English translation of Theon (and other *progymnasmata*) is based on Spengel but revised with the release of the works of Butts, Patillon, and Bolognesi. See Spengel, *Rhetores Graeci*; Butts, "'Progymnasmata' of Theon."

A consistent system for citing Theon's *Progymnasmata* is lacking. In my citations, I follow the system used by Kennedy and Patillon, which cites Spengel's page numbers. If citing a direct quotation, I then provide Kennedy's or Patillon's page number in brackets with their name. The Greek text of Theon ends abruptly in the middle of the exercise on law. The remaining sections (i.e., on reading aloud, listening to what is read, paraphrase, elaboration, and contradiction or counterstatement) exist only in Armenian with French and English translations. When citing from those sections, Kennedy marks the reference with a "P" to indicate that he has translated from Patillon's French translation of the Armenian. I follow Kennedy in this practice as well.

12. Gibson, "Learning Greek History," 105; Kennedy, *Classical Rhetoric*, 27; Morgan, *Literate Education*, 225.

13. Webb, "*Progymnasmata* as Practice," 291–92; Cribiore, *Gymnastics of the Mind*, 231.

tives, personae and values to appeal to.... [The exercises were] a source of techniques and material to be adapted to the task at hand."[14]

While Theon's *progymnasmata* is the earliest extant treatise on the exercises today,[15] *Rhetorica ad Alexandrum* uses the term προγυμνάσματα, suggesting the use of some sort of preparatory exercises in education as early as the fourth century BCE.[16] Michael John Roberts says this reference refers to "preparatory exercises in general, without implying the fully developed syllabus of the rhetorical schools of the Empire."[17] Both Roberts and Kennedy suggest that it was probably not until the second century BCE that a more systematic set of *progymnasmata* was developed, as passages from the anonymous *Rhetorical ad Herennium* and Cicero's *De inventione* suggest.[18]

The evidence for the *progymnasmata* is widespread not just chronologically, but also geographically. The exercises were practiced or known by the orators in Rome (Cicero, *De or.* 1.34.154; Quintilian, *Inst.* 1.9.2–6), were used by students throughout Egypt (as evinced by exercises found in the papyri),[19] and were written about by authors in Alexandria (Theon), Antioch (Libanius and Aphthonius), and Constantinople (Nicolaus).[20] Both Latin and Greek writers refer to the exercises. Thus, Kennedy's com-

---

14. Webb, "*Progymnasmata* as Practice," 290–91. To show the adaptability of the skills learned in the *progymnasmata*, Webb gives an example from Ps.-Dionysius of Halicarnassus' *Art of Rhetoric*, where "the thesis topic on marriage furnishes arguments for the desirability of marriage for use in wedding speeches" (291, n. 6).

15. See below on the dating of Theon.

16. "Consequently, the qualities common to all the species and the modes of employing them being known to us from what has been said previously, if we habituate and train ourselves to repeat them on the lines of our preparatory exercises (προγυμνάσματα), they will supply us with plenty of matter both in writing and in speaking" (*Rhet. Alex.* 28.1436a25 [Rackham, LCL]).

17. See Roberts, *Biblical Epic*, 6. Cf. Webb, "*Progymnasmata* as Practice," 293; Kennedy, *Progymnasmata*, xi. Kennedy notes that while Aristotle does not discuss the preliminary exercises in his *Rhetorica* or his other writings, "he does discuss rhetorical forms which later appear among the exercises, including fable, maxim, narrative, encomion, vivid description [ecphrasis], and thesis."

18. Roberts, *Biblical Epic*, 7; Kennedy, *Progymnasmata*, xi. See *Rhet. Her.* 1.8.12; 4.42.54–4.44.58; Cicero, *Inv.* 1.19.27. Cribiore, *Gymnastics of the Mind*, 210, suggests that it was not until the first century CE that "grammatical theory became a fixed part of the school curriculum."

19. See Morgan, *Literate Education*, 53–64, for a catalog of the contents of the school text papyri found in Egypt.

20. See below for more on Theon, Aphthonius, Libanius, and Nicolaus.

ments on the popularity of the *progymnasmata* are warranted: "By at least the first century BC, virtually all Greek and Roman students were practiced in progymnasmatic exercises in grammar or rhetorical schools."[21]

It is not entirely clear, however, where in the educational process the *progymnasmata* came into play—an obscurity that may be a result of a debate amongst ancient educators about their proper place.[22] Evidence from Quintilian suggests that teachers of rhetoric and teachers of grammar disagreed over who should teach the *progymnasmata* (*Inst.* 2.1.1–13). Quintilian recommends that the *grammaticus* teach at least fables, paraphrase, aphorisms, chreia, and ethologiae[23] (1.9.1–6), while the rhetor should teach narrative, refutation and confirmation, encomnia and invective, commonplace, theses, and law (2.4). Suetonius, a near contemporary of Quintilian, however, suggests that the *grammaticus* used to teach many of the exercises to students so as not to "turn over their pupils to the rhetoricians wholly ignorant and unprepared," but that by his time this practice had been abandoned (*Gramm.* 4 [Rolfe, LCL]).[24] Marrou describes the situation well:

> [A]s the more advanced rhetoric became increasingly technical and more and more exacting, it became a matter of necessity for higher education to hand preparatory exercises over to the secondary school and so, by force of circumstances, they were "usurped" by the grammarian. The rhetors, of course, did not take this lying down—though the Latin rhetors who came at a much later stage of educational development did not stand on their dignity quite so much—but the Greek ones never gave up the whole field of the προγυμνάσματα to their humble rivals, and only allowed them the most elementary portions.[25]

---

21. Kennedy, *Classical Rhetoric*, 27.

22. Cribiore and Morgan both treat the *progymnasmata* in their respective chapters on rhetoric, while Marrou and Kennedy see them as part of both the intermediate education and the rhetorical training. See Marrou, *History of Education*, 238–39, 272, 276; Kennedy, *Classical Rhetoric*, 27. Our lack of knowledge about the transition from the grammarian to the rhetor contributes to this confusion. See Cribiore, *Gymnastics of the Mind*, 224.

23. Russell argues that ethologiae likely means "description of character" or "speech in character" (like *ēthopoiia*). See Russell's comments in Quintilian, *Institutio oratoria*, 210–11, n. 4. This understanding accords with the exercises that appear toward the beginning of the list in the *progymnasmata* treatises (see below).

24. Cited in Webb, "*Progymnasmata* as Practice," 296.

25. Marrou, *History of Education*, 238–39.

From this information, it seems best to conclude that the use of the *progymnasmata* began in grammar schools and continued into the early stages of rhetorical training. Ruth Webb describes them as "the transition from the study of grammar and the reading of texts . . . to writing and speaking."[26] Wherever they fell in the educational process, they were "preliminary" to declamation. This understanding matches other evidence that suggests that "learning was organized into tightly connected links, each joined to the previous and giving a base to the next."[27]

Once the progymnasmatic building blocks had formed the base, a student would study more advanced rhetoric. The rhetorical handbooks represent the type of material an advanced student would learn in preparation for various facets of civic life. The teaching at this level centered on analyzing the five components of speech making: invention, arrangement, style, memory, and delivery.[28] Though few advanced this far in education, the contents of the handbooks demonstrate how ancient composers (be it of oral or written projects) conceived of their works and how audiences might receive them. We will now look at the pertinent sources in more detail.

Focusing on the Sources: Extant *Progymnasmata* and Rhetorical Handbooks

The *Progymnasmata*

We have access to several ancient *progymnasmata*,[29] all of which were originally written in Greek, through two types of sources: (1) treatises

---

26. Webb, "*Progymnasmata* as Practice," 289. Cf. Patillon and Bolognesi, *Aelius Théon*, xvii, who also call the exercises "une transition entre l'enseignement du *grammatikos* et celui du *rhetor*."

27. Cribiore, *Gymnastics of the Mind*, 222.

28. Aristotle focused primarily on invention, but also discussed arrangement, style, and, briefly, delivery (*Rhet.* 3.1). The five divisions had taken place by the time *Rhetorica ad Herennium* was written in the first century BCE (*Rhet. Her.* 1.2.3). Cicero and Quintilian utilized these divisions as well, though with minor variations (Cicero, *De or.* 1.31.142–43; Quintilian, *Inst.* 3.3.1).

29 This study includes the earliest extant Greek *progymnasmata*—those of Theon, Ps.-Hermogenes, Libanius, Aphthonius, and Nicolaus—which date between the first and fifth centuries of the Common Era. The presence of one of these *progymnasmata* at the end of the first century indicates that the ideas therein were in circulation during the time that Luke wrote his Gospel. As mentioned in the previous chapter, I am not arguing that Luke knew Theon's work but that Theon's work is representative of the

for students or teachers that describe the exercises and contain some examples of the exercises, and (2) collections of exercises.[30] The first are preserved in the works of Theon,[31] Ps.-Hermogenes, Aphthonius, and Nicolaus; the second are preserved in the works of Libanius and in papyri from Egypt.

Theon

The earliest treatise on the *progymnasmata* is believed to have been written by Aelius Theon, a rhetor from Alexandria who lived during the first century CE. The manuscripts of this work only identify the author as Theon, but an entry in a tenth-century Byzantine encyclopedia on Aelius Theon of Alexandria identifies Theon as an author of *progymnasmata* and works on Xenophon, Isocrates, and Demosthenes. This overlap leads most scholars to consider Aelius Theon as "the leading candidate for author of this work."[32] Theon's references to Theodorus of Gadara and Dionysius of Halicarnassus establish a *terminus a quo* in the late first century BCE for the work. Additionally, Quintilian, writing at the end of the first century CE, refers to the works of someone named Theon on stasis theory (3.6.48) and figures of speech (9.3.76). Though it is impossible to be sure, many believe these references refer to the Theon who wrote the *progymnasmata*, which, if accepted, would establish a *terminus ad quem* for this *progymnasmata* in the first century CE. Similarities between Theon's work and Quintilian's discussion of the exercises further

---

education taught in the first century. Of all the *progymnasmata*, I rely most heavily upon Theon, partly because his work is the most extensive and partly because of his early date. The other progymnasmatic treatises, though later in date, are still helpful in that they show the enduring legacy of many of the ideas from the first century and because of the continuity of the rhetorical instruction throughout the Roman period. On this continuity, see Murphy, "Roman Writing Instruction," 69–76.

30. I follow Gibson, *Libanius's Progymnasmata*, xxi–xxii, on this division of the types of sources.

31. Butts points out that Theon "does not refer to his own work as *progymnasmata*. His terminology varies between *gymnasma* and *gymnasia*. It is probably that these exercises did not take on the name *progymnasmata* on a wide scale until the time of Aphthonius when his set of exercises was prefixed to the *technē* of Hermogenes." Butts, "'Progymnasmata' of Theon," 8. Cf. Cribiore, *Gymnastics of the Mind*, 221; Hock and O'Neil, *Chreia in Ancient Rhetoric*, 12–15.

32. Kennedy, *Progymnasmata*, 1. For more on the identification of Theon, see also Stegemann, "Theon," 2037–54.

support a first-century date.[33] Though we cannot be absolutely certain, I follow the scholarly consensus in maintaining that the evidence points toward a first-century CE date, with authorship likely by Aelius Theon of Alexandria.[34] Theon's treatise is thus "the earliest surviving work on exercises in composition."[35]

Most of Theon's treatise exists in Greek, but the Greek textual tradition[36] does not accurately reflect all of Theon's original components or order. The Greek tradition makes three significant changes to what scholars believe to be Theon's original: (1) it transposes material on refutation and confirmation from the end of the chapter on narrative to its own chapter[37]; (2) it rearranges the order of the chapters; (3) it omits the five chapters on reading aloud, oral presentation, paraphrase, elaboration, and contradiction.[38] Scholars have reconstructed Theon's Greek original from an Armenian translation of the Greek that was completed before the changes were made in the Greek.[39] James Butts, in his critical edition of the Greek text of Theon, explains that these changes happened "because the work

---

33. On the similarities see Patillon and Bolognesi, *Aelius Théon: Progymnasmata*, xiv–xvi; Butts, "'Progymnasmata' of Theon," 3–6. Neither of these authors suggests literary dependence between Theon and Quintilian.

34. For a summary of the issues surrounding the dating of Theon, see Butts, "'Progymnasmata' of Theon," 2–6; Heath, "Theon and the History," 129–60. Heath acknowledges that the scholarly consensus dates Theon in the first century CE but argues for a fifth-century date for Theon.

35. Kennedy, *Progymnasmata*, 1.

36. On the textual history of Theon's *progymnasmata*, see Butts, "'Progymnasmata' of Theon," 23–70; Patillon and Bolognesi, *Aelius Théon*, cxiv–clvi.

37. Spengel follows the Greek tradition by including a separate chapter on refutation and confirmation. Kennedy follows Butts and the Armenian tradition by leaving the section on refutation and confirmation as part of the chapter on narrative. Butts believes that the Armenian most likely preserves Theon's original order because of both external and internal evidence. He lists six pieces of internal evidence and argues that, externally, the Armenian "preserves a textual tradition that is earlier and better than the Greek tradition." See Butts, "'Progymnasmata' of Theon," 9–10.

38. Ibid., 17. On the transposition of material, see 8–11; on the rearrangement of chapters, see 11–17; on the omission of material from the end of the treatise, see 17–19.

39. Crucial to this reconstruction were the works of Lana and Patillon and Bolognesi. See Lana, *I "progimnasmi" di Elio Teone*; Patillon and Bolognesi, *Aelius Théon*. Lana was crucial in restoring the original order of the chapters in Theon and in providing a detailed study of the Greek textual tradition. Patillon, with assistance from Bolognesi on the Armenian, reconstructed the Greek text on which the Armenian was based.

of Theon was transformed from a treatment of the subject intended for teachers into a school text intended for students. This transformation was modeled on those texts that were later more popular: e.g., the *progymnasmata* of Hermogenes, Aphthonius, and Nicolaus."[40] Thus, though it is not reflected in the Greek tradition, Theon originally treated refutation and confirmation in the chapter on narrative and included chapters on reading aloud, oral presentation, paraphrase, elaboration, and contradiction. Furthermore, he originally treated the exercises in the following order (after an untitled prolegomenon and a discussion of the education of young students): chreia, fable, narrative, commonplace, description, speech-in-character, encomion, comparison, thesis, law, reading aloud, oral presentation, paraphrase, elaboration, and rebuttal.[41]

Ps.-Hermogenes

Another extant progymnasmatic treatise was traditionally attributed to Hermogenes of Tarsus, who lived in the second century CE.[42] This Hermogenes wrote at least two textbooks on rhetoric—one on *stasis* and one on *ideai*—that were popular in Byzantine times, but most scholars today doubt that Hermogenes of Tarsus wrote the *progymnasmata* often associated with his name. Though some medieval writers attributed it to him (e.g., John of Sardis, c. 800 CE), others attributed it to Libanius. Its manuscript tradition is different from those works of Hermogenes, whose authenticity scholars do not question. The *progymnasmata* mentions Aelius Aristides (second century CE) and is known to Nicolaus (late fifth century CE); these references establish the boundaries on its dating. Kennedy tentatively dates it in the third or fourth century CE.[43] Priscian, a Roman grammarian, relied heavily on this work for his Latin *progymnasmata*, composed around the beginning of the sixth century, which suggests that these exercises attributed to Hermogenes were still in use several centuries after their composition. Because this work likely did not

---

40. Butts, "'Progymnasmata' of Theon," 20.

41. This stands in contrast to the order in which they appear in all the Greek manuscripts: fable, narrative, chreia, refutation and confirmation, commonplace, encomion, comparison, speech-in-character, description, thesis, law. See ibid., 11, 17. On the order that Theon recommend for classroom practice, see ibid., 19–20.

42. Introductory information on Hermogenes is from Kennedy, *Progymnasmata*, 73–74.

43. Ibid., 72.

come from the hand of Hermogenes, I follow authors like Craig Gibson and refer to the author of this work as Ps.-Hermogenes.[44]

Aphthonius

Next is the work of Aphthonius, the student of Libanius (treated below). Aphthonius studied under Libanius in Antioch in the second half of the fourth century CE. His work survives in several manuscripts and was used as a source for *progymnasmata* and textbooks in both Armenian and Latin.[45] Its popularity is attested by its inclusion in the Hermogenic corpus alongside Hermogenes' *On Stasis* and *On Ideas of Style* and other works attributed to Hermogenes.

Nicolaus

The final treatise on *progymnasmata* was penned by Nicolaus (c. 410–after 491). Nicolaus, though originally from Lycia, studied in Athens and taught rhetoric in Constantinople; his teaching career spanned most of the last quarter of the fifth century. Nicolaus includes all of the exercises discussed by Ps.-Hermogenes and Aphthonius, though he adds a preface in which he discusses the definition, species, and divisions of rhetoric. For Nicolaus, the *progymnasmata* were necessary because rhetoric was too difficult for young students to manage—the exercises provided a way of practicing the individual parts of rhetoric rather than the whole.[46]

The Contents and Organization of the Treatises

Generally speaking, the contents of the treatises by Theon, Ps.-Hermogenes, Aphthonius, and Nicolaus are similar in many ways. They all contain material on fable, narrative, chreia, maxim, refutation and confirmation, topos (or commonplace), ecphrasis, prosopopoeia (or ethopoeia), encomion and invective, synkrisis, thesis, and law. They usually begin with a definition of the exercise under consideration. For example, Ps.-Hermogenes begins his chapter on chreia as follows: "A chreia

    44. Gibson, "Learning Greek History."
    45. Kennedy, *Progymnasmata*, 89.
    46. On Nicolaus, see Kennedy, *Greek Rhetoric*, 66–69. Cf. Stegemann, "Nikolaos," 424–57.

(*khreia*) is a recollection (*apomnêmoneuma*) of a saying or action or both, with a pointed meaning, usually for the sake of something useful" (*Prog.* 6 [Kennedy, 76]). Theon and Aphthonius begin with similar definitions. While some authors spend more time on definitions than others, each author eventually offers ways to practice the exercise. Of course, each author does this differently, but there is significant overlap between them. For example, three of the authors recommend that a student restate or paraphrase the chreia (Theon, *Prog.* 101; Ps.-Hermogenes, *Prog.* 7; Aphthonius, *Prog.* 23). Ps.-Hermogenes and Aphthonius both also recommend praising the speaker, as well as supplying the cause of and something contrary to the chreia, a comparison, and an example.

There are significant differences between these works, however. Theon, for instance, has several chapters not present in the others that focus specifically on pedagogy (cf. Nicolaus' preface). Theon's preface includes a discussion on the sequence in which the exercises should be employed (*Prog.* 59–65), and he devotes an entire chapter to the education of the young (*Prog.* 66–72). He also has chapters on exercises not present in the others: reading aloud, oral presentation, paraphrase, elaboration, and contradiction (*Prog.* 102P–112P). Even when one excludes those extra chapters, Theon is still significantly longer than Ps.-Hermogenes and Aphthonius. Nicolaus' work is lengthy as well, in large part due to his interaction with other *progymnasmata*.[47]

Furthermore, the authors organize their material somewhat differently.[48] Theon, for example, treats maxim with chreia, rather than giving it its own chapter (*Prog.* 96). Ps.-Hermogenes and Aphthonius distinguish between ethopoeia and prosopopoeia (the latter being one type of the former), whereas Theon seems unaware of this distinction (Ps.-Hermogenes, *Prog.* 20; Aphthonius, *Prog.* 44; Theon, *Prog.* 115). Theon discusses only the latter. Finally, with regard to the exercises that all four authors treat, the order of chapters varies.[49] Ps.-Hermogenes, Aphthonius, and Nicolaus follow the same order, with only a few variations: (1)

47. Nicolaus indicates that his work is based on previous accounts. Kennedy argues that "verbal echoes suggest that he may have known the works attributed to Theon and to Hermogenes, but, perhaps surprisingly, he seems not to have used Aphthonius's work, at least not directly." See Kennedy, *Progymnasmata*, 130.

48. Cribiore, *Gymnastics of the Mind*, 223, notes that even though the order of exercises varied, it did "follow an apparent progression in difficulty."

49. Regarding Theon, I am referring to the order that scholars believe to be the original—the one preserved in the Armenian, not the Greek, textual tradition. See above for a fuller discussion of Theon's order.

Aphthonius treats refutation and confirmation as two chapters, while Ps.-Hermogenes and Nicolaus treat them together; (2) Ps.-Hermogenes does not treat invective. Theon treats chreia before fable and narrative, and, as previously mentioned, treats maxim with chreia, rather than giving the former its own chapter. Furthermore, Theon discusses refutation and confirmation in his chapter on narrative, rather than giving them their own chapter(s). Topos (or commonplace) follows these chapters in Theon as it does in the others, but the order of the next four exercises is different between the two. Theon treats ecphrasis and prosopopoeia before encomion/invective and synkrisis, while the other three treat them after. All four put thesis and law next, although Theon follows these chapters with his extra five. Table 1 summarizes this data.

Table 1. Contents of the *progymnasmata* organized by author

Theon	Ps.-Hermogenes	Aphthonius	Nicolaus
Preface			Preface
On the Education of the Young			
Chreia (includes maxim)	Fable	Fable	Fable
Fable	Narrative	Narrative	Narrative
Narrative (includes refutation & confirmation)	Chreia	Chreia	Chreia
	Maxim	Maxim	Maxim
	Refutation & Confirmation	Refutation	Refutation & Confirmation
		Confirmation	
Topos	Common-place	Common-place	Common-place

Theon	Ps.-Hermogenes	Aphthonius	Nicolaus
Ecphrasis	Encomion	Encomion	Encomion & Invective
		Invective	
Prosopopoeia	Synkrisis	Synkrisis	Synkrisis
Encomion and Invective	Ethopoeia	Ethopoeia	Ethopoeia
Synkrisis	Ecphrasis	Ecphrasis	Ecphrasis
Thesis	Thesis	Thesis	Thesis
Law	Law	Law	Law
Reading aloud			
Oral presentation			
Paraphrase			
Elaboration			
Contradiction			

Libanius

In addition to these treatises on the *progymnasmata* by Theon, Ps.-Hermogenes, Aphthonius, and Nicolaus, we also have works that are simply exercises or collections of exercises. The work of Libanius is the prime example of the latter. In contrast to some of the authors already discussed, we know much about Libanius.[50] Libanius (c. 314–393 CE) grew up in Antioch, studied in Athens (336–40), and taught rhetoric in Constan-

50. Gibson describes Libanius as "one of the best known and best documented public figures of the later Roman Empire" (xvii). In addition to his *progymnasmata*, his surviving works include an autobiography, sixty-three speeches, over 1500 letters, fifty-one declamations, and introductions to Demosthenes' orations. For more on Libanius' life, see Gibson, *Libanius's Progymnasmata*, xvii–xxv; Foerster and Münscher, "Libanios," 2485–551.

tinople, Nicomedia, and, finally, Antioch. Among his famous students were John Chrysostom, Theodore of Mopsuestia, and most likely Basil and Gregory of Nazianzus.

Libanius' *progymnasmata* is the most extensive collection of exercises that survive from antiquity, with a total of 144 exercises. Libanius includes exercises on fable, narration, anecdote, maxim, refutation and confirmation, common topics, encomion and invective, comparison, speech in character, description, thesis, and introduction of a law, but the number of exercises of each topic is not balanced. For instance, he includes only one exercise on the introduction of a law but forty-one on narration. Libanius' work is particularly valuable in that it shows us what the exercises actually looked like. For example, while Theon provides important information about prosopopoeia (i.e., speech in character)—what it is, examples of types of prosopopoeia, crucial components of prosopopoeia—Libanius shows us prosopopoeia in action. Theon's examples of prosopopoeia only provide the questions that prompt the exercise (e.g., "What words would a man say to his wife when leaving on a journey? Or a general to his soldiers in time of danger?" (*Prog.* 115 [Kennedy, 47]). Libanius, however, provides both the prompt ("What words would a eunuch say when he falls in love?") and a paragraph-long answer to the prompt (*Prog.* "Speech in Character 26" [Gibson 421–23]).

Remains from Egypt

Though much less systematized than Libanius, we also have pieces of teachers' handbooks and pupils' exercises preserved on papyri, ostraca, tablets, parchment, and private letters found in Egypt. In contrast to the elite literary sources that have often been the sole source of information on ancient education, these works provide evidence from the lower strata of society.[51] Extensive "sub-elite" sources are not plentiful outside of Egypt, but since recent studies have shown that "Egypt was remarkably similar to other Eastern provinces,"[52] the educational materials found there can be used as a window into the education practices of the larger Mediterranean world.

---

51. Morgan, *Literate Education*, 45–46.

52. Cribiore, *Gymnastics of the Mind*, 6, 247. Cf. Morgan's defense of Egypt as accurately representing education in the larger Greco-Roman world in Morgan, *Literate Education*, 44–46.

Of the 410 school texts surviving from Egypt, only nineteen are early rhetorical exercises.[53] Instead most contain elementary exercises like the alphabet and word lists or entailed copying or reciting gnomic sayings. The difference in numbers between elementary texts and texts containing rhetorical exercises is expected, however, since far more students received elementary education than intermediate or advanced. Papyri with rhetorical exercises survived in Upper Egypt, Arsiniote, Karanis, Soknopaious Nesos, Oxyrhynchus, Hermopolis, and Thebes from the third century BCE through the Byzantine period (though more than half are prior to the third century CE).[54] The diversity of rhetorical exercises preserved reflects the descriptions of the exercises in Theon, Ps.-Hermogenes, Aphthonius, and Nicolaus.[55] Of interest to this study is the preservation of several paraphrases of ancient literary texts, which I discuss below. These paraphrases offer us the ability to compare what theorists or educators like Quintilian and Theon say about paraphrase with what actual paraphrases of texts looked like in practice. First, however, we need to survey the rhetorical handbooks relevant to this study.

The Rhetorical Handbooks

Another set of sources for this study are the Greek and Latin rhetorical handbooks.[56] Hundreds of rhetorical handbooks were written in antiqui-

---

53. Morgan says, "None of the rhetorical exercises on papyrus can be classified as belonging to a more advanced level than that covered in the *progymnasmata* by myth or story or in Quintilian by paraphrases of Aesop, *sententiae*, *chriae*, and *ethologiae*. Most of them are paraphrases, more or less elaborate, of literary texts." See Morgan, *Literate Education*, 203.

54. For figures on the geographical, chronological, and numerical distribution of the over 400 schooltext papyri, see ibid., 53–67. Morgan discusses the rhetorical exercises specifically on 56–57 and 61. See also Table 10 (306–7) on what texts come from what cities at what time.

55. Ibid., 70–71.

56. Aune expresses concerns over the "tendency to use Latin rhetorical handbooks from the Western Empire, particularly Quintilian, as tools for analyzing Greek compositions written in the Eastern Empire (i.e., the letters of Paul), because they are from the first century CE, assuming that Greek and Latin rhetoric must be essentially identical." While this concern is worth considering, Mitchell's response eases this concern. She points to "the remarkable stability of Hellenistic rhetoric through into the Byzantine period, the well-known and easily documented dependence of the Latin rhetorical handbooks on Greek exemplars, and the extent to which a figure like Cicero himself traveled to the east and hence was not an isolated figure on the Italian

ty, but only a handful survive today.⁵⁷ These handbooks provided instruction on the different facets of rhetoric—invention, arrangement, style, memory, and delivery—and were used primarily for training orators.⁵⁸ Kennedy notes, however, that ancient critics like Demetrius, Dionysius of Halicarnassus, and Longinus also used the handbooks as a basis for analyzing other forms of discourse.⁵⁹

Aristotle

One of the first systematic treatments of rhetoric was Aristotle's *Rhetorica*, which he wrote from Athens sometime around 330 BCE. In books 1 and 2, Aristotle discusses thought (διάνοια) (later known as invention [εὕρεσις]), and in book 3 he discusses style (λέξις), arrangement (τάξις), and delivery (ὑπόκρισις). Later rhetorical theorists systematized these four items (along with memory) into what became the standard five stages of rhetoric.⁶⁰ Relevant to this study is Aristotle's discussion of "inartificial proofs" (πίστεις ἄτεχνοι), and witnesses in particular (*Rhet.* 1.2.2; 1.15.15–17 [Freese, LCL]), which fall under the invention stage.

Cicero

One of antiquity's most prolific Latin writers was Cicero, who was active in the first century BCE. Several of his works provide information for this study: *De inventione, De oratore,* and *Topica*.⁶¹ Cicero describes *De inventione* as a series of "unfinished and crude essays, which slipped out of the notebooks" sometime during his youth (*De or.* 1.2.5 [Sutton & Rackham, LCL]).⁶² The work focuses on rhetorical genre (deliberative, epideictic, and forensic) and the various components of a speech (ex-

---

peninsula." See Aune, *Westminster Dictionary*, 421; Mitchell, "Rhetorical Handbooks," 351, n. 8.

57. Kennedy, "Historical Survey of Rhetoric," 19.

58. Quintilian, for example, explains that the purpose of his work is "to educate the perfect orator" (*Inst.* 1.pref.9).

59. Kennedy, *New Testament Interpretation*, 13.

60. Kennedy, "Historical Survey of Rhetoric," 20.

61. For a more thorough introduction to these works, see Kennedy, *Art of Rhetoric*, 103–48, 205–29, 239–53; Eisenhut, *Einführung in die antik Rhetorik*, 61–66.

62. While he planned to discuss all five parts of rhetoric, Cicero completed only two books on invention.

ordium, narrative, partition, confirmation, refutation, peroration) (*Inv.* 1.19). Later in life (56 BCE.), Cicero wrote *De oratore*, which he viewed as a "more polished and compete" work on the topics he had treated earlier in *De inventione* (*De or.* 1.2.5). *De oratore* takes the form of a discussion on the ideal orator among Crassus (whom Cicero identifies as himself), Antonius, Scaevola, and Caesar Strabo. Finally, Cicero wrote *Topica* in an attempt to explain Aristotle's *Topica*.[63] The work treats not only the topics of arguments, but also testimony, the types of rhetoric, and the divisions of a speech. For this study, these works supply information on refutation, confirmation, paraphrase, and divine testimony.

Rhetorica ad Herennium

A work that resembles *De inventione* in many ways is *Rhetorica ad Herennium*.[64] This work was erroneously attributed to Cicero until the late fifteenth century because of its similarities to *De inventione*, which predates *Rhetorica ad Herennium* (86–82 CE) by only a few years. This handbook explicates the five stages of rhetoric (invention, arrangement, style, memory, and delivery), and is useful here because of its discussion on how to refute and confirm charges.

Quintilian

Of prime importance to this study is Quintilian's *Institutio oratoria*—the longest extant Latin writing on rhetoric, dubbed by Fuhrmann "the most important document of literary classicism in Rome."[65] The twelve books comprising *Institutio oratoria* describe the ideal training of an orator from childhood through his career. Quintilian directly relied on Cicero and several other classic rhetoricians, equipping him to include histori-

---

63. Scholars point out, however, that the illustrations and examples hardly resemble Aristotle's work. For a fuller treatment, see Hubbell's discussion in Cicero, *Topica*, 377–78.

64. For a comparison of the methodologies of these two works, see Fuhrmann, *Das systematische Lehrbuch*, 41–69, esp. 47–54, 61–67. On the similarities between the works see Gaines, "Roman Rhetorical Handbooks," 163–80; Kennedy, *Art of Rhetoric*, 126–38.

65. Fuhrmann, *Die antike Rhetorik*, 71 (translation mine). For an introduction to Quintilian and *Institutio oratoria*, see Murphy and Meador, "Quintilian's Educational and Rhetorical Theory," 179–81.

cal surveys of many of the subjects he discusses (e.g., *Inst.* 2.14.4; 2.15.5; 6.2.32). Quintilian discusses each of the techniques that form the basis of this study—refutation and confirmation, rhetorical figures, synkrisis, narration, and paraphrase.

Other Works

Finally, though they are not rhetorical handbooks, Suetonius' *De grammaticis*, Pliny the Younger's epistle to Fuscus Salinator, and Plutarch's *Parallel Lives* provide supplementary information for this study. All three date near the turn of the first century CE; the former two were written in Latin, and the latter in Greek. *De grammaticis* was part of a larger work called *De viris illustribus*, only parts of which survive. Suetonius, a Roman biographer, introduces the subject of grammar and explains what teachers taught certain subjects and exercises, including paraphrase. Pliny, a senator, praetor, and consul who had studied rhetoric under Quintilian, published several books of his letters. His letter to Fuscus Salinator tells us about the practice of paraphrase. Finally, Plutarch's *Parallel Lives* provides us with a classic example of synkrisis.

The Exercises and Techniques

Before we turn to the discussion of the exercises in the relevant sources, a note about my treatment of these exercises is in order. The *progymnasmata* writers and the rhetorical theorists view refutation and confirmation differently enough (i.e., the former treat them as an exercise; the latter as a division of a speech) to merit organizing that section around the sources—first what the *progymnasmata* say about refutation and confirmation, then what the theorists say about them. However, there is enough uniformity within each of the subgroups of sources (i.e., the *progymnasmata* and the theorists) to warrant a topical treatment of the techniques within each subgroup.

In contrast to refutation and confirmation, however, the comments on synkrisis, narration, and paraphrase are quite similar between the two groups.[66] Because of the overlap between the *progymnasmata* and

---

66. This is despite the fact that in the *progymnasmata* narration refers to exercises in writing narratives while in the handbook tradition it usually refers to one part of a speech (the *narratio*). Despite these differences, the comments on them are remarkably

the handbooks on these techniques (e.g., both discuss the same narrative virtues), it seems best to organize these sections topically (e.g., what paraphrase is, the different types of paraphrase) rather than by author. Of course, this organization is susceptible to the criticism of ignoring the differences in language and date of the individual authors.[67] However, despite this potential criticism, this organization scheme is the most logical and efficient one, as it avoids repetition of material and provides the reader with a picture of each technique rather than a picture of each author. The reader can rest assured that this presentation represents a synthesis of the material that was researched author by author, and attempts to respect the distinctions between the authors, even if it does not treat the authors one by one.

Refutation and Confirmation

The first exercises or techniques under consideration here are refutation (ἀνασκευή; *refutatio* or *reprehensio*) and confirmation (κατασκευή; *confirmatio* or *probatio*).[68] All of the extant *progymnasmata* discuss refutation and confirmation as exercises for students. In addition to functioning as exercises, refutation and confirmation were also one of the divisions of a speech, sometimes earning their own division and sometimes treated as a subdivision of the *argumentio* (πίστις).[69] Here we are more interested in how one would refute or confirm an argument or a charge (be it in an

---

similar. Both the *progymnasmata* and the handbooks view paraphrase as an exercise. The *progymnasmata* say almost nothing about rhetorical figures, so the organization of that section is not an issue.

67. See, for example, Aune's list of several problems that can arise when using the rhetorical handbooks for NT interpretation. He points out that some have "the tendency to read the extant rhetorical theorists synchronically, without due regard for development over the centuries." See Aune, *Westminster Dictionary*, 421. For a response to these potential abuses, see Mitchell, "Rhetorical Handbooks," 350–52.

68. See Martin, *Antike Rhetorik*, 124, on the different titles.

69. Rhetorical theorists did not agree on how exactly to divide the parts of a speech, and the parts of a speech often depended on what genre of speech one was giving (i.e., epideictic, forensic, or deliberative). For a summary of how different theorists divided a speech, see ibid., 124–25; Lausberg, *Handbook of Literary Rhetoric*, §262. N.B. that Quintilian refers to the *confirmatio* as the *probatio* (translated by Russell as "proof"; *Inst.* 3.9.1), while Cicero refers to the *refutatio* as the *reprehensio* (translated by Hubbell as "confirmation"; *Inv.* 1.19). Cf. ibid., §430.

exercise or in a speech) than in where in a speech a refutation or confirmation should go or if either constituted their own division.

We will first look at the exercises on refutation and confirmation in the *progymnasmata*. Ps.-Hermogenes defines refutation (ἀνασκευή) as "an overturning of something that has been proposed," and confirmation (κατασκευή) as the opposite (*Prog.* 11 [Kennedy, 79]); cf. Aphthonius, *Prog.* 27). Several of the writers agree that one should refute or confirm something that is in doubt instead of spending time on matters that are clearly true or clearly false (Ps.-Hermogenes, *Prog.* 11; Aphthonius, *Prog.* 27; Nicolaus, *Prog.* 29). Ps.-Hermogenes and Nicolaus treat refutation and confirmation together, Aphthonius and Libanius treat them separately (though back to back), and Theon treats them not as their own exercise, but as a skill developed across different exercises—narrative, theses, fables, etc.[70] This integration witnessed by Theon indicates that a student would have to be well-versed in both refutation and confirmation in order to complete the requirements of secondary education, and it reveals that there was a certain amount of adaptability in the practices of refutation and confirmation. Here I treat refutation and confirmation together because of how closely related they are.[71]

Theon lists several headings (κεφάλαια) or topics (τόπων)[72] from which a student could refute something or someone: the unclear, the impossible, the not-at-all natural, the incredible, the inappropriate, the unbeneficial, the deficient, the false, the inexpedient, the useless, the shameful, the unnecessary, the contradictory, the unjust, the unworthy, the implausible, the redundant, the unfamiliar, the inconsistent, and the

---

70. For more on refutation and confirmation in each of these exercises in Theon, see fables (*Prog.* 74, 76–78), narratives (*Prog.* 93–96), chreia (*Prog.* 104), theses (*Prog.* 120–25), and law (*Prog.* 129–30). Although Kennedy includes the most extensive discussion on refutation and confirmation under Theon's exercise of narrative, some manuscripts of Theon and all the other extant *progymnasmata* (i.e., those of Ps.-Hermogenes, Aphthonius, Nicolaus, and Libanius) treat them as their own exercise (discussed above). Ps.-Hermogenes treats them as their own exercise and in his discussion of thesis. Whether these exercises received their own chapter or were a part of the narrative section does not impact this study.

71. E.g., Theon lists ways to refute a fable, then says, "one should confirm in the opposite way" (κατασκευαστέον δὲ ἐκ τῶν ἐναντίων) (Theon, *Prog.* 76 [Kennedy 26; Patillon 35]; cf. Theon, *Prog.* 95, 121; Ps.-Hermogenes, *Prog.* 11; Aphthonius, *Prog.* 30; Nicolaus, *Prog.* 33; Cicero, *Inv.* 1.42.78).

72. Theon uses both of these terms, sometimes in the same discussion (see, e.g., κεφάλαια in *Prog.* 121 [Patillon, 84] and τόπων in *Prog.* 122 [Patillon, 86]). Both of these references are in his discussion on how to confirm theses.

false.⁷³ One would confirm someone or something from the opposite of these headings—such as the possible, the appropriate, the reverent, the necessary, the honorable, and the profitable. While it is not necessary to list every heading for refutation and confirmation here, the overlap between the headings listed by various *progymnasmata* writers is notable. The differences in lists of headings suggests that their lists were not meant to be exhaustive.⁷⁴ These topics were valuable to students because they provided a flexible storehouse of ideas for analyzing and constructing arguments on a variety of subjects.⁷⁵

When refuting a narrative, Theon recommends students practice the "elements" of which all action consisted: person, action, place, time, manner, and cause (*Prog.* 94 [Kennedy, 41]; cf. Nicolaus, *Prog.* 30; Quintilian, *Inst.* 5.10.33–53). He demonstrates how a student could practice all of the elements using the heading "the incredible" in the story about Medea. Mentioning only a few here, one could "argu[e] from the person, that it is incredible that a mother would harm her children, . . . from the place, that she would not have killed them in Corinth where lived Jason, the father of the children; . . . from the manner, that she would have tried to escape notice and would not have used a sword, but poison, especially since she was a sorcerer" (*Prog.* 94 [Kennedy, 41]). Elsewhere, when discussing the confirmation of the thesis that a wise man should engage in politics, Theon recommends not using the elements, but rather utilizing as many headings as possible—that engaging in politics is possible, in accordance with nature, easy, appropriate, just, pleasing to the gods, sweet to the dead, necessary, honorable, profitable, safe, and the start of greater and more beautiful things (*Prog.* 123–24).⁷⁶ This latter exercise resembles the refutation and confirmation exercises in Libanius, which interacted with a thesis (e.g., "that the account of the wrath of Achilles is plausible" [*Prog.* "Confirmation 2" (Gibson, 127)]) using various topics or headings.⁷⁷

---

73. This list is a combination of the topics extracted from the exercises listed in note 70. For similar lists see Ps.-Hermogenes, *Prog.* 11; Aphthonius, *Prog.* 27–28, 30; Nicolaus, *Prog.* 30.

74. E.g., Ps.-Hermogenes (*Prog.* 11 [Kennedy, 79]) lists "the advantageous," while Theon does not.

75. Webb, "*Progymnasmata* as Practice," 312.

76. For a more complex example of choosing proper arguments in Quintilian, which is too long to recount here, see Quintilian, *Inst.* 5.10.109–18.

77. For more on refutation and confirmation in Libanius, see Schouler, *La tradition*

These sample exercises show the versatility and the creativity involved in the exercises of refutation and confirmation. The exercises could be short or long. At times students would practice developing one refutation in depth (e.g., the various ways to show how a narrative was incredible) and at others they would practice confirming or refuting something in as many ways as possible (e.g., using several topics to confirm that a wise man should engage in politics). Additionally, Theon advises that "a more advanced student should include in each of the topics just mentioned the evidence of famous men, poets and statesmen and philosophers ... [and] any histories that agree with what is being said" (*Prog.* 122 [Kennedy, 57]).[78] In other words, the more advanced students could supply material from outside sources to strengthen their case. Thus, the exercise could be adapted to the level of the student.

The rhetorical handbooks have much to say about refutation and confirmation as well, no doubt because they were viewed as indispensable parts of forensic speeches.[79] Only Quintilian mentions refutation and confirmation as exercises in the vein of the *progymnasmata*. Along with narratives, encomia, invectives, commonplaces, theses, and laws, Quintilian discusses refutation and confirmation as part of the exercises to be taught by the rhetor (*Inst.* 2.4.18–19).[80] Like Theon, Quintilian connects refutation and confirmation with narrative and suggests that the elements of action—time, place, person, etc.—are fruitful tools for refuting and confirming.

More common among the rhetorical handbooks, however, is a discussion of confirmation and refutation as part of the invention of an argument—usually an argument to be used in court. Of the handbooks surveyed here, Cicero offers the most helpful definitions of refutation and confirmation. He defines confirmation (*confirmatio*) as the part of a speech that "by marshalling arguments lends credit, authority, and support to our case" (*Inv.* 1.24.34 [Hubbell, LCL]). Refutation (*reprehensio*), in contrast, was the part of a speech "in which arguments are used to impair, disprove, or weaken the confirmation" (*Inv.* 1.42.78). The confirmations and the refutations, then, competed with one another and—similar to the exercises in the *progymnasmata*—drew upon similar topics (*loci*)

---

hellénique, 1:86–97.

    78. Cf. Aristotle, *Rhet.* 1.15.13–17, and Cicero, *Top.* 20.78, discussed below.

    79. Fuhrmann, *Die antike Rhetorik*, 89.

    80. Here Quintilian actually uses the Greek ἀνασκευή and κατασκευή.

for invention.⁸¹ Cicero explains, "[A]ny proposition can be attacked by the same methods of reasoning by which it can be supported.... Therefore the rules for the invention and embellishment of arguments may properly be transferred from what has been said before [i.e., on confirmation] to this part of the oration [i.e., the refutation]" (*Inv.* 1.42.78). Thus, the rhetorical theorists—like the writers of the *progymnasmata*—believed that refutation and confirmation were two sides of the same coin.⁸²

Quintilian lists several ways of countering a charge: "the defence advocate may deny, justify, seek to transfer the case, make excuses, plead for mercy, soften, extenuate, divert the charge, or scorn and ridicule it" (*Inst.* 5.13.3). Other forms of refutation include discrediting witnesses, questioning the legal procedure, and making the opponent's arguments seem "contradictory, irrelevant, unbelievable, superfluous, or favorable to our side rather than to the opponent's" (*Inst.* 5.13.7, 8, 17).⁸³ Another available option for refuting and confirming a charge was to appeal to previous judgments, either on similar cases or on the same case by a different ruler (*Rhet. Her.* 2.13.19; Cicero, *Inv.* 1.42.79; Quintilian, *Inst.* 5.2.2).

Lastly, we turn to the role of witnesses in refutation and confirmation. Aristotle divided proofs (πίστεις) into two types—artificial and inartificial—and was followed by later rhetorical theorists in this division.⁸⁴ Inartificial proofs (ἄτεχνοι) are "all those which have not been furnished by ourselves but were already in existence, such as witnesses, tortures, contracts, and the like," while artificial proofs (ἔντεχνοι) are those constructed by the orator—the speaker's character (ἦθος), appeal to the emotions (πάθος), and logical reasoning (λόγος) (*Rhet.* 1.2.2; cf. 1.15.1; Cicero, *De or.* 2.27.118).⁸⁵ Quintilian follows Aristotle in this classification and even mentions the "almost universal acceptance of Aristotle's primary

---

81. In his treatise on topics, Cicero explains that topics provided a system for inventing arguments, "so that we might come upon them by a rational system without wandering about" (*Top.* 1.2). He continues, "If we wish to track down some argument, we ought to know the places from which arguments are drawn" (*Top.* 2.7).

82. Cf. note 183 above.

83. For several more ways to refute or confirm an argument, see Cicero, *Inv.* 1.42.79–1.50.94. Cf. Martin, *Antike Rhetorik*, 126–29.

84. For a summary of what different theorists said about inartificial proofs, see ibid., 97–101. Artificial proofs are sometimes called technical proofs; inartificial proofs are sometimes called nontechnical proofs.

85. Though he does not call them artificial proofs, Cicero describes *ethos*, *pathos*, and *logos* similarly in *De or.* 2.27.115.

classification of Proofs" at the time of his writing (*Inst.* 5.1.1).[86] Quintilian also points out that "the major part of forensic disputes rests on these [i.e. the inartificial proofs]" (*Inst.* 5.1.2). Here we are most interested in the inartificial proofs—particularly the witnesses—because of the prominent role of witnesses in Luke's passion narrative and because of the forensic nature of Jesus' trial and death in Luke.[87]

Both Aristotle and Cicero treat witnesses (μάρτυς/*testis*) as a type of inartificial proof.[88] Aristotle distinguishes between two kinds of witnesses—ancient and recent. The former includes poets and persons of repute (e.g., Homer), interpreters of oracles, and proverbs. The latter includes "all well-known persons who have given a decision on any point" and those who could be at risk by the trial (e.g., if they are found to be perjurers) (*Rhet.* 1.15.15–16).[89] He also mentions that "witnesses from a distance" (οἱ δ' ἄπωθεν) are very trustworthy (πιστότατοι) (*Rhet.* 1.15.17). Those who share the risk of the trial are only valuable for establishing if something happened, not the quality of the act (i.e., if it was just), but witnesses from a distance are reliable even for establishing the quality of the act.

Cicero also distinguishes between two types of testimony—testimony from humans and testimony from the gods—both of which derived their authority from their virtue. For humans, virtuous people include those "endowed with genius, industry and learning and those whose life has been consistent and of approved goodness" (*Top.* 20.78). Also considered virtuous were those who hold public office and serve the state as well as orators, philosophers, poets, and historians. The gods, on the other hand, were virtuous by nature and thus constituted the most

---

86. He provides both the Greek and Latin terms for the two types of proofs: ἄτεχνοι = *inartificiales*; ἔντεχνοι = *artificiales*. Cf. Cicero, *De or.* 2.27.116; *Top.* 4.24; *Part. or.* 2.6.

87. Parsons points out that "there are some striking linguistic and conceptual similarities between Theon's comments [on refutation and confirmation] and Luke's stated purpose to provide Theophilus with 'confirmation' (ἀσφάλειαν, *asfaleian*, a term, along with its cognates, that also appears in Theon, ἀσφαλής—124.9; 126.21; ἀσφαλεία—122.8) of the 'things that have been fulfilled among us' (Luke 1:1–4)." See Parsons, *Luke: Storyteller*, 25–26.

88. Quintilian also treats witnesses as a type of proof (*Inst.* 5.7), but his discussion has little to add to what Aristotle and Cicero say.

89. Aristotle gives the following as an example: "Eubulus, when attacking Chares in the law courts, made use of what Plato said against Archibus, namely, 'that the open confession of wickedness had increased in the city'" (*Rhet.* 1.15.15).

authoritative witness.⁹⁰ One could appeal to the testimony of the gods via oracles or things embodying the works of the gods (e.g., the heavens, the flight of birds, heavenly and earthly portents, the entrails of animals, and dreams) (*Top.* 20.77).⁹¹

In sum, refutation and confirmation held a prominent place in both the *progymnasmata* and the rhetorical handbooks. In the *progymnasmata*, the aim was to teach students how to overturn or strengthen an argument that had been proposed, whether in the form or a thesis, a law, a chreia, or something else. Students learned a versatile set of the topics or headings by which to refute or confirm an argument and could adapt this skill to various levels of difficulty. In the rhetorical handbooks, refutation and confirmation were discussed as the part of a forensic speech that either supported or impaired a case. Orators were encouraged to draw inspiration from the topics of invention—like those they had learned in the *progymnasmata*—but they were also taught to counter charges in other creative ways: by seeking to transfer a case, by appealing to previous judgments, and by producing witnesses, be they human or divine, ancient or modern.

Rhetorical Figures

The *progymnasmata* writers give little attention to rhetorical figures,⁹² but figures receive significant attention in the rhetorical handbooks under the third component of speechmaking: style (λέξις/*elocution*).⁹³ After inventing and arranging the argument, a rhetorician would focus on the style of the work, which entailed "the adaption of suitable words and sentences to the matter devised" (*Rhet. Her.* 1.2.3 [Caplan, LCL]). This phase

---

90. McConnell, *Topos of Divine Testimony*, 49–50. Cf. *Top.* 19.73; 20.76.

91. In *Inst.* 5.7.35, Quintilian also mentions divine testimony as a type of witness; however, his comments do not add anything to what Cicero said.

92. One of the few figures mentioned in the *progymnasmata* is asyndeton. Theon describes it as a way of narrating facts, but does not discuss its function (*Prog.* 90). This example from Theon suggests, however, that rhetorical figures did play some role in intermediate education, even if not to the same degree as they did in later rhetorical training. Even students who did not advance past the intermediate stage would have had some introduction to rhetorical figures.

93. For more on style in ancient rhetoric, see Lausberg, *Handbook of Literary Rhetoric*, §538–1054; Martin, *Antike Rhetorik*, 145–345; Rowe, "Style," 121–57.

in the process was followed by memory and delivery.[94] Under the division of style, the rhetoricians usually discussed figures in relation to ornamentation or adornment, and they divided the figures into three subtypes: tropes, figures of speech, and figures of thought.[95] Since grammarians and philosophers debated which figures went into which subtypes[96] and since the function of a figure depends on its context rather than its classification, I will not go into the distinction between the subtypes and will simply refer to all three generically as figures.[97]

The ancient rhetoricians identified a host of rhetorical figures. A discussion of all of these figures is unnecessary, since only a handful of figures appear in Luke's passion narrative.[98] Important to this study, instead, is the function of ornamentation, which speaks to the function of rhetorical figures. For Quintilian, ornamentation is never simply for the sake ornamentation: "True beauty," he explains, "is never separated from usefulness" (*Inst.* 8.3.11). Ornamentation is useful and important because "[t]hose who find it a pleasure to listen are both more attentive and readier to believe" (*Inst.* 8.3.5). Thus, rhetorical figures—one way of ornamenting a speech or writing—help listeners pay attention and make them favorably disposed to a speaker or an argument.

The ancient rhetoricians rarely describe the function of individual figures, though they do on a few occasions. One such occasion is in the discussion of *apostrophe* in two different rhetorical handbooks. The

---

94. On the divisions see Aristotle, *Rhet.* 3.1; *Rhet. Her.* 1.2.3; Cicero, *De or.* 1.31.142–43; Quintilian, *Inst.* 3.3.1.

95. Reich describes the three subtypes of figures as follows: "Tropes, which deal with single words, figures of speech, which deal with the artful ordering of multiple words, and figures of thought which deal with the artful ordering of thoughts." See Reich, *Figuring Jesus*, 4. Cf. Quintilian, *Inst.* 8.6.1; *Rhet. Her.* 4.13.18.

96. Described in Quintilian, *Inst.* 8.6.1.

97. I follow Reich in this regard.

98. For the ancient discussion of figures, see *Rhet. Her.* 4; Quintilian, *Inst.* 8–9. For modern discussion of ancient figures, see Reich, *Figuring Jesus*, 8–18; Rowe, "Style," 124–50; Martin, *Antike Rhetorik*, 270–315; Lausberg, *Handbook of Literary Rhetoric*, §552–910. Reich combines the figures from these sources into an alphabetized list with primary source references, definitions, and examples. Rowe also provides lists of the figures with references, definitions, and examples, and he attempts to classify them. Martin provides definitions and references and organizes them into tropes (die Tropen) and figures (die Figuren), the latter of which is divided into figures of thought (die Sinnfiguren) and figures of speech (die Wortfiguren). Lausberg—the most exhaustive of these works—uses the same categories as Martin and provides definitions and references.

author of *Rhetorica ad Herennium* explains that *apostrophe* "is the figure which expresses grief or indignation by means of an address to some man or city or place or object" (4.15.22), while Quintilian's example of *apostrophe* conveys praise and admiration (9.3.24-25). These differing descriptions lead Reich to conclude—rightly, I believe—that "the function of a figure must be based on context."[99] He then summarizes various functions of a rhetorical figure: the broadest function is emphasis, acting as a "pay attention here" sign; other functions include making speech pleasing to the ear, making it memorable or powerful, and inviting audience participation.[100]

In sum, rhetorical figures were viewed as a prime way to ornament a piece of writing or a speech and were used as a tool to increase the argument's persuasiveness. Such ornamentation helps the speaker or writer catch and keep the audience's attention, make the hearer disposed to the speaker, emphasize a specific point or make it more powerful, and invite the audience to participate.[101]

Synkrisis

Synkrisis (σύγκρισις; *comparatio*) is an exercise discussed in both the *progymnasmata* and the rhetorical handbooks, though the *progymnasmata* treat it more thoroughly. Theon defines synkrisis as "language setting the better or the worse side by side" (*Prog.* 112 [Kennedy, 52]; cf. Ps.-Hermogenes, *Prog.* 18; Aphthonius, *Prog.* 42; Nicolaus, *Prog.* 60). The *progymnasmata* writers agree that one could compare two or more persons, occasions, places, or concepts, among other things. Theon adds that one should only compare things that were not wholly different—i.e., comparison is best "where we are in doubt which should be preferred because of no evident superiority of one to another" (*Prog.* 113 [Kennedy, 53]).[102] At times one subject would prove superior while the other was

---

99. Reich, *Figuring Jesus*, 19. Cf. Kennedy's similar observation: "Figures in the abstract do not have single definable effects; the impact has to be determined from the context." Kennedy, *New Testament Interpretation*, 29.

100. Reich, *Figuring Jesus*, 19-20.

101. In chapters 3, 4, and 5 we will discuss more specifically the function of rhetorical figures that Reich has identified in Luke's Gospel.

102. On the differences between the *progymnasmata* writers on whether you should compare things that are dissimilar or only those that are similar, see Martin, "Philo's Use of Syncrisis," 274-77, complete with a lucid chart listing the various types

inferior, and at times the subjects would appear equal (Ps.-Hermogenes, *Prog.* 19; Nicolaus, *Prog.* 60).

Theon explains that synkrisis, or comparison, was used across the rhetorical genres (judicial, epideictic, deliberative) and thus, like the other exercises in the *progymnasmata,* was versatile and adaptable (*Prog.* 61). That all of the *progymnasmata* writers treat synkrisis immediately after encomion and invective suggests a relationship between the exercises, as do the comments of Ps.-Hermogenes, Aphthonius, and Quintilian. Ps.-Hermogenes recommends that a student use the encomiastic topics when composing a synkrisis (*Prog.* 19),[103] and Aphthonius even classifies synkrises as either a double encomion, a double invective, or an encomion/invective (*Prog.* 42; cf. Nicolaus, *Prog.* 59–60). Quintilian, who discusses synkrisis briefly under encomion and invective in his chapter on the *progymnasmata,* sees synkrisis as a type of encomion or invective that "doubles the material and handles not only the nature of virtues and vices but their degree" (*Inst.* 2.4.21). This relationship is important because it helps us understand the function of synkrisis—something that few of the *progymnasmata* writers spell out specifically. Typically they are more concerned with how to make comparisons than with the purpose of making them, likely because the exercises functioned as a foundation for all sorts of discourse. By virtue of the relationship between synkrisis and encomion and invective, we see that synkrisis was used as a tool for extolling or criticizing someone or something.

Because of its relation to encomion and invective, students derived topics for comparison from the topics used in encomion and invective.[104] These topics were commonly categorized as goods of the mind, goods of the body, and external goods (Theon, *Prog.* 109; cf. Ps.-Hermogenes,

---

of synkrises. Because we are only concerned with comparison of similar things in Luke's passion narrative (i.e., a double encomion of two people with similar virtues)—a comparison which all the writers support—this debate is not particularly important for this study.

103. Ps.-Hermogenes also notes the relationship between synkrisis and commonplace (*Prog.* 18 [Kennedy, 83]). Apparently "some authorities" saw synkrisis, commonplace, encomion, and invective as so related that they treated them together rather than as separate exercises. Nicolaus makes a similar observation (*Prog.* 59).

104. For more on the relation between the encomiastic topics and synkrisis, see Focke, "Synkrisis," 332–39; Martin, "Philo's Use of Syncrisis," 277–79. Focke (348–51) also discusses the relationship between synkrisis and historiography (e.g., the use of synkrisis by historians like Herodotus and Polybius). While this connection could be fruitful for the study of Luke-Acts, it is beyond the scope of this project.

Prog. 15–16; Aristotle, *Rhet.* 1.5.4; *Rhet. Her.* 3.6.10; Cicero, *De or.* 3.29.115).[105] The topics most relevant to this study include a good death (one of the topics of external goods) and virtues (ones of topics of goods of the minds).[106] Students were taught not just to discuss a person's virtues, but also the actions that resulted from them, such as "those done for others rather than ourselves; and done for the sake of the honorable, not the expedient or the pleasant" (Theon, *Prog.* 110 [Kennedy, 51]). Theon explained two different ways that students could arrange these topics for comparison: "either we give an account separately of each of the things to be compared, or combine them in one account, judging one better than the other" (*Prog.* 115 [Kennedy, 55]).

Exercises in synkrisis took different forms. Both Nicolaus and Aphthonius compare Achilles and Hector, but they do so differently. Nicolaus provides a one-line comparison: "The man who fled in front was good, but by far a better man pursued" (*Prog.* 61 [Kennedy, 163]) to show that one subject seems greater when compared to something great. Aphthonius provides a more extended example—comparing the various virtues of Achilles to the virtues of Hector—and in doing so he explains the larger function of the comparison. He explains, "In seeking to compare virtue to virtue, I shall measure the son of Peleus against Hector; for virtues are to be honored for themselves, but *when measured against each other they become more worthy of imitation*" (*Prog.* 43 [Kennedy, 114]; emphasis added). He then goes on to compare their place of birth, ancestry, training, prestige in war, and death.

As with the other exercises, the *progymnasmata* writers envisioned students using synkrisis for their larger rhetorical goals.[107] One famous example of synkrisis in the ancient world is Plutarch's *Parallel Lives*, written near the end of the first or the beginning of the second century CE. The work is a series of biographies that pairs a famous Greek figure with a famous Roman figure. It is a classic example of synkrisis and is particularly important because Plutarch intimates the goal of his comparison, which is worth quoting in full:

---

105. For other ancient authors' attestation to this division, see Butts, "The 'Progymnasmata' of Theon," 481, n. 7. Cf. Martin, "Philo's Use of Syncrisis," 277.

106. For a discussion of the other topics, see Martin's argument that Luke used the topics from the *progymnasmata* as a compositional template for his Gospel: Martin, "Progymnasmatic Topic Lists," 18–41.

107. Focke traces the origin of Plutarch's comparisons in *Parallel Lives* back to the *progymnasmata* exercises on synkrisis. See Focke, "Synkrisis," 357–58.

I began the writing of my "Lives" for the sake of others, but I find that I am continuing the work and delighting in it now for my own sake also, using history as a mirror and *endeavouring in a manner to fashion and adorn my life in conformity with the virtues therein depicted*. For the result is like nothing else than daily living and associating together, when I receive and welcome each subject of my history in turn as my guest, so to speak, and observe carefully "how large he was and of what mien," and select from his career what is most important and most beautiful to know. "Ah oh! what greater joy than this canst thou obtain," and more *efficacious for moral improvement*? . . . But in my own case, the study of history and the familiarity with it which my writing produces, enables me, since I always cherish in my soul the records of the noblest and most estimable characters, *to repel and put far from me whatever base, malicious, or ignoble suggestion my enforced associations may intrude upon me, calmly and dispassionately turning my thoughts away from them to the fairest of my examples*." (*Aem.* 1–3 [Perrin, LCL]; emphasis added)

Elsewhere Plutarch explains the value of reading about virtuous people: "Virtuous action so disposes a man that he no sooner admires the works of virtue than he strives to emulate those who wrought them" (*Per.* 2 [Perrin, LCL]).[108] These comparisons, then, aim not only at educating the readers on the subject, but also at producing moral virtue in the writer and readers.[109] This explanation is consistent with the explanation of purpose that Aphthonius offered for his synkrisis of Hector and Achilles—to provide models for imitation.

One further characteristic of Plutarch's *synkrisis* is significant for this study: the priority of character development over strict chronology. Andrew Clark notes that "for Plutarch chronology and development over time are of secondary importance."[110] Since the primary aim is presenting a figure's character, these other considerations become secondary. Clark adds,

---

108. Clark, *Parallel Lives*, 88–89. Clark points to one of Plutarch's statements about the value of putting figures in parallel: "Actually it is not possible to learn better the similarity and the difference between the virtues of men and women from any other source than by putting lives beside lives and actions beside actions" (Plutarch, *Mulier. virt.* 243 B, C [Babbit, LCL]).

109. Wardman, *Plutarch's Lives*, 26; Duff, *Plutarch's Lives*, 309; Frazier, *Histoire et morale*, 173–273.

110. Clark, *Parallel Lives*, 83.

Plutarch deliberately rearranged material from his sources to make it illustrate the overriding themes or morals he wished to emphasize. This involved the re-shaping of whole episodes, the moving of material to a different context, the ready simplification of complex detail, the use of exaggeration to sharpen contrasts, the fabrication of details, and the borrowing of characteristics from familiar stereotypes.[111]

In sum, synkrisis was a common rhetorical technique, practiced in intermediate education and employed in classic literary works like Plutarch's *Parallel Lives*. It entailed comparing two or more persons or things to show superiority, inferiority, or equality and drew from the topics of encomia and invectives to accomplish this purpose. The *progymnasmata* writers allowed for flexibility in arrangement so that students could adapt the exercise to their own needs, one of which was to promote virtue in the readers by providing models for imitation, as attested both by extant exercises (e.g., Aphthonius) and extant literary works that employed synkrisis (e.g., Plutarch's *Parallel Lives*). Finally, synkrisis allowed for the subordination of chronology for the sake of emphasizing a particular theme or moral.

Narration

Next we will look at techniques used in composing a narrative. This entails defining narrative, looking at the components of a narrative, and examining the agreed-upon virtues of narration. Theon defines narrative (διήγημα[112]) as "language descriptive of things that have happened or as though they have happened" (*Prog.* 78 [Kennedy, 28; Patillon, 38]; cf. Ps.-Hermogenes, *Prog.* 4; Aphthonius, *Prog.* 22; Nicolaus, *Prog.* 11; *Rhet. Her.* 1.3.4; Cicero, *Inv.* 1.29.27). To this definition Quintilian adds that the

111. Ibid., 99.

112. Parsons notes, "Theon appears to use the terms διήγησις (*diēgēsis*) and διήγημα (*diēgēma*) interchangeably (see 5.2–4), while other writers, such as Hermogenes (4.9–12), distinguish between the two arguing that διήγημα (*diēgēma*) refers to the elementary exercise and διήγησις (*diēgēsis*) is equivalent to the 'statement of facts' portion of a speech (the *narratio*). To further complicate matters, when Theon does seem to distinguish between the two terms it is in direct opposition to Hermogenes' distinction, e.g., for Theon διήγησις (*diēgēsis*) refers to the elementary exercise of story-writing and διήγημα (*diēgēma*) is the 'statement of facts' part of a speech (see 60.5; Patillon, 2)." Parsons, *Luke: Storyteller*, 22, n. 47. Cf. Robbins, "Narrative in Ancient Rhetoric," 371, who also argues that Theon uses the terms interchangeably.

narrative is "designed to be persuasive" (*Inst.* 4.2.31); its purpose is not simply to acquaint the hearer with the facts, "but rather to ensure that he agrees with us" (*Inst.* 4.2.21).[113] A sufficient narrative contains each of the following: person, action, place, time, manner of action, and the cause of the events. Lacking even one of these makes the narrative deficient or incomplete (Theon, *Prog.* 79; Aphthonius, *Prog.* 22; Nicolaus, *Prog.* 13).

A successful writer is attentive to the virtues of narration, which were somewhat standardized across the rhetorical tradition. Theon (*Prog.* 79), Aphthonius (*Prog.* 22), and Nicolaus (*Prog.* 14) all list σαφήνεια (clarity), συντομία (conciseness or brevity), and πιθανότης (credibility or plausibility) as virtues of narration. Quintilian advocates for similar virtues in the narrative section of a court speech: it ought to be "lucid (*lucidus*), brief (*brevis*), and plausible (*very similis*)" (*Inst.* 4.2.31; cf. *Rhet. Alex.* 30; *Rhet. Her.* 1.9.14; Cicero, *Inv.* 1.28). Aphthonius adds Hellenism (i.e., purity of Greek), and Nicolaus notes that some add charm and grandeur. We will look at the most popular three—clarity, conciseness, and plausibility—in more detail.

A narrative's clarity stems from the order of the events and the language the author uses. Theon describes clarity as it pertains to the order of the narrative by using Thucydides' *Peloponnesian Wars* as an example:

> It [the narration] becomes clear . . . whenever one does not narrate many things together but brings each to its completion. Some critics blame Thucydides for not doing this. Since he divides his history into summers and winters he is often forced to switch to another event that happened in the same season before the whole of an incident is ended; then he narrates the rest of the subject as done during another winter or summer. Sometimes he needed even three or four seasons until he came to the end of the subject that he was describing from the beginning, always taking up again the events that happened in each season as begun in the first account, so that, taken together, the facts are unclear and hard to remember. (*Prog.* 80 [Kennedy, 30])

---

113. Quintilian has in mind the narration that formed one part of a court speech. While Luke's passion narrative is something other than part of a court speech, its juridical nature—particularly with its alternating refutations and confirmations (see chapters 3 and 4)—suggests that Quintilian's instructions on the narration in a court speech can provide helpful information. Cf. Robbins, "Narrative in Ancient Rhetoric," 368, who reminds us that "[e]mbedded in the narrational texture of each story [i.e., the Gospels], however, is an argumentative texture."

Thus, according to Theon, one should keep related events together for the sake of clarity, even at the expense of other organizational structures that might be in place. Dionysius of Halicarnassus also criticizes Thucydides for the same reason. After describing Thucydides' organization by summers and winters, Dionysius explains that the readers cannot follow the sequence of events; the readers gets confused because events that belong together are separated and thus cannot easily be recalled (*De Thuc.* 9).[114] In addition to confusing the time or order of events, Theon also notes that narrating the same thing twice also confuses hearers and thus ought to be avoided (*Prog.* 80). Parsons explains how Theon seems to understand order: "By order in the narrative, Theon does not imply any kind of strict historical or chronological order. Theon does seem to distinguish between unintentionally 'mixing up . . . the order of the events' . . . , which he says 'one must guard against' . . . and the elementary exercise of intentionally 'changing the order of the events' (5.299, Patillon, 50), of which he approves."[115] Quintilian also approved of "narrat[ing] events in the order that is most advantageous," even if that meant not following a chronological order (*Inst.* 4.2.83).[116] Finally, poetic and coined words, tropes, archaisms, foreign words, and homonyms decrease clarity (Theon, *Prog.* 81; cf. Quintilian, *Inst.* 1.5.1–8).

The second virtue of narration, conciseness or brevity, concerns not just length, but quality. Theon explains, "Conciseness is language signifying the most important of the facts, not adding what is not necessary nor omitting what is necessary to the subject and the style" (*Prog.* 83 [Kennedy, 32]). Quintilian's definition of brevity is similar: "Brevity however is not 'saying less than one ought to say,' but 'not saying more'" (*Inst.* 4.2.43). It entails "prun[ing] away everything which can be removed without in any way damaging either the process of judgment or our own interest" (*Inst.* 4.2.40). Quintilian warns against being too brief, however, as it risks both leaving out essential information and being inelegant (*Inst.* 4.2.44, 46). Conciseness goes hand in hand with clarity, as it "arises from the contents when we do not combine many things together [and when we] do not mix them in with other things" (Theon, *Prog.* 83 [Kennedy, 32]).

---

114. Moessner, "Appeal and Power," 109–10; Meijering, *Literary and Rhetorical Theories*, 139–40.

115. Parsons, *Luke: Storyteller*, 44.

116. For a fuller discussion of rhetorical order (καθεξῆς), particularly as it relates to Luke, see Moessner, "Meaning of καθεξῆς," 1513–28; Parsons, *Luke: Storyteller*, 45–57; Gorman, "Crank or Creative Genius?," 62–81.

Theon explains that the nature of the events being narrated and the effect those events would have on hearers should determine how briefly to narrate something: events that would distress the hearers, like death, should be narrated briefly, while "pleasant-sounding things" do not require such brevity (*Prog.* 80 [Kennedy, 29]).[117]

Theon views the third virtue, plausibility, as a narrative's "most special feature" (*Prog.* 79 [Kennedy, 29]). Making a narrative plausible entails "employ[ing] styles that are natural for the speakers and suitable for the subjects and the places and the occasions" (*Prog.* 84 [Kennedy, 33]). He also notes that plausibility includes "guard[ing] against confusing the times and order of events" (*Prog.* 80 [Kennedy, 30]), which shows that clarity and plausibility go hand in hand. For Quintilian, a narrative is credible if authors do four things: "(1) if we consult our own hearts first and so do not say anything contrary to what is natural; (2) if we give motives and reasons before events (not *all* events, but those on which the inquiry turns); (3) if we set up characters appropriate to the actions which we wish to be believed . . . , [and] (4) if we also specify places, times, and the like" (*Inst.* 4.2.52).

In sum, a successful narrative describes things that happened or as though they happened with the goal of persuading the hearer to agree with the author. The best narratives contain person, action, place, time, manner of action, and the cause of events; they aim for clarity, brevity, and plausibility, which relate to the order of the events, the language the author uses, and the contents that the author chooses to include.

Paraphrase

Theon describes paraphrase as the practice of "changing the form of expression while keeping the thoughts" (*Prog.* 107P [Kennedy, 70]). Paraphrase included subtracting words or thoughts, altering syntax,[118] adding words or thoughts, substituting words, or, more often than not, a combination of these things (*Prog.* 107P).

---

117. Theon provides examples of the *Iliad* and the *Odyssey* to demonstrate his point.

118. According to Kennedy, *Progymnasmata*, 70, n. 208, syntactical paraphrase entailed keeping the same words but rearranging their order and thus was more akin to rearrangement than actual changes in syntax. Cf. Lausberg, *Handbook of Literary Rhetoric*, §1099–1103.

Quintilian's understanding is similar to that of Theon's. When discussing the things taught by the grammar teacher (*grammaticus*) to students who were too young for the rhetor, Quintilian describes paraphrase as follows: "Verse they should first break up, then interpret in different words, then make a bolder paraphrase, in which they are allowed to abbreviate and embellish some parts, so long as the poet's meaning is preserved" (*Inst*.1.9.2). Elsewhere, Quintilian discusses paraphrase among "the best written exercises for those who are developing their facility" (*Inst*. 10.5.1).[119] Here he explains that paraphrase entails adding force to the thoughts, supplying information that was left out, and deleting redundancies (*Inst*. 10.5.4). Thus, to paraphrase Theon and Quintilian, the ancient exercise of paraphrase entailed addition, subtraction, substitution, and/or syntactical variation of an original text while preserving the thoughts of the original.

Paraphrase could be either a simple exercise practiced at the beginning of intermediate education or a complex exercise practiced by those who were already accomplished orators.[120] At the end of his discussion

---

119. As the examples below show, Patillon is right in saying that paraphrase, "far from being a mechanical exercise, is challenging intellectual gymnastics that requires great mental agility." See Patillon and Bolognesi, *Aelius Théon: Progymnasmata*, cvii (translation mine).

120. Roberts distinguishes between the grammatical and rhetorical paraphrase. Characteristics of the former are that it is exegetical, a school exercise, and has "no stylistic pretensions." Examples of the grammatical paraphrase include Pack 2. 1172 and 1176, but we will not discuss these here. My discussion below of Archilochus' paraphrase of Homer mentioned by Theon suffices as a representative of this type. Roberts distinguishes between two types of rhetorical paraphrase, both of which had some degree of stylistic sophistication. First were school exercises, which either (a) entailed paraphrasing a single short passage in various ways using the *modi tractandi* (e.g., Sopater's Μεταποιήσεις) or (b) entailed paraphrasing a long passage only once with the motive of *aemulatio* (e.g., *Bodl. Gr. Inscr.* 3019, discussed below). The second type of rhetorical paraphrase was the literary paraphrase, which either (a) were exegetical in nature with a technical subject (e.g., Themistius, Eutecnius), or (b) were "artistic compositions intended for independent circulation" (e.g., the biblical epics, which are the object of Roberts' study). The exegetical type is exemplified by technical treatises that attempted to explain or interpret a work. They are of little interest here because they differ so significantly from the Gospels. While Roberts' classification can be helpful in some ways, it is more detailed and more systematic than is needed here, particularly since several of the types of paraphrase are irrelevant to this study. Furthermore, such classification is liable to make us forget that the boundaries between the types of paraphrase were fluid. See Roberts, *Biblical Epic and Rhetorical Paraphrase*, 39–60, especially the chart on 39.

In contrast, Butts distinguishes between only two types of paraphrase: "that which

of paraphrase, Theon summarizes the progression from shorter, simple paraphrases to longer, more complex ones: "Begin with the simplest thing, for example, with exercise of memory, then pass to paraphrasing some argument in a speech, then to paraphrasing some part of the speech, either the prooemion or narration. Thus our young men will gradually become capable of paraphrasing a whole speech, which is the result of perfected ability" (*Prog.* 110P [Kennedy, 71]). It is presumably this longer, more complex paraphrase that Quintilian has in mind when he says that paraphrase "is difficult even for the fully trained teachers; any pupil who handles it well will be capable of learning anything" (*Inst.* 1.9.3). Thus, paraphrase was an exercise that could be adapted to the level of the one practicing it, which may account for its popularity among ancient teachers and learners.[121] It will be helpful to look at examples of paraphrase at various points along the spectrum from elementary to advanced in order to understand the different types of paraphrase. We begin with an elementary example.

Theon recommends that teachers introduce the exercise on paraphrase "from the beginning [of when a student began the preliminary exercises]" (ἀπ' ἀρχῆς; *Prog.* 65 [Kennedy, 9; Patillon, 9]).[122] The type of paraphrase that a student would practice "from the beginning" likely entailed recasting a line or two from a poet in new words. Theon gives several examples of this type of paraphrase, one of which we will analyze here. Theon quotes the following from Homer and Archilochus and says that the latter is a paraphrase of the former (*Prog.* 62 [Kennedy, 6; Patillon, 5]):

---

occurred in the school of the grammarian which consisted of saying with different words exactly what one found in the text to be paraphrased and that which belonged to the school of rhetoric which consisted of artistically developing from another viewpoint merely the same thought in one's text." See Butts, "'Progymnasmata' of Theon," 18. Building off of Butts, I find it most helpful to view the types of paraphrase along a continuous spectrum from short and simple to long and complex.

121. As we will see, it is mentioned explicitly by Theon and Quintilian. Cicero, Pliny, and Suetonius, though not naming the exercise specifically, describe an exercise that sounds much like paraphrase. We also find several examples of paraphrase in the papyri from Egypt.

122. Suetonius mentions paraphrase as an exercise teachers would have their students practice so that "they might not turn over their pupils to the rhetoricians wholly ignorant and unprepared" (*Gramm.* 4). While this reference does not give us details about what paraphrase entailed, it does suggest that at some point it was viewed as an exercise that students should practice at an intermediate level before they studied with the rhetor.

Τοῖος <γὰρ> νόος ἐστὶν ἐπιχθονίων ἀνθρώπων,
Οἷον ἐπ' ἦμαρ ἄγῃσι πατὴρ ἀνδρῶν τε θεῶν τε

Such is the mind of men who live on earth
As the father of men and gods grants it for the day
(Homer, *Odyssey* 18.136–37)

―――

Τοῖος ἀνθρώποισι θυμὸς Γλαῦκε Λεπτίνεω πάϊ,
γίγνεται θνητοῖς, ὁκοῖον Ζεὺς ἐφ' ἡμέρην ἄγει

Such, Glaucus, son of Leptines, is the mind
Of mortal men as Zeus brings it for the day
(Archilochus, Frag. 131)

It will be helpful to tease out just what Archilochus did with Homer's lines. Archilochus begins with the exact same word as Homer (Τοῖος) but changes almost everything else in some way. First, Archilochus addresses the quotation to Glaucus, an address not included by Homer. Second, while Archilochus maintains the word ἄνθρωπος, he changes its case from genitive to dative and moves it forward in the sentence. Furthermore, he replaces Homer's νόος, ἐπιχθόνιος, and εἰμί with synonyms—θυμός, θνητός, and γίγνομαι—as well as providing the proper name Ζεύς for Homer's πατὴρ ἀνδρῶν τε θεῶν τε. Finally, Archilochus keeps the words of Homer's phrase ἐπ' ἦμαρ ἄγῃσι in the same order (ἐφ' ἡμέρην ἄγει), but he moves the phrase to the end of the quotation, changes the mood of ἄγω from subjunctive to indicative, and switches the ἦμαρ—the prevailing word used for "day" in Homer—to ἡμέρα.

It is not hard to see why Theon provides this as an example of paraphrase. It includes addition (e.g., addressing Glaucus), substitution (e.g., "Zeus" for "the father of men and gods"), and syntactical variation or rearrangement (e.g., moving ἄνθρωπος from the last word of the line to the second word of the line). Despite all these changes, the paraphrase preserves the thoughts of the original—namely, that the human mind is the way it is because Zeus grants it as such for the day. It also allows for the new work to retain some of the exact words and phrases from the original.

Although this example from Theon, among others,[123] would be considered small in scale since it was a paraphrase of only two lines of Hom-

---

123. Theon lists examples of Demosthenes and Aeschines paraphrasing two lines of Homer (*Prog.* 62–63). Elsewhere Theon describes Demosthenes' paraphrase of

er, Theon also mentions examples of paraphrase done on a larger scale. For example, Theon points out that Philistus "borrowed (μετενήνοχε) almost the whole account of the war with Athens from Thucydides" for his history of Sicily (*Prog.* 1.63 [Kennedy, 7]).[124] Unfortunately most of Philistus' work is lost, and the fragments that did survive are too small to enable us to see just what this paraphrase looked like. Nonetheless, this example proves that Theon had both large and small scale paraphrases in mind for his students; it also shows that Theon conceived of paraphrases of both prose and poetry.

A more helpful example of a longer and more advanced paraphrase comes to us from a tablet in Egypt—the *Bodleian Greek Inscription* 3019 from the third century CE.[125] This work is the longest paraphrase surviving from Egypt—it paraphrases the first twenty-one lines of the *Iliad* and results in a work that is three times as long as the portion being paraphrased.[126] Space prohibits an analysis as detailed as the one above from Theon, but several aspects of the paraphrase deserve mention. The author of the inscription expands Chryses' speech, transposes elements of the original either for emphasis or for "logical continuity,"[127] and elaborates stylistically on Homer's original through anaphora, *interpretatio*, a tricolon crescendo, parallelism, and period.[128] It walks the line between being

Thucydides: "Thucydides (1.142.1) said, 'in war, opportunities are not abiding,' while Demosthenes (4.37) paraphrased this, 'opportunities for action do not await our sloth and evasions'" (*Prog.* 108P [Kennedy, 70]). Butts explores the nature of these paraphrases. See Butts, "The 'Progymnasmata' of Theon," 132–35.

124. Butts notes that Theon's choice of μεταφέρω "seems to imply that Philistus used Thucydides' account *verbatim*, that he copied Thucydides. But judging from T[heon]'s later reference to Isocrates and Lysias . . . , it is doubtful that the relationship between Philistus and Thucydides was understood by T[heon] to be one characterized by *verbatim* citations. . . . If, however such were to be T[heon]'s understanding, such an appraisal of the work of Philistus would undoubtedly be unfair." See ibid., 132.

125. While other shorter paraphrases are extant, I am less interested in them for a few reasons: (1) the examples provided in Theon, like the Archilochus' paraphrase of Homer or Demosthenes' paraphrase of Thucydides, are very similar to one another. Those of a larger scale allow us to see the diversity of ways in which paraphrase was completed. (2) Luke's reworking of Mark's passion narrative is most akin to a "large scale" paraphrase, so those are of most interest here.

126. Because of the length, I will not reproduce the text here. Morgan, *Literate Education*, 205–6, reproduces the Greek text and English translation of the first half of *Bodl. Gr. Inscr.* 3019. For the full Greek text, however, see Parsons, "School-Book," 133–49.

127. Morgan, *Literate Education*, 207.

128. For analyses of this inscription, see Roberts, *Biblical Epic*, 47–50; Morgan,

"an act of creative composition and an elementary exercise ... [and] does not seek to keep slavishly close to the original."[129] As such, it is an example of a student taking steps away from the elementary exercise toward more advanced composition and thus becoming more independent.

Cicero also provides evidence of a larger scale paraphrase. Though a lack of details prevents us from knowing how long the original text or the paraphrase was, that which is described by Cicero (in the voice of Crassus) certainly points to a paraphrase much longer than those of a few lines of Homer. His description is worth quoting in full:

> For my part, in the daily exercises of youth, I used chiefly to set myself that task which I knew Gaius Carbo, my old enemy, was wont to practise: this was to set myself some poetry, the most impressive to be found, or to read as much of some speech as I could keep in my memory, and then to declaim upon the actual subject-matter of my reading, choosing as far as possible different words. But later I noticed this defect in my method, that those words which best befitted each subject, and were the most elegant and in fact the best, had been already seized upon by Ennius, if it was on his poetry that I was practising, or by Gracchus,[130] if I chanced to have set myself a speech of his. Thus I saw that to employ the same expressions profited me nothing, while to employ others was a positive hindrance, in that I was forming the habit of using the less appropriate. (*De or.* 1.34.154)

Admittedly, Cicero does not identify this practice as paraphrase, but it sounds so much like the exercise described in Theon and Quintilian that scholars consider him to be describing paraphrase.[131] Elsewhere Cicero mentions Carbo as one who was "industrious, painstaking, and in the habit of devoting much attention to declamatory exercises and compositions" (*Brut.* 27.105 [Hendrickson, LCL]), which further suggests that Cicero had some form of the exercise of paraphrase in mind. The significance of these references to Carbo—a mature orator—practicing paraphrase is that they suggest that students were not the only ones who practiced paraphrase (though, of course, Crassus testifies that he

---

Literate Education, 205–9. Roberts (49) actually calls Homer's original "quite jejune" in contrast to the paraphrase!

129. Morgan, *Literate Education*, 208.

130. Sutton and Rackham note that C. Gracchus' speeches "were studied as models in the rhetorical schools of the Empire." See their commentary in Cicero, *De oratore*, 106.

131. See, e.g., Roberts, *Biblical Epic*, 8–9.

practiced it in his youth).¹³² Pliny also provides witness to the use of paraphrase by accomplished orators through his recommendation of the practice in his letter to Fuscus Salinator, an orator who had already begun his career (*Ep.* 7.9). Accomplished orators could continue to use and benefit from the exercise.

If we are willing to grant that Cicero is referring to paraphrase, his description confirms a few of the things we learned from Theon and Quintilian about paraphrase. First, a student could paraphrase either poetic texts (Homer is described by Theon; Ennius is described by Cicero) or prose texts (Thucydides is described by Theon; Gracchus' speech is described by Cicero). Secondly, paraphrase entailed choosing different words than the text being paraphrased. Cicero eventually found this second point problematic—he seems to think that Ennius or Gracchus, for example, had employed more appropriate words than he could, which ultimately led him to abandon the exercise. Instead, he opted to translate Greek speeches into Latin,¹³³ which he found to be a more profitable exercise (*De or.* 1.34.155).

Cicero's view that paraphrase was unhelpful may be a reflection of a view to which both Theon and Quintilian respond. The comments of Theon and Quintilian suggest that not everyone in antiquity saw the value of the exercise of paraphrase. According to Theon, these detractors viewed paraphrase as useless, claiming that once something had been said well, it could not be said well a second time. Theon strongly opposes this notion, claiming instead that thoughts are stirred in a variety of different ways: "Sometimes we are making a declaration, sometimes asking a question, sometimes making an inquiry, sometimes beseeching, and sometimes expressing our thought in some other way" (*Prog.* 62 [Kennedy, 6]). Quintilian shares Theon's perception of the utility of paraphrase and was outraged at the suggestion that something is said

---

132. Ibid., 8. Roberts also believes that Quintilian's reference to Sulpicius, who was "said to have practised no other form of exercise" (*Inst.* 10.5.4), is evidence that mature orators practiced paraphrase. See ibid., 18. Mature orators seemed to have practiced other exercises as well. For instance, Quintilian tells us that Cicero practiced theses "when he was already a leading public figure" (*Inst.* 10.5.11).

133. Pliny also notes the merits of translating Greek into Latin or Latin into Greek (*Ep.* 7.9.1). Quintilian discusses exercises in translation in his section on written exercises—the section in which paraphrase appears. In fact, his discussion on translation immediately precedes that on paraphrase. Cf. Lausberg, *Handbook of Literary Rhetoric*, §1098. On the relationship between translation and paraphrase, see Roberts, *Biblical Epic*, 9.

best the first time. Quintilian's passion about the subject merits a quotation of his defense of paraphrase:

> I do not want Paraphrase to be a mere passive reproduction, but to rival and vie with the original in expressing the same thoughts. I therefore disagree with those who forbid paraphrases of Latin speeches, on the ground that all the best expressions have been anticipated and anything we put in another way is bound to be worse. In fact we do not always need to despair of being able to find something better than the original, nor did nature make eloquence such a poor starved thing that any given subject can only be well handled once! Or are we to suppose that, while actors' gestures can so often vary the effect of the same words, oratory has *less* power, so that things are said which leave nothing more to be said on the same subject? But grant that what we discover is neither better than the original nor equal to it: there is still a place for the second best. Do we not ourselves often speak twice or more on the same theme, sometimes even in successive sentences? Is it conceivable that we can compete against ourselves but not against others? If there were only one way of saying a thing well, we might legitimately suppose that our predecessors blocked the road for us; but in fact there are countless ways, and many roads lead to the same destination. Brevity and fullness both have their charms; metaphor and literal language both have their merits; straightforward speech does well for some things, a figured variation for others. And finally, the actual difficulty of the exercise is very useful. . . . It will be useful not only to paraphrase the work of others, but to modify our own in various ways, deliberately taking up some thoughts and turning them in as many ways as possible, just as one shape after another can be made out of the same piece of wax.[134] (*Inst.* 10.5.6–9)

These comments by Theon and Quintilian, along with the widespread witness to the practice of paraphrase, suggest that paraphrase was an immensely popular exercise amongst ancient students and mature orators alike, despite the existence of a few detractors.

But this quotation teaches us other things about paraphrase as well, things confirmed by Theon and other writers. First, we see that authors would often paraphrase their own works for practice (Quintilian, *Inst.*

---

134. Pliny likewise used a memorable metaphor to describe paraphrase: "to graft new limbs, in fact, on a finished trunk without disturbing the balance of the original" (*Ep.* 7.9.6 [Radice, LCL]).

10.5.9; Theon, *Prog.* 62; Pliny, *Ep.* 7.9.1),[135] not just others'. Second, when they did paraphrase others, it often was viewed as a competition of sorts. Quintilian uses competitive terms (*certamen* and *aemulatio*; 10.5.5) to describe the relationship between the paraphrase and the original, and Pliny actually describes it as a contest (*certamen*): "[W]e see many people entering this type of contest [i.e., choosing a passage written by someone else and trying to improve it] with great credit to themselves and, by not lacking confidence, outstripping the authors whom they intended only to follow" (*Ep.* 7.9.4).

In sum, paraphrase was an exercise that entailed changing the form of a text through addition, subtraction, substitution, or variation, all the while preserving the original's meaning. Because paraphrase was versatile—it could be short or long, simple or complex, of poetry or of prose—beginning students and accomplished orators alike practiced it. Paraphrase was competitive in nature—it sought to compete with an original text, whether it belonged to the paraphraser or to someone else. This competition aimed at saying what the original said in a better way. While the evidence shows that some doubted the utility of paraphrase, its widespread use suggests that it was a quite popular exercise.

Relationship between the Exercises

Students were equipped to apply the techniques learned in the *progymnasmata* in a variety of situations and often in an integrated way. While it may appear from the structure of the progymnasmatic treatises that students practiced the exercises in isolation, a closer look reveals that they often overlapped with one another. The following are specific examples illustrating this interconnectedness. First, Theon recommends that when practicing with a chreia, a student should expand and compress (i.e., paraphrase) the chreia and should "refute and confirm" it (ἀνασκευάζομεν καὶ κατασκευάζομεν) (Theon, *Prog.* 101 [Kennedy, 19; Patillon, 24]). Theon continues, "for we try to express the assigned chreia, as best we can, with the same words (as in the version given us) or with others in the clearest way." Second, Theon treats refutation and confirmation as

---

135. Cf. also Plutarch, *Dem.* 8.2, where Plutarch explains that Demosthenes paraphrased (μετάφρασις) his own and others' speeches. Roberts notes, "The reference is difficult to evaluate, but, if Plutarch's information is reliable, we must suppose that Demosthenes, at least, recognized the value of the paraphrase as a stylistic exercise." Roberts, *Biblical Epic*, 7.

part of his discussion of narration, suggesting an interconnectedness between them. Third, Quintilian and all of the *progymnasmata* writers instructed students to draw upon the topics in an encomion or invective for their synkrisis. The latter presumed knowledge of the former. Fourth, in *Bodl. Gr. Inscr.* 3019, discussed above, the author greatly expands Chryses' speech (which was only five lines in Homer), suggesting that ethopoeia fell under the category of paraphrase. Fifth, that same paraphrase demonstrates that ornamenting with rhetorical figures was part of paraphrasing, even if rhetorical figures were almost only discussed in the rhetorical handbooks. Sixth, Quintilian suggests that theses, refutation, confirmation, and commonplaces were valuable to those who were paraphrasing another work (*Inst.* 10.5.12).[136] Thus, students learned not only the specific techniques but also how to integrate them with one another toward their larger rhetorical goals.

The last three examples suggest that many of the exercises or techniques that students practiced could be viewed as ways of paraphrasing. In fact, the overlap between paraphrase and other exercises provides for Roberts the reason why paraphrase is not present in extant *progymnasmata* other than Theon's. He explains, "We may surmise that the inclusion of the paraphrase among the *progymnasmata* was felt to be an anomaly. The standard *progymnasmata* were defined by the subject they treated, the paraphrase was a technique that could be applied to the treatment of any subject.... In a sense, then, the *progymnasmata* could be subsumed under the genus of paraphrase, since they all involved stylistic elaboration of a predetermined subject."[137]

Chapter Summary

Here I have presented the tools for a rhetorical analysis of Luke's passion narrative. I have demonstrated the transitional role that the *progymnasmata* played in ancient education—it functioned as the base upon which more advanced education was built by helping students develop skills in invention, expression, and the ability to work with sources. I have also synthesized the material on refutation and confirmation, rhetorical figures, synkrisis, narration, and paraphrase from the *progymnasmata* and

---

136. For other examples of the overlap between exercises, see Webb, "*Progymnasmata* as Practice," 299.

137. Roberts, *Biblical Epic*, 23.

the rhetorical handbooks, placing us in a position to better analyze how Luke composed his passion narrative, how he worked with source material, how he arranged his narrative, and how an ancient audience might have received his work.

I now turn to chapters 3 and 4, where I explore how these rhetorical techniques inform our understanding of the composition of Luke's passion narrative. The techniques associated with refutation and confirmation help us understand how Luke arranged his narrative and how he seeks to underscore the judicial nature of the entire passion narrative and thus the political dimension of Jesus' innocence. The rhetorical figures also contribute toward Luke's characterization of Jesus as innocent. The types and function of synkrisis outlined in this chapter help us decipher why Luke constructs parallels between Jesus in the passion narrative and Stephen and Paul in Acts. Finally, the techniques associated with narration and paraphrase help us understand why Luke edits Mark in certain ways and informs our understanding of what sources Luke may or may not have used in addition to Mark.

3

Scene 1: Pre-Trial Hearing (22:66–71) and Formal Trial (23:1–25)

Introduction

THIS CHAPTER AND THE following one are an analysis of Luke's passion narrative with insights from the ancient rhetorical tradition—particularly the techniques of refutation and confirmation, rhetorical figures, synkrisis, paraphrase, and narration, all of which I described in the preceding chapter. This rhetorical analysis reveals that Luke organizes his passion narrative into two large scenes: the first scene includes the pre-trial hearing (22:66–71) and the formal trial before Pilate (23:1–25), and the second scene includes the transition to the cross (23:26–32) and the informal trial at the cross (23:33–49).[1] This chapter treats scene one; chapter 4 treats scene two.

1. Scholars debate which portions of the passion narrative should be considered a trial and which should not. Many scholars argue that 22:66–71 is not a trial. Walaskay, for instance, says it is "not a trial at all, but the chaotic prelude to a lynching which even Roman jurisprudence could not overcome." See Walaskay, "Trial and Death," 82. Walaskay and others point to the lack of witnesses, testimony, and a formal verdict in 22:66–71 as evidence that this appearance before the Jewish leadership is not a trial. Tyson, *Death of Jesus*, 128, makes a similar assessment of 22:66–71. Others, like Matera and Gaston, argue that only part of the passion narrative is a trial. Matera sees 22:66—23:25 as a four-scene trial: Jesus before the Sanhedrin (22:66–71), Jesus before Pilate (23:1–7), Jesus before Herod (23:8–12), and Jesus before Pilate again (23:13–25). Gaston, however, argues that the scenes that make up 22:66—23:12 are not trials. Rather, only in 23:13–25 "can we speak of even the semblance of a trial, and it is a trial before the people who are both judge and executioner. Pilate (and to a lesser degree Herod) appears in the role of defence attorney desperately trying to dissuade the people from their undertakings." See Matera, "Luke 23,1–25," 535–51; Matera, "Luke 22,66–71," 45; Gaston, "Anti-Judaism," 148. In contrast to these studies, I argue that Jesus is on trial throughout the whole of Luke's passion narrative (22:66—23:49). Though some sections of the narrative lack some formal elements of a trial, whether Jesus is innocent

Within and across these two scenes, Luke uses refutations and confirmations of the charges against Jesus as an organizing principle for his narrative. Ultimately this is a debate about Jesus' innocence. Luke consistently employs the topics of refutation and confirmation found in the rhetorical tradition as a way of structuring the entire narrative as a trial. An outline of Luke's passion narrative, based on these refutations and confirmations, is as follows:

I. Scene 1: The Pre-Trial Hearing (22:66–71) and the Formal Trial (23:1–25)
   A. Setting the Stage: The Pre-Trial Hearing (22:66–71)
   B. The Formal Trial—The Pilate Scene (23:1–25)
      1. The Accusations (23:1–3)
      2. Refutation 1: Pilate (23:4)
      3. Confirmation 1: The Jewish Leaders (23:5)
      4. Refutation 2: Herod and Pilate (23:6–16)
      5. Confirmation 2: The Chief Priests, Rulers, and People (23:18–21)
      6. Refutation 3: Pilate (23:22–25)

II. Scene 2: The Transition to the Cross (23:26–32) and the Informal Trial (23:33–49)
   A. Transition: From the Trial to the Cross (23:26–32)
   B. The Informal Trial—The Crucifixion Scene (23:33–49)
      1. Confirmation 3: Rulers (23:33–35)
      2. Confirmation 4: Soldiers (23:36–38)
      3. Confirmation 5: First Criminal (23:39)
      4. Refutation 4: Second Criminal (23:40–43)
      5. Refutation 5: Darkness and Rending of the Veil (23:44–46)
      6. Refutation 6: The Centurion (23:47–49)

I will proceed through the trials in order, discussing the relevant rhetorical techniques as they arise.

---

or guilty—i.e., the main question of a trial—is the focus of 22:66—23:49.

Beyond the refutation-confirmation scheme outlined above, ornaments such as rhetorical figures adorn Luke's narrative and serve as clues to parts of the narrative that Luke wants to emphasize.[2] In the analysis below, I will highlight these ornaments and discuss their contribution to Luke's larger narrative. Luke also sets up parallels between Jesus and characters in Acts,[3] though these parallels do not function as his organizing principle. Many scholars have noted these parallels,[4] but the rhetori-

---

2. Reich describes emphasis as the "broadest function of a figure" (19). Beyond this broad function, Reich's analysis shows that Luke uses rhetorical figures on the lips of Jesus for at least three more specific reasons: (1) to portray Jesus "as an educated man who speaks with the high rhetorical style of the social elites" which would "make his speech and message easy to follow and pleasing to the ear"; (2) "to draw the gospel audience to his side and to cause them to become participants in the gospel message"; and (3) to make Jesus' "socially subversive and role-revising message" both powerful and memorable. See Reich, *Figuring Jesus*, 20–21.

3. The primary parallels (based on the criteria described below) are between Jesus and Paul. Some parallels exist between the trials and deaths of Jesus and Stephen (most notably their dying words and their hearing before the Sanhedrin), but the narratives as a whole meet fewer of the criteria. On other parallels between Jesus and Stephen (i.e., outside the passion narrative), see Moessner, "'Christ Must Suffer,'" 227–34.

For the most part, I see the relationship between Jesus' passion narrative and Stephen's stoning as different than one of parallels (though I do acknowledge a few parallels). Stephen's story hearkens back to Jesus' Lukan passion in several ways: (1) by referring to Jesus as ὁ δίκαιος (Acts 7:52; cf. Luke 23:47); (2) by referring to Jesus' presence at the right hand of God (Acts 7:55–56; Luke 22:69); and by specifically naming his accusers' ancestors as those who betrayed and murdered Jesus (7:52). These points are *connections* between the two stories but not parallels. In some instances, instead of creating parallels between the two, Luke actually transfers some of the details about Jesus' trial in Mark to Stephen's trial in Acts. For example, the accusation about Jesus threatening to destroy the temple is in Mark 14:58 and Acts 6:14 but not in Luke's passion narrative. In other ways, one could say that Luke actually creates parallels between Stephen's trial and Jesus' *Markan* trial (e.g., the false witnesses [Mark 14:56–59; Acts 6:13]; the charge of blasphemy [Mark 14:64; Acts 6:11]). On Acts as a potential sequel to many Gospels, not just Luke, see Parsons, *Acts*, 12–15.

The differences between the stories of Jesus and Stephen (e.g., an organized execution according to Roman law versus a mob lynching; the lack of Roman officials in Stephen's story; the lack of emphasis on the innocence theme) make me hesitant to make too much of the parallels with Stephen. Nonetheless, I will discuss the parallels with Stephen below, though they are few, because they are somewhat related to the purpose of the synkrisis between Jesus and Paul and because they help explain some of Luke's compositional activity. I contend, however, that the primary narrative comparison for Luke's account of Jesus' passion is the story of Paul's trials.

4. See, e.g., Mattill, "Jesus-Paul Parallels," 15–46; Radl, *Paulus und Jesus*; Talbert, *Literary Patterns*; Moessner, "Christ Must Suffer." Reviews of works that treat the parallels between Luke and Acts (or within either of these two books) have rightly called for the authors to intimate criteria for judging parallels so as not to let the

cal function of the parallels is debated. Here I will bring the rhetorical tradition's explanation of the function of synkrisis to bear on Luke's presentation of Jesus in his passion narrative.[5]

In addition to analyzing Luke's final product—organized with refutations and confirmations, adorned with rhetorical figures, and designed with parallels to Acts—I will demonstrate that the final shape of Luke's passion narrative is explicable without recourse to a non-canonical written source.[6] The techniques of paraphrase and narration described in the ancient rhetorical tradition problematize the assumption that differences between Luke and Mark—be they large or small—must be attributed to an alternate source. Such an assumption ignores the ingenuity and freedom encouraged in ancient writers, particularly as it related to improving their sources. Instead, rhetorical training, even at an intermediate level, encouraged writers to improve their source(s) in the direction of clarity, conciseness, and plausibility through addition, subtraction, and rearrangement. Luke's editing of Mark's passion narrative fits squarely within these guidelines. Therefore, I will explore many of the ways that

---

modern scholar's creative imagination overestimate Luke's crafting. See, e.g., Paul Sevier Minear, review of Talbert, *Literary Patterns*, 85–86; Praeder, "Jesus-Paul," 23–39.

In establishing what is and what is not a parallel between Jesus and characters in Acts, I have relied on the "criteria for acceptable parallels" intimated by Andrew Clark in his *Parallel Lives*. He looks at both internal controls (the material in Luke and Acts and how previous scholars have treated it) and external controls (relying on Theon's instructions on synkrisis and Plutarch's example in *Parallel Lives*) (73–101). Criteria for acceptable parallels include similar content, similar literary form, similar sequence, similar structure, similar theme, and disruption of the text where the parallel is introduced. While not all of these criteria must be present at one time, the more the better (e.g., "Similarity in *content* is too vague a criterion to stand on its own, though it may complement other similarities" [75]). As detailed below, across the stories of Jesus and Paul (and to a lesser extent the stories of Jesus and Stephen) we see similar content (including sometimes almost verbatim language), a similar literary form (a trial and/or death narrative), similar sequences (appearances before the council and various rulers), similar themes (witness and innocence), and potentially the disruption of the text (e.g., one could argue that Luke "disrupts" the hearing before Pilate with the Herod episode, which is not present in Mark). This last criterion is certainly not required, but its presence may signal a parallel. Clark adds, "particularly detailed parallels extra to the main parallel . . . must be assessed individually according to their merits. The presence of an overall parallel does not guarantee that all minor parallels which may be suggested will also be valid" (111).

5. I explore the parallels between Luke and Acts in this chapter and the next; in chapter 5 I discuss those parallels in relation to the larger function of synkrisis.

6. See "Methodology" in chapter one for my understanding of the Synoptic Problem.

Luke redacts Mark and will try to understand these redactions in light of the techniques of paraphrase and narration. However, the nature of this study does not require an explanation for every single change that Luke makes to Mark in the process of composing his narrative.[7] As I will discuss more fully in chapter 5, the skills that an author would have acquired from practicing the popular exercise of paraphrase easily account for adjustments in syntax,[8] word substitutions,[9] or minor additions or deletions.[10] As we saw in the example that Theon gives of Archilochus paraphrasing Homer (*Prog.* 62), even a student who had only learned the most basic principles of paraphrase was capable of altering syntax (e.g., changing the case or mood of words or rearranging them), using synonyms, and adding thoughts. The resulting paraphrase, though maintaining the meaning of the original, preserved few of the words of the original. Thus, even those students who were near the beginning of their education were not only capable of altering their sources in various ways for the sake of variety or to achieve their own point, but they were even encouraged to do so. Based on this understanding, it seems unnecessary to appeal to unknown sources for minor differences between Luke and Mark. Instead, I will focus on the changes most commonly cited as a reason to posit an additional passion source.[11]

In this chapter and the next, then, I will analyze Luke's passion narrative one unit at a time, noting how the techniques of refutation and confirmation, rhetorical figures, synkrisis, narration, and paraphrase illuminate our understanding of Luke's larger rhetorical goals. Before we turn to the individual units, however, it will be helpful to note how Luke's larger arrangement of his passion narrative differs from Mark's.[12]

---

7. Several studies devoted to Luke's redaction of Mark account for these changes in great detail. See, e.g., Brown, *Death of the Messiah*; Neyrey, *Passion according to Luke*; Büchele, *Der Tod Jesu*.

8. E.g., Luke's Σίμωνά τινα Κυρηναῖον in place of Mark's τινα Σίμωνα Κυρηναῖον (Luke 23:26; Mark 15:21).

9. E.g., Luke's ἑκατοντάρχης in place of Mark's κεντυρίων (Luke 23:47; Mark 15:39).

10. E.g., Luke adding οὗτος to Mark's τί γὰρ ἐποίησεν κακόν (Luke 23:22; Mark 15:14).

11. Of course, even scholars who agree that Luke used an additional source do not always arrive at that conclusion via the same texts. Contrast Perry and Taylor, for instance. Both believe that Luke had a source in addition to Mark for his passion narrative. Perry thinks that Luke 23:1–16 comes from this source (which he refers to as J), while Taylor (speaking of vv. 6–16) says, "[t]here is little to suggest the use of a source" here. Perry, *Sources of Luke's Passion Narrative*, 45; Taylor, *Passion Narrative*, 87.

12. Though the boundaries of this study are Luke 22:66—23:49, it is necessary

The Big Picture: A Comparison of the Arrangements of Mark and Luke

Table 2 compares the order of events in the passion narratives of Mark and Luke. Italics signify Luke's rearrangement of Mark; underlining signifies Luke's additions to Mark; gray shading signifies common order between Mark and Luke.

On a macro-level, we see that Luke retains most of Mark's material, though some of it is in a different order. For instance, Luke places Peter's denials immediately after they enter into the courtyard, whereas Mark waits to narrate Peter's denials until after Jesus' appearance before the council (and notes in 14:66 that the scenes happen concurrently). Luke also places the initial mocking of Jesus (Mark 14:65//Luke 22:63–65) before the pre-trial hearing (Mark 14:55–64//Luke 22:66–71). Later in the narrative, Luke moves the mocking by the soldiers to before Jesus is handed over for crucifixion; he also moves the tearing of the temple veil to before Jesus' death.[13]

The question, of course, is how to interpret these differing arrangements—did Luke borrow his arrangement from a different source or did he simply rearrange Mark? Some, like Vincent Taylor, find the first option most plausible. Taylor argues that the best way to explain these differences in structure is to posit that Luke, when writing his Gospel, inserted Markan material into the framework of a different source, Proto-Luke (Luke's earlier combination of Q and L).[14] The alternative source, then, is the origin of Luke's order rather than Mark.

---

here to include the events beginning in 22:47 in order to properly show how and why Luke rearranges Mark's material.

13. In this section I discuss the rearrangements in Mark 14:53–72//Luke 22:55–71; I will discuss the others in their respective sections below.

14. Taylor, *Passion Narrative*, 124–25. Cf. a similar mentality in Jeremias. Jeremias argues that prior to the passion narrative Luke "painstakingly" follows Mark's order, except for two deviations. However, in the Last Supper account (though not included in this study, the Last Supper is often included in discussions of the passion narrative), there are several deviations, and thus, 22:14f "is no longer built upon a Markan basis, but comes from *Urlukas*." This example demonstrates the outworking of Jeremias' stated principle: "deviations in the order of the material must therefore be regarded as indications the Luke is not following Mark," but rather another source. See Jeremias, *Eucharistic Words*, 99. Jeremias does not describe this source in as much detail as Taylor. He simply refers to it as "Luke's special source" (97) or "*Urlukas*" (99).

Table 2. Order of events in the passion narratives of Mark and Luke

	Mark	Luke	
Evening	Jesus' arrest (14:43–52)	Jesus' arrest (22:47–53)	Evening
	Jesus is escorted to high priest; Peter follows (14:53–54)	Jesus is escorted to high priest; Peter follows (22:54)	
	Jesus appears before the chief priests and council; questioned about being Messiah & Son of the Blessed One (14:55–64)	*Peter denies Jesus (22:55–62)*	
	Jesus is mocked, beaten, and told to prophesy (14:65)	*Jesus is mocked, beaten, and told to prophesy (22:63–65)*	
	Peter denies Jesus (14:66–72)	*Jesus appears before the chief priests and council; questioned about being Messiah & Son of God (22:66–71)*	
Morning	Chief priests, elders, scribes, and whole council bring Jesus to Pilate (15:1)	The whole multitude brings Jesus to Pilate (23:1)	Morning
	Jesus "testifies" before Pilate (15:2–5)	Jesus "testifies" before Pilate (23:2–5)	
		<u>Pilate sends Jesus to Herod (23:6–10)</u>	
	The crowd demands Jesus' crucifixion from Pilate (15:6–15)	<u>Herod and</u> soldiers mock Jesus; dress him in shining clothes (23:11–12)	
	Soldiers mock Jesus; dress him in purple (15:16–20)	*The crowd demands Jesus' crucifixion from Pilate (23:13–25)*	
	Simon carries Jesus' cross (15:21)	Simon carries Jesus' cross (23:26)	
		<u>Jesus is followed by and speaks to a crowd (23:27–31)</u>	

SCENE 1: THE PRE-TRIAL HEARING AND FORMAL TRIAL 81

	Mark	Luke	
3rd Hour	Jesus is crucified (15:22–32)	Jesus is crucified (23:32–33)	Morning
		Jesus converses with the two criminals (23:34–43)	
6th hour	Darkness comes over the land (15:33)	Darkness comes over the land (23:44–45)	6th hour
9th Hour	Jesus' last words and death (15:34–37)	*Temple veil torn* (23:45)	9th Hour
	Temple veil torn (15:38)	*Jesus' last words and death* (22:46)	
	Centurion's confession (15:39)	Centurion's confession (22:47)	
	Crowds watch (15:40–41)	Crowds watch (23:48–49)	
Later on the Day of Preparation	Jesus is buried (15:42–47)	Jesus is buried (23:50–56)	Later on the Day of Preparation

Others, however, opt for the second option and argue that the differing order does not necessitate a separate source. Linnemann, for example, argues that Luke transposed Mark for reasons of theology, apologetics, and plausibility. She notes that Luke's one meeting of the council (22:66–71, in the morning) is more plausible than Mark's two meetings of the council (14:53–65 at night; 15:1 in the morning). This change also "removed the unusual and illegal interrogation at night."[15]

These two examples (Taylor and Linnemann) represent the assumptions that lie behind the different sides of the source issue. Taylor and those who posit an independent source behind Luke's passion narrative (besides the canonical gospels) assume that variations from Mark imply

15. Linnemann, *Studien zur Passionsgeschichte*, 98 (translation mine). She does not offer an explanation of Luke's theological or apologetic reasons for rearranging the material.

the use of another unknown source. Linnemann and those who posit that Luke simply worked with Mark (or other canonical gospels and oral tradition) assume that differences between Luke and Mark—big or small—are the result of Luke's own theological and rhetorical goals.

In arriving at an answer on what sources Luke may have used, it is important to ask about the function of the differences between the two narratives. Overall, the structural changes that Luke makes to Mark result in a narrative that focuses on Jesus without interruption. That is, by moving Peter's denials and the first mocking of Jesus to before the Jewish trial, nothing interrupts the repeated proclamations of Jesus' guilt or innocence, enabling the hearers to focus on this important Lukan theme.[16] Furthermore, with this new arrangement Luke links the proceedings before the Jewish leaders with the proceedings before Pilate and Herod,[17] which allows the repeated refutations and confirmation of the charges to immediately follow the accusations. Finally, Soards points out two other effects of Luke's rearrangement of Mark: "(1) Jesus' courage is accentuated by having Peter's cowardice precede. (2) Deep irony is inherent in Luke's narrative when Peter remembers that Jesus had prophesied his denials, and then, the men holding Jesus imply he is no prophet with their mocking game."[18]

In light of what the rhetorical tradition says about clarity, conciseness, and plausibility in a narrative, the differences in arrangement between Luke and Mark described above can reasonably be attributed to Luke's reworking of Mark. We remember that Theon warns against narrating the same thing twice, as it can confuse hearers (*Prog.* 80), and he also notes that clarity comes "whenever one does not narrate many things together but brings each to completion" (*Prog.* 80 [Kennedy, 30]).

---

16. I trace the development of this theme in the remainder of this chapter and in the next.

17. Matera, "Luke 22,66–71," 49. Matera also notes that Luke's arrangement here creates consistency with Acts, where none of the trials take place at night. Rather, in several cases, prisoners are arrested and imprisoned at night and not brought to trial until the morning (Peter and John in Acts 4:3–5; the apostles in Acts 5:18–21 [the high priest calls for them in the morning, not knowing that an angel released them during the night]; Paul in Acts 22:30). He concludes, "It would appear that Luke viewed a night trial as something improbable and irregular, and hence not even his polemic against the Jewish leaders allowed him to follow Mark at this point. In effect, Luke's preference in Acts for a morning assembly of the council is further evidence that he is responsible for the arrangement of events in this section" (50).

18. Soards, "Literary Analysis," 91.

SCENE 1: THE PRE-TRIAL HEARING AND FORMAL TRIAL 83

Luke may have seen Mark's narrative as potentially confusing to hearers, with two different meetings by the council at two different times.[19] And, though Mark's choice to narrate the trial and Peter's denials as if happening simultaneously has its own rhetorical effect,[20] Luke seems to be concerned with keeping the lens on Jesus by moving Peter's denials to before the mocking and trials.[21] This rearrangement results in a narrative that brings Peter's story to completion before moving on to Jesus, a technique that Luke uses elsewhere in his editing of Mark.[22] Finally, Luke may have also been motivated to redact Mark's order out of a concern for plausibility because a trial during the evening—especially on the evening of Passover—may have appeared suspicious to some hearers.[23]

The other units that Luke rearranges need comment on a micro-level as well, so I will address those rearrangements in the sections that follow. In the remainder of the chapter, I will analyze Luke 22:66—23:25—from the pre-trial hearing through the trial before Pilate—following Luke's

---

19. Brown, however, suggests the possibility of Mark's early morning gathering of the council (15:1) as the terminus of their earlier gathering (14:53–65). See Brown, *Death of the Messiah*, 420.

20. See Marcus, *Mark 8—16*, 1021, on Mark's enhancement of the drama by having the two scenes unfold simultaneously.

21. Brown, *Death of the Messiah*, 423. Brown's commentary is worth repeating in full, with numbers referring to the sequence in each Gospel: "Why bother the readers with Mark's complicated sequence of Jesus (#1), Peter (#2), Jesus (#3,4), Peter (#5), Jesus (#6)? Why not more simply have Jesus brought to the high priest's house (#1), Peter following and denying Jesus three times (#2,3), and then Jesus mocked and interrogated (#4,5,6)? Why bother with complicated simultaneity, interrupting the interrogation of Jesus to narrate the denials of Peter, and then retracing one's steps to the interrogation to tell the readers that it was finishing about the same time as the denials, namely, morning? Why not tell the Peter story as an undivided whole that took place at night? (This would have the added advantage that Jesus could be mentioned at the end, both as a transition to the interrogation and by implication as present during the denials and thus able to extend forgiveness to Peter on the spot . . . .) And why not describe the legal procedure against Jesus as an undivided whole, taking place in the morning where it finished in any case? A Luke who did not hesitate to improve on Mark's order at the beginning of the Gospel, finishing the story of [John the Baptist] to his arrest before telling the story of Jesus, and placing the history of Simon Peter's mother-in-law before Simon followed Jesus rather than afterwards, did not hesitate to improve on it at the end of the Gospel, especially when the improvement would match the pattern in Acts (4:3,5) where Peter and John, arrested at night, were kept in custody till the next day."

22. See, e.g., the examples from Brown in the previous note.

23. Neyrey, *Passion according to Luke*, 71; Linnemann, *Studien zur Passionsgeschichte*, 98; Matera, "Luke 22,66–71," 48.

narrative (rather than Mark's) since Luke's portrayal of Jesus is of ultimate interest here.

Setting the Stage: Pre-Trial Hearing (22:66–71)

After Jesus' arrest and Peter's denials, the night concludes with those who were holding Jesus beating and insulting him. The pre-trial hearing begins the next morning (ὡς ἐγένετο ἡμέρα; 22:66) when the elders of the people, including both the chief priests and the scribes, lead Jesus before their council (συνέδριον), similar to how they brought Stephen before the council (συνέδριον; Acts 6:12).

The interrogation entails two inquiries about Jesus' identity—whether he is the Messiah or the Son of God. The council's first inquiry is framed as a conditional sentence with a command: "If you are the Messiah, tell us" (εἰ σὺ εἶ ὁ χριστός, εἰπὸν ἡμῖν; 22:67). To this inquiry Jesus responds with his own conditional sentence: "If I tell you, you will not believe; and if I ask, you will not answer" (ἐὰν ὑμῖν εἴπω, οὐ μὴ πιστεύσητε· ἐὰν δὲ ἐρωτήσω, οὐ μὴ ἀποκριθῆτε; 22:67–68).[24] In this first part of his response, Jesus employs three different rhetorical figures.[25] First, we see that Jesus twice uses repeated negation. In both of the conditional sentences, he uses οὐ μή, which Bullinger argues functions to "show the accuracy of the Lord's foreknowledge."[26] Second, these first two sentences of Jesus' response are examples of isocolon—a figure that consists of cola of equal or almost equal number of syllables.[27] The first two clauses have six syllables and the second two have seven, resulting in a rhythmically bal-

---

24. On these words' contribution to the motif of Jesus as the prophet rejected by his homeland, see Neyrey, *Passion according to Luke*, 72–73. He notes how these words are fulfilled not only in this trial scene, but also throughout Luke's Gospel.

25. This is not the first instance in Luke of this same group of leaders—the elders, chief priests, and scribes (though contrast πρεσβύτερος in 20:1 with πρεσβυτέριον τοῦ λαοῦ in 22:66)—debating with Jesus and being shown up by his rhetorical figures. In 20:1–7 they question Jesus' authority to teach in the temple. He responds with a counter-question: whether the baptism of John was of divine or human origin. Reich classifies this as an example of the figure hypophora, in which "one asks questions of adversaries, or of oneself, and answers with what ought or ought not to be said, making oneself look good, and the adversary look bad." See Reich, *Figuring Jesus*, 13. By using hypophora to reduce his opponents to aporia (being at a loss), the audience is drawn to the Lukan Jesus and becomes a proponent of his message. See ibid., 66–69, 77–78.

26. Bullinger, *Figures of Speech*, 341.

27. Reich, *Figuring Jesus*, 14. Cf. *Rhet. Her.* 4.20.27; Quintilian, *Inst.* 9.3.80.

anced response.[28] Finally, successive alternating phrases begin with the same word (ἐὰν), an instance of epanaphora, which *Rhetorica ad Herennium* associates with charm, impressiveness, and vigor (4.8.19).

These three figures not only "make [Jesus'] speech and message easy to follow and pleasing to the ear,"[29] which would in turn make the audience favorable to his case, but they also combine "as a means of defeating his narrative interlocutors."[30] Reich gives ample examples of this phenomenon occurring elsewhere in Luke,[31] each of which draws the audience to Jesus' side over his opponents. Thus, from the outset of the trial, the audience is favorably disposed to Jesus' side of the case through the figures that Luke places on Jesus' lips. Furthermore, such an eloquent response on Jesus' part would draw attention to the content of what he is claiming, namely, that no matter what Jesus says, his accusers will find him guilty.[32] This foreshadows the debate over his innocence that follows and makes sense of why Jesus never defends himself to those in power in the rest of the narrative.[33] Instead, the rest of the narrative is full of other characters defending his innocence.

The rest of Jesus' response to their inquiry is also rhetorically savvy. Jesus does not just assert their unwillingness to believe or answer him; he also makes an affirmative statement about the Son of Man: he will, from now on, be seated at the right hand of the power of God (22:69). Fitzmyer describes Jesus' use of Ps 110:1 here as a rhetorical strategy that enables him to indirectly "assert his victory over his adversaries" (i.e., he will sit at the right hand of the power of God). This lack of a direct, affirmative answer—similar to the one he offers in response to their next question—shows that Jesus is too smart to walk into their trap.[34] Reich also highlights Jesus' unwillingness to directly answer their question by pointing

---

28. ἐ-ὰν ὑ-μῖν εἴ-πω (6), οὐ μὴ πισ-τεύ-ση-τε (6)· ἐ-ὰν δὲ ἐ-ρω-τή-σω (7), οὐ μὴ ἀ-πο-κρι-θῆ-τε (7).

29. Reich, *Figuring Jesus*, 20, describes this as one of the three functions of rhetorical figures on the lips of Jesus in Luke.

30. Ibid.

31. Ibid., 67–96.

32. Tannehill offers an analysis of Jesus' relationship with the authorities in Luke, showing that Jesus' response to them here is based on prior encounters with them earlier in the narrative. See Tannehill, *Narrative Unity*, 187–99, especially 190–91.

33. While not to those in power, Jesus' words to the women in 23:28 ("weep not for me") could be seen as an implicit defense of his innocence.

34. See Fitzmyer, *Gospel according to Luke*, 1462–63.

out that Jesus' use of "Son of Man" is an instance of antonomasia—"the trope in which one designates by an accidental epithet a thing that cannot be called by its proper name."³⁵

This first evasive answer from Jesus prompts the council to pose a second clarifying question—"Then are you the Son of God?" (22:70). The leaders' question suggests that they drew this conclusion from Jesus' statement about the Son of Man.³⁶ To the question about his being the Son of God Jesus responds with an equally evasive statement: "You yourselves are saying that I am" (ὑμεῖς λέγετε ὅτι ἐγώ εἰμι; 22:70).³⁷ Fitzmyer explains that Jesus' response is a "half-yes" answer—it does not refuse to answer; "it implies an affirmation, yet stresses that it is their way of putting it."³⁸ He notes the irony in Jesus' answer, which is highlighted by the contrasting pronouns ὑμεῖς and ἐγώ—they may say that he is the Son of God, but in reality they deny it. This response to the council is the first and only time in the passion narrative that Jesus speaks to those who think he is guilty. All of his other words (to Pilate in 23:3; to the women

---

35. Reich, *Figuring Jesus*, 9. Cf. *Rhet. Her.* 4.31.42; Quintilian, *Inst.* 8.6.29–30. Cf. 22:48.

36. Fitzmyer, *Gospel according to Luke*, 1463. Based on Dan 7:13 Schweizer even claims that "'Son of Man' designates the one who is exalted to God and can therefore be equated with 'Son of God.'" Schweizer, *Good News according to Luke*, 348.

37. Bock interprets this answer as "both a positive reply and a circumlocution." See Bock, *Luke*, 363.

38. Fitzmyer, *Gospel according to Luke*, 1468. Walaskay reads Jesus' responses differently. Jesus answers the question about messiahship obscurely, Walaskay says, but Jesus' response to the question about divine sonship is "most pointed." He interprets this to mean that "Jesus' only claim to leadership was a religious one." Luke aims to emphasize the culpability of the Jews in Jesus' death, so he "wants his readers to be certain that the charge, if any, to be brought before Pilate should have *only* a religious content, which he would have—out of ignorance more than anything else—summarily dismissed." See Walaskay, "Trial and Death," 82–83.

Nolland, on the other hand, offers yet another interpretation. He suggests that the gist of Jesus' response to their question about him being the Son of God suggests it might best be punctuated as a question—"Are you saying that I am?" However, I agree with Culy, Parsons, and Stigall that the leaders' response ("What further testimony do we need? For we ourselves have heard [it] from his lips!") suggests that Jesus' response is a statement—even if an ambiguous one—rather than a question. See Nolland, *Luke 18:35—24:53*, 1111; Culy et al., *Luke: A Handbook*, 701.

in 23:28–31; to the Father in 23:34, 46; to the second criminal in 23:43[39]) are to those who find him innocent.[40]

The pre-trial hearing concludes with a rhetorical question from the council: "What further testimony do we need? For we ourselves have heard [it] from his lips!" (22:71). This rhetorical question draws attention to two things. First, it highlights the theme of testimony (μαρτυρία), a crucial theme in the rest of the story, and thus has a similar function to many of the other rhetorical figures in the narrative.[41] Second, it reinforces the point that Jesus just made. He told them that if he answered their questions, they would not believe him. Then when he answered their question by saying that *they* say that he is the Son of God (something Jesus never directly affirmed), they claimed to have heard it from Jesus himself. Thus, unlike the figures on Jesus lips,[42] which portrayed him as rhetorically savvy and helped him defeat his interlocutors,[43] here the figure in the council's response actually proves Jesus' point and makes them look rash.

Ultimately, Luke does not specifically list any charges against Jesus during this meeting with the council. At the conclusion of the meeting, the hearer knows that the Jews are upset about issues related to Jesus' identity, but the formal charges are not mentioned until the next scene where Jesus is before Pilate.

In this scene before the council Luke makes several changes to Mark's account. Beyond changing the time from evening until morning,[44] as

---

39. I exclude Jesus' words in 23:34 because I do not think they were originally part of Luke. See "Confirmation 3" in chapter 4 for a fuller discussion.

40. Pilate and the second criminal explicitly declare Jesus' innocence (23:4, 14–15, 22, 41). Contra Neyrey who argues that the women are weeping for the ruin of their children and not over Jesus, I agree with Soards that the women's breast-beating, wailing, and (especially) Jesus' words to them suggest they are mourning at Jesus being wrongly executed. Soards points out that the rare verbs κόπτω and θρηνέω in 23:27 typically signal mourning in other contexts in Luke and Acts. See Soards, "Tradition, Composition, and Theology in Jesus' Speech," 230; Neyrey, *Passion according to Luke*, 112.

41. Reich describes emphasis as one of the primary purposes of rhetorical figures. A figure functions as "a verbal marker or warning sign, as if to say: 'pay attention here.'" Reich, *Figuring Jesus*, 19.

42. Cf. 22:48, 52; 23:31 for rhetorical questions on the lips of Jesus nearby in the narrative.

43. For more on Jesus' defeating his interlocutors through the use of rhetorical figures, see the section on rhetorical figures in chapter 5.

44. This difference in time along with the difference in order "points to the use of a source" for Taylor. Unfortunately, Taylor does not explain why "the reference to the

discussed in the preceding section, one of Luke's more notable changes to Mark's account relates to the dialogue between Jesus and the accusers. In Mark, witnesses give false testimony against Jesus then the high priest asks Jesus if he has a response to them, but Jesus remains silent (14:61). The high priest then asks in one question if Jesus is the Messiah, the Son of the Blessed One (14:61). Jesus' only words in the scene in Mark are in response to this question. He answers explicitly, "I am" (ἐγώ εἰμι), then tells them that they will see the Son of Man sitting at the right hand of the Power and coming with the clouds of heaven" (14:62).

When composing his narrative, Luke splits the high priest's question about Jesus' identity in Mark into two separate questions—one about the Messiah and one about the Son of God, and, as discussed above, Jesus provides equivocal answers to both.[45] To the question about his messiahship, Jesus responds with words not in Mark: "If I tell you, you will not believe; and if I ask, you will not answer" (22:67–68).[46] Luke's Jesus then proceeds to the Son of Man saying, drawn from Mark, adding to Mark that the Son of Man will be seated "from now on" at the right hand of the power "of God" (22:69) and deleting Mark's reference to the Son of Man coming with the clouds of heaven.[47] The addition of the highly figured

---

early morning suggests the use of a special source or tradition," but instead just asserts it. See Taylor, *Passion Narrative*, 81. Here I show that the difference in time and the difference in order do not necessitate positing a source in addition to Mark. Rather, Luke's concern for consistency and a streamlined narrative prompt him to make these changes to Mark.

45. Brown argues that one needs a "divinely revealed knowledge to interpret 'the Messiah' correctly as a title that fully identifies Jesus as the Son of God." This explains the angelic connection between the Davidic Messiah (Luke 1:32) and Son of God (1:35), as well as the demons' proclamation of Jesus as Son of God, which they were able to make, Luke explains, because they knew he was the Messiah (4:41). Brown points out that humans recognize Jesus as Messiah in Luke (by Peter in 9:20; implicitly by John the Baptist in 3:15–16), but that the divine recognizes him as Son of God (3:22; 9:35). Thus, the Jewish leaders, not endowed with divine knowledge of who Jesus is, separated the two titles. Brown adds that this split "has the historicizing effect of suggesting a distinction between 'Messiah' as understood by Jews and the Christian understanding of 'the Son of God.'" See Brown, *Death of the Messiah*, 471–72.

46. Marshall suggests that this response may have in mind the Jewish leaders' refusal to dialogue with Jesus in 20:1–8. See Marshall, *Gospel of Luke*, 850.

47. Bovon explains these changes: "Unlike the parousia [in Mark], the exaltation [in Luke] has the advantage of already having happened (because of the formula ἀπὸ τοῦ νῦν, 'from now on,' the future 'will be' [ἔσται has the value of an immediate future]). It is not visible, as the parousia will be, but it calls forth the certainty that encourages, and that is enough for faith." Bovon, *Luke 3*, 245.

conditional sentences, discussed above, portrays Jesus as rhetorically savvy, attracts the hearers to his side, and draws attention to the fact that his opponents will not believe what he says. Furthermore, by adding "from now on," Luke, through Jesus, foreshadows Jesus' ultimate vindication. Neagoe explains, "[the force of ἀπὸ τοῦ νῦν] is that Luke was concerned to tell his readers that, by virtue of Jesus' glorification (of which they were soon going to read in Luke's narrative), God himself had pronounced the ultimate verdict on the Christological claim which is now on trial (Ac. 2.2–4; 3.13–15), and the evidence of this verdict is *already* available in the event of Jesus' resurrection-exaltation."[48]

To the question about Jesus' identity as Son of God (ὁ υἱὸς τοῦ θεοῦ; 22:70)—a slight change from Mark's "son of the Blessed One" (ὁ υἱὸς τοῦ εὐλογητοῦ; 14:61)—Luke's Jesus responds with, "You yourselves are saying that I am" (ὑμεῖς λέγετε ὅτι ἐγώ εἰμι; 22:70). As Luke splits Mark's one question into two, he also split Mark's one answer into two. Additionally, he also alters Mark's title for Jesus. Instead of Mark's "Son of the Blessed One," Luke has "Son of God," which provides consistency with connections Luke made elsewhere between Jesus' messiahship and his status as God's son (see, e.g., 4:41).[49] Furthermore, Luke takes the first part of Mark's answer (ἐγώ εἰμι) and reworks it for Jesus' answer to the question about being God's Son. Rather than providing a clear and bold answer as does Mark's Jesus, Luke's Jesus puts the answer back on the questioner—"*You* are saying that I am." By doing this, he refuses to walk into his accusers' trap. Ultimately, Luke's splitting of Mark's question and answer into two questions and two answers accomplishes two goals: (1) it allows Luke to focus on each component of Jesus' identity[50]; and (2) it gives Luke's Jesus twice as many opportunities to pull the audience to his side through his rhetorically savvy answers.

Also significant are the several key elements that Luke omits from Mark's hearing before the council: the council's search for testimony against Jesus (14:55); the false testimony against Jesus (14:56–59); the high priests' asking Jesus why he does not answer (14:60); the high priests'

---

48. Neagoe, *Trial of the Gospel*, 66.

49. Matera, "Luke 22,66–71," 56.

50. As he does elsewhere in his Gospel (e.g., 1:32–35; 4:41). Ibid., 55–56. Neyrey adds that the separation "call[s] attention here to the foundational confession of Jesus by his Church." See Neyrey, *Passion according to Luke*, 72. Neagoe notes that this split question "enabled Luke to cast the episode into the form of such a pregnantly Christological dialogue." See Neagoe, *Trial of the Gospel*, 65.

tearing his clothes (14:63a); the blasphemy charge (14:64); and the official condemnation that Jesus deserved death (14:64).[51] When viewed as a whole, we see that Luke draws most of the material that he reworks for his own account from the central section of Mark's version: 14:61b–63.

What do we make of these omissions? The first block that Luke omits, Mark 14:55–59, is related to the false testimony brought against Jesus, including the claim that Jesus said he would destroy and rebuild the temple. Luke's concern for Jesus to secure his audience's support via figured speech and his concern to present the testimony in a formal way may have motivated him to omit these verses.[52] Luke's editorial activity elsewhere—e.g., his moving the hearing from the evening to the morning and his having government officials repeatedly proclaim Jesus innocent—shows his larger concern with a formal trial. While Mark's narration of the council's gathering of false witnesses shows the injustice of what is done to Jesus and the desperation of the Jewish leaders, these are not Luke's primary concerns.[53] Luke's own concerns explain the omission of the temple charge, as Collolly-Weinert explains: "Considering Luke's other efforts in this context to affirm Jesus' innocence and messianic stature as benign, prophetic king, any charges of impiety toward the national religious shrine now would thwart Luke's main concerns here. . . . In his wish to stress Jesus' innocence, Luke can well avoid suggesting that Jesus provoked his own fate by opposing the temple."[54] As argued above, Luke

---

51. Luke also moves Mark's mocking, beating, and demands to prophesy (15:65) to before the pre-trial hearing (22:63–65), as shown in the chart above. Since this material is outside of the stated bounds of this study, I mention only briefly that this rearrangement functions to keep all of the formal trial material together (i.e., an editorial motivation similar to that of his rearrangement of Peter's denial). For more on Luke's rearrangement of this scene, see Brown, *Death of the Messiah*, 568–86, esp. 581–86.

52. Neyrey suggests that Luke's concern for formality is also evident by his not saying that the meeting took place in the high priest's private chambers (Mark 14:54). Neyrey, *Passion according to Luke*, 71.

53. These concerns, however, are not completely absent from Luke. See, e.g., 22:2, where the leaders seek to put Jesus to death out of fear of the people. Furthermore, Luke does not abandon the notion of false witnesses entirely. Instead of placing them in Jesus' story, however, he transfers them to Stephen's arrest (Acts 6:11–13), which, in many ways, has the informal tenor of Mark's passion narrative complete with the search for false testimony (6:13) and stoning by an enraged mob (7:54–58).

54. Connolly-Weinert, "Assessing Omissions," 365. He points to 19:47–48; 20:1, 19; 21:5–7; 22:53, as other evidence where Luke tries to "dissociate the Temple itself from the true source of opposition to Jesus" (361). Brown also mentions the possibility that Luke removed the false charge about Jesus claiming to destroy and rebuild the temple from Mark because he "want[ed] to make it clear to the readers that in his own

sets up the whole passion narrative as a trial of Jesus, but that formal trial does not begin until the assembly brings formal charges against Jesus to Pilate—someone with the official authority to rule on the charges. Once Luke's trial begins, however, he sets out the refutations and confirmations of the accusations in an orderly way.

Furthermore, as I will discuss below, Luke downplays Mark's theme of Jesus' silence out of a desire to emphasize another theme: Jesus' innocence. He does not remove the notion altogether; instead, he relocates Jesus' silence to the Herod pericope, where Jesus is actually silent.[55] Since Luke wanted Jesus to draw the audience to Jesus' side early in the narrative through the use of rhetorical figures, Jesus speaks more in this scene in Luke than he does in Mark. This larger speaking role makes a reference to Jesus' silence (and the high priest's question about his silence) unfitting for his narrative. Thus, Luke's omission of Mark 14:60–61b makes sense in light of his larger rhetorical goals and his concern for consistency in his narrative.

The other omissions are from the end of Mark's narrative of the hearing: the high priests' tearing his clothes, the blasphemy charge, and the condemnation that Jesus deserves death (14:63–64).[56] All three of these elements are a result of Jesus' bold admission (ἐγώ εἰμι) to being the Messiah and the Son of the Blessed One in Mark (14:62). Jesus' veiled answers to the questions in Luke would make such reactions overly dramatic and out of place. Instead of including these elements from Mark, Luke simply retains Mark's rhetorical question ("What further witnesses do we need?" [τί ἔτι χρείαν ἔχομεν μαρτύρων]; 14:63), only slightly modified: "What further testimony do we need?" (τί ἔτι ἔχομεν μαρτυρίας χρείαν; 22:71). Besides moving Mark's χρείαν to the end of the question (possibly for the sake of alliteration between ἔτι and ἔχομεν), the only other change Luke makes is substituting Mark's μαρτύρων with μαρτυρίας. This shift from "witness" (μάρτυς) to "testimony" (μαρτυρία) is natural since there were no outside witnesses in Luke's account.[57] Besides these slight alterations

---

lifetime Jesus was not against the temple." See Brown, *Death of the Messiah*, 436.

55. For more on this, see "Accusations" and "Refutation 2" below.

56. For some, these omissions suggest a source in addition to Mark. Schweizer, for instance, holds that Luke's choice not to include the Jewish leaders' death sentence from Mark 14:64 signifies that "[h]e is obviously following a different account." Schweizer, *Good News according to Luke*, 349.

57. Bovon also points out that Luke's μαρτυρία may have been inspired by Mark 14:55–56. See Bovon, *Luke*, 242, n. 23.

to Mark, Luke found Mark's material fitting for his larger goals, so he retained it (cf. Mark 15:14//Luke 23:22).

The Formal Trial—The Pilate Scene (23:1–25)

The Accusations (23:1–3)

At the conclusion of the pre-trial hearing, the assembly or multitude (ἅπαν τὸ πλῆθος αὐτῶν) brings Jesus before Pilate. Their initial charges are threefold: (1) he misleads the Jewish people; (2) he forbids payment of taxes to the emperor; and (3) he hails himself Messiah, a king (23:2).[58] The first charge presumably relates to Jesus' teaching (cf. 23:5, 14), which was met with opposition from the scribes and Pharisees earlier in the narrative (e.g., 19:47; 20:1–8, 20).[59] The second charge recalls Luke 20:20–26, where the chief priests and scribes sent spies to trap Jesus by asking if it is lawful to pay taxes to Caesar. His response, "Give to Caesar what is Caesar's and to God what is God's," suggests that this charge is patently false.[60] Finally, the third charge flows from the earlier trial before the Sanhedrin (22:66–71), where they ask Jesus if he is the Messiah (though the word "king" [βασιλεύς] is not specifically used).[61] Tyson points out that while others have hailed Jesus Messiah in Luke, Jesus has made no such claim.[62]

---

58. Some see these not as three separate charges but as one charge (misleading the people, repeated in 23:5, 14) with two examples (forbidding payment of taxes and hailing himself Messiah). See, e.g., Grundmann, *Das Evangelium nach Lukas*, 422; Büchele, *Der Tod Jesu*, 27–28; Fitzmyer, *Gospel according to Luke*, 474; Brown, *Death of the Messiah*, 838. Those seeing three charges include Marshall, *Gospel of Luke*, 852; Bock, *Luke*, 365; Bovon, *Luke 3*, 253. While I think they are three separate charges, ultimately this distinction does not affect my argument.

59. Schmidt notes that Luke presents Jesus' teaching the people as the locus of his ministry, and that "misleading the people" would have been "a realistic appraisal of the effect of Jesus' teaching on the people, as experienced by the chief priests and scribes. Luke had emphasized the people as the audience of Jesus' teaching, and the resulting fear the leaders have of their people. Therefore, to charge that as a result of Jesus' teaching the people had been estranged from their leaders is surely not a fabrication. Jesus had indeed diverted the people from their leaders, and done so by taking over their temple." See Schmidt, "Luke's 'Innocent' Jesus," 112–15 (quotation on 115).

60. Bock, *Luke*, 365; Meynet, *L'Évangile selon Saint Luc*, 227. Schmidt, "Luke's 'Innocent' Jesus," 115–16, argues for a more cautious interpretation, saying that "Jesus' refusal to singularly endorse Caesar [was interpreted by the priests and scribes] as an act of defiance. We can label this a misinterpretation, but not a deliberate falsehood."

61. Tannehill, *Narrative Unity of Luke-Acts*, 195.

62. Tyson, *Death of Jesus*, 125–26. See 2:11, 4:41; 20:41–44; 22:67–68. See also the

In the time between the former scene and this one, there has been a shift from theological accusations (Messiah; Son of God) to more overtly political ones (perverting the nation; forbidding payment of taxes; calling himself king)—though the two cannot be separated entirely.[63] This shift may have been the accusers' attempt to present Jesus in opposition to Pilate in hopes of prompting Pilate to rule in their favor.[64] Pilate's clarifying question (23:3) suggests that he views the accusations as political in nature.[65] He asks Jesus simply, "Are you the king of the Jews?" to which Jesus responds, "You are saying so" (σὺ λέγεις; 23:3)—an evasive answer similar to the one given to the council when asked if he was the Son of God (ὑμεῖς λέγετε ὅτι ἐγώ εἰμι; 22:70).

In these charges we see the first parallels between the trials of Jesus and Paul.[66] The similarities are detailed in table 3:[67]

---

comments in "Confirmations 3, 4, and 5" in chapter 4.

63. Brown, *Death of the Messiah*, 739. Cf. Walaskay, "Trial and Death," 84.

64. Bock, *Luke*, 365.

65. Cassidy points out, "The basic thrust of the charges is that Jesus had adopted a stance similar to the Zealots. He was, the Sanhedrin members assert, seeking to throw off Roman rule and establish himself as king over the Jews of Palestine." While Jesus did call for new social patterns, he did not accept the Zealot's notion of resisting Roman rule through armed force. Nor was he attempting to establish an earthly political kingdom in the sense that Pilate would have imagined. Cassidy, *Jesus, Politics, and Society*, 65–66 (quotation on 65). Most commentators believe that these charges are false (and that Luke's hearers would understand them as such in light of Luke's larger narrative). See, e.g., Schmid, *Das Evangelium nach Lukas*, 342; Cassidy, *Jesus, Politics, and Society*, 65; Brown, *Death of the Messiah*, 739–40.

66. In addition to these charges, the Asian Jews also accuse Paul of preaching against the law and the temple (Acts 21:28) and defiling the temple by bringing Greeks into it (Acts 21:28; cf. 24:5). Luke does not intimate any charges against Jesus related to the temple in his Gospel, but false witnesses in Stephen's trial say that they heard Stephen saying that Jesus would destroy the temple and change the customs that Moses handed down to them (Acts 6:14). Thus, there are parallels between these charges against Jesus and Paul (regarding the temple and the customs of Moses), but these specific ones are not mentioned in relation to Jesus until Acts.

67. The titles of these accusations (the left hand column) are Mattill's; the translations of the verses are mine. Moessner categorizes the charges somewhat differently under the headings of "law," "people," and "Caesar." See Moessner, "Christ Must Suffer," 253–54. He also points out that for both Jesus and Paul, "the Temple forms the fulcrum of hostility against those 'prophets and apostles sent to' her" (252).

Table 3. Parallel charges against Jesus and Paul

Accusation	Against Jesus	Against Paul
Perverting the [Jewish] nation	Jesus is "misleading our people" (Luke 23:2)	Paul is "one who arouses dissension among all the Jews throughout the world" (Acts 24:5)
Opposing Caesar's decrees	Jesus is "forbidding the payment of taxes to the emperor" (Luke 23:2)	Paul (and Silas) "act contrary to the decrees of Caesar" (Acts 17:7)
Claiming sovereignty for Christ in opposition to Caesar	Jesus "say[s] that he is the Messiah, a king" (Luke 23:2)	Paul (and Silas) are "saying that there is another king, Jesus" (Acts 17:7)

As with many of the parallels between Luke and Acts, the specifics of these charges are not intimated in Mark's passion narrative. Here and elsewhere in Luke's passion narrative, however, Luke takes a verse from Mark and amplifies it by putting words on the lips of a character.[68] Mark simply says, "And the chief priests accused him of many things" before Pilate (15:3), but Luke takes the opportunity to narrate their specific accusations (23:2)—that Jesus misleads the people, forbids payment of taxes to Caesar, and hails himself Messiah, a king. As described above, the content of these accusations is drawn from Luke's earlier narrative, much of which was drawn from Mark.[69] Thus, it is no stretch to see 23:2 as Luke's adaptation of Mark 15:3 and material that he had drawn from earlier in Mark's narrative. By reworking the material in this way, he not

---

68. Luke also does this with Mark 15:8 and 15:32. In the former, Mark says that the crowd asked Pilate to release Barabbas. Luke takes this and turns it into direct discourse: "Away with this man! Release Barabbas for us!" See "Confirmation 2" below. In the latter, Mark simply says that those who were crucified with Jesus taunted him. Luke gives words to those crucified with him (Luke 23:39–43). See "Refutation 4" and "Confirmation 5" in chapter 4.

69. On Jesus misleading the people, see Mark 11:18//Luke 19:47; Mark 11:27-33//Luke 20:1–8. On payment of taxes to Caesar, see Mark 12:13–17//Luke 20:20–26. On hailing himself Messiah, see Mark 14:62//Luke 22:67.

SCENE 1: THE PRE-TRIAL HEARING AND FORMAL TRIAL   95

only achieves one of his other goals of creating parallels between Jesus and Paul, but he also supplements Mark's narrative because it lacked an indispensable part of a Roman trial: the presentation of complaints.[70]

In 23:3, Luke follows Mark's narrative more closely, offering a near verbatim quotation of Pilate's question and Jesus' answer:

Mark 15:2: Καὶ ἐπηρώτησεν αὐτὸν ὁ Πιλᾶτος·

σὺ εἶ ὁ βασιλεὺς τῶν Ἰουδαίων; ὁ δὲ ἀποκριθεὶς αὐτῷ λέγει· σὺ λέγεις.

Luke 23:3: ὁ δὲ Πιλᾶτος ἠρώτησεν αὐτὸν λέγων·

σὺ εἶ ὁ βασιλεὺς τῶν Ἰουδαίων; ὁ δὲ ἀποκριθεὶς αὐτῷ ἔφη· σὺ λέγεις.

Though keeping this material almost verbatim, Luke reorganizes the scene for the sake of clarity.[71] Compare their arrangements in table 4.

---

70. Bovon, *Luke 3*, 253. Bovon points to Cicero, *Rosc. com.* 20 as evidence that "every Roman trial begins with a presentation of the complaints made." Cf. Sherwin-White, *Roman Society*, 24–25.

71. For Marshall, the close agreement between Mark 15:2 and Luke 23:3 "makes the non-Marcan character of the surrounding narrative all the plainer and strongly suggests that Luke has used another source for his account of the proceedings before Pilate, although he has edited it in his own style. If Luke were drawing on Mk., it would be inexplicable why he had left this one verse unedited." See Marshall, *Gospel of Luke*, 852.

On the contrary, Luke's leaving Mark 15:2 unedited while significantly reworking other material is explicable with an understanding of the techniques associated with paraphrase. When working with a source, an author would retain what was fitting for his argument but rework material that need improved. See chapter 5 for a more complete discussion of this practice with relation to Luke's redaction of Mark. Bovon, who advocates for a special source for parts of Luke's passion narrative, views 23:1–5 as "an editorial reworking of Mark." See Bovon, *Luke 3*, 250.

Table 4. Luke's reorganization of Mark 15:1–5

Mark 15:1–5	Luke 23:1–5
The council hands Jesus over to Pilate (15:1)	The multitude hands Jesus over to Pilate (23:1)
Pilate asks Jesus if he is King of the Jews (15:2a)	The multitude accuses Jesus of three specific charges (23:2)
Jesus answer equivocally (15:2b)	Pilate asks Jesus if he is King of the Jews (23:3a)
The chief priests accuse Jesus of many things (15:3)	Jesus answers equivocally (23:3b)
Pilate questions Jesus again, wondering why he has no answer to their charges (15:4)	Pilate refutes the charges (23:4)
Jesus does not respond, and Pilate is amazed (15:5)	They accuse him of stirring up the people in all Judea (23:5)

In Luke's account, Pilate's question about Jesus being king of the Jews naturally flows out of the third charge—that he hails himself king. In Mark, Pilate's question seems to come out of nowhere. Luke's rearrangement, then, can be considered an improvement of Mark's order, as the initial accusations provide the basis for Pilate's question.

Furthermore, Luke removes Mark's comment about Jesus not responding to Pilate (15:5), a point that Mark also made in 14:61 when Jesus was before the High Priest (which Luke also omitted). Luke instead tells of Jesus' silence just once when he is before Herod (23:9). This can be seen as an instance of one of Luke's editorial tendencies—narrating only once material that is in Mark twice.[72] This tendency could be viewed

---

72. Cadbury, "Four Features," 89. He explains, "[T]he apparent tendency in Luke to avoid parallel scenes must be mentioned. The Gospel [i.e., Luke's Gospel], if we may assume that it used Mark, not only omits the second of Mark's accounts of feeding the multitude, but appears to cancel his account of Jesus in his home town (Mark 6:1–6), and of his anointing by a woman (Mark 14:3–9), and perhaps other sayings or scenes in Mark by introducing, before he comes to these scenes, independent versions (Luke 4:16–30; 7:36–50, etc.). Matthew on the contrary appears to repeat passages

as Luke's concern with brevity, which Quintilian describes as "prun[ing] away everything which can be removed without in any way damaging either the process of judgment or our own interest" (*Inst.* 4.2.40).[73] When the final products are compared, Luke's placement of Jesus' silence in the Herod pericope makes sense, since Jesus does not actually say anything to Herod (in contrast to when he is before the council and Pilate, where he does speak, both in Mark and Luke). Thus, with regard to the charges against Jesus, Pilate's questioning of Jesus, and Jesus' silence before his accusers, Luke can be described as editing Mark in the direction of clarity and brevity.

With the charges specifically stated, Luke spends the remainder of the passion narrative refuting and confirming these charges through various characters. In some cases the concern is to support or counter the specific charges directly (e.g., 23:14, 35), but in most cases the concern is the broader issue of whether Jesus is guilty or innocent (e.g., 23:41, 47).[74]

Refutation 1: Pilate (23:4)

Once Jesus responds to Pilate's question about his role as the king of the Jews, Pilate offers the first of several refutations of the charges against Jesus. He states simply, "I find in this man no cause (for accusation)" (23:4). Here we see Luke, through Pilate, employing one of the topics used for refutation that was common in the rhetorical tradition: Pilate points out the inadequacy of the Jews' charge, saying that they have no basis for their accusations. Additionally, Luke constructs Pilate's response here in a way that would have been pleasing to the ear and that would have caught his hearers'

---

from Mark a second time."

Theon notes that narrating the same thing twice can confuse the reader (*Prog.* 80). While that may have been the motivation for Luke's removal of Mark's doublets elsewhere, I do not think that is what is going on here, as Mark's narrating Jesus' silence twice would not likely confuse the readers to the degree that repeating whole scenes might. There is a place for repetition for the sake of emphasis, but Luke does not want to emphasize Jesus' silence as Mark did, and he may have been concerned about narrating that Jesus was silent when he had just spoken (as happens in Mark).

73. I do not deny that Mark's repetition of stories would have its own rhetorical effect and contributed to his larger purposes. Familiarity with the rhetorical tradition, however, helps explain why Luke might not have found Mark's repetition suitable for his own purposes.

74. Cadbury is right that Luke is more interested in the verdict than the charges. See Cadbury, *Making of Luke-Acts*, 309.

attention. His words make use of the figure assonance: οὐδὲν εὑρίσκω αἴτιον ἐν τῷ ἀνθρώπῳ τούτῳ.[75] Reich notes that this figure can "carry force on behalf of the speaker."[76] Thus, Luke's drawing his hearers' attention to Pilate's proclamation through the use of assonance suggests that the content of the proclamation is a key theme in the narrative that follows.[77]

This first refutation of the charges, like many that follow it, is a Lukan addition to Mark. Prior to the Barabbas scene, Pilate's role in Mark is to emphasize Jesus' lack of response to his accusers. Beyond asking Jesus if he is the king of the Jews, as he does in Luke, Pilate's interaction with Jesus in Mark is twofold: (1) He asks Jesus, "Do you not have an answer? See how many things they accuse you of!" and (2) Jesus' lack of response results in (ὥστε) Pilate's amazement (15:5). Thus, in Mark Pilate's response and his amazement both function to emphasize Jesus' silence before his accusers and the response of those who witness it.[78]

Luke does not choose to emphasize this theme,[79] but instead emphasizes the theme of Jesus' innocence. Luke does, however, take a cue from Mark to employ Pilate as one of the many voices for his own theme. Luke substitutes Pilate's words about Jesus' silence in Mark for the first

---

75. Although not mentioned in the rhetorical handbooks, alliteration/assonance were known in the ancient world. Cf. Reich, *Figuring Jesus*, 37–39; Lausberg, *Handbook of Literary Rhetoric*, §935, 1246.

76. Reich, *Figuring Jesus*, 38.

77. Reich shows Luke using assonance (and paronomasia) toward a similar end in the parable of the sower—to catch the hearers' attention and to emphasize the main subject of the parable. The emphasis helps the audience pay attention. See ibid., 38–39.

78. The prominence of Jesus' silence in Mark is often noted. See Collins, *Mark*, 703–4. In addition to specifically narrating that Jesus was silent, Mark develops the theme of Jesus' silence less directly by placing few words on his lips (especially noticeable when compared to Luke). Jesus speaks two words in Mark 15:3 but does not speak again until the cry of dereliction in 15:34. His only other speech after his arrest is at his appearance before the council in 14:62, and even that pericope states that Jesus was silent and did not answer (14:61). This lack of speech stands in contrast to Luke's narrative where Jesus speaks more extensively before the council (22:67–69, 70), as well as before Pilate (23:3, albeit briefly), to the wailing women (23:28–31), to the second criminal (23:43), and finally to the God (23:46).

79. If Luke is indebted to the noble death tradition, as some believe he is, Luke may have downplayed Jesus' silence in Mark because accounts of noble deaths often include speeches from the main character. Collins points to the accounts of Eleazar's death in 2 and 4 Maccabees and the accounts of the various leaders in the *Acts of the Alexandrians*, where the one threatened with death gives a speech of some sort. See ibid. Also see "Translation of δίκαιος" in chapter 1 for a fuller discussion of Luke and the noble death tradition.

of Pilate's three declarations of Jesus' innocence—one adorned with the figure of assonance to draw attention to the theme he is beginning to develop.[80] With this substitution of material, Luke sets up Pilate as the first of several people to refute the charges against Jesus.

Confirmation 1: The Jewish Leaders (23:5)

In response to Pilate's refutation of their charges, the chief priests and the crowds (τοὺς ὄχλους)[81] respond by confirming their charges against Jesus: "He stirs up the people by teaching throughout all Judea" (23:5). Here we see the accusers adding force to their earlier charges by emphasizing how geographically widespread Jesus' influence has been: he causes trouble "... throughout all of Judea, starting from Galilee [and coming] as far as this place" (23:5; cf. Theon, *Prog.* 94; Nicolaus, *Prog.* 30; Quintilian, *Inst.* 5.10.37–42). Not only is Jesus guilty, but the effects of his wrongdoing are even greater than they had mentioned before.

Mattill categorizes this charge against Jesus as "stirring up sedition" and sees a parallel with Paul in Acts 24:5, where Tertullus, the high priest Ananias' attorney, calls Paul "a ringleader of the sect of the Nazarenes."[82] Beyond the similarity in the nature of the charge, the emphasis on the widespread effects of Jesus' wrongdoing parallels the accusation against Paul mentioned above—that he is an agitator among *all* the Jews *throughout the world* (Acts 24:5; emphasis added). Essentially, the accusers confirm their accusations by emphasizing their extensive impact.

Regarding its relation to Mark, this verse is similar to 23:2. There Luke took Mark 15:3 ("and the chief priests accused him of many things") and expanded it into specific charges against Jesus. Luke edits

---

80. We remember from chapter 2 that the paraphrase in the *Bodleian Greek Inscription* 3019 concerned itself with stylistically elaborating on the original by adding figures of speech that were lacking in the original. Here and in several other places (e.g., 22:67–68; 23:28–31) Luke's additions to Mark include figures of speech.

81. Based on the usages of ὄχλος and λαός in the passion narrative, Weatherly argues that τοὺς ἀρχιερεῖς καὶ τοὺς ὄχλους in 23:4 refers to "a sizable, unorganized gathering of the leadership, led by the high priests." He points out that the ὄχλος who arrested Jesus in 22:47 "is explicitly composed of high priests, captains of the temple and elders (22:52)" and that 23:10 specifies that the chief priests and scribes are the accusers. See Weatherly, *Jewish Responsibility*, 63–64 (quotation from 64, n. 1). Cf. Kodell, "Luke's Use of *laos*," 328, who argues that Luke uses λαός when he wants to distinguish between the people and the leaders.

82. Mattill, "Jesus-Paul Parallels," 33.

Mark similarly in 23:5. In order to construct his refutation-confirmation organizational scheme, Luke adds specifics to Mark 15:3 in order to provide the first confirmation of the charges against Jesus: "He stirs up the people by teaching throughout all Judea . . . " (23:5).

Refutation 2: Herod and Pilate (23:6–16)

At the mention of Galilee, Pilate asks if Jesus is a Galilean.[83] When his suspicions are confirmed, he sends Jesus to Herod Antipas since Jesus would have been under his jurisdiction.[84] We remember from Quintilian that transferring a case was one way in which the defense could counter a charge (*Inst.* 5.13.3).[85] Thus, even before he vocally refutes the charges again in 23:14–15 and 23:22, Pilate counters the charges against Jesus though his actions—by transferring the case to Herod.

Herod has a history with Jesus in Luke. Luke narrates that Herod was perplexed (διαπορέω) by Jesus and the things he heard about him, which prompted him to seek to see Jesus (9:7–9). Luke specifically connects the passage in ch. 9 with Jesus' appearance before him in the passion narrative by noting Herod's joy at seeing Jesus "for he had been wanting to see him for a long time" (23:8). The hearer no doubt experiences some apprehension when discovering that Jesus will go before Herod, however, since the

---

83. Darr notes that in addition to binding the Herod scene with the previous one, the reference to Galilee also connects Jesus' passion with his Galilean ministry. Luke connects Galilee and Jerusalem, the ministry and the passion, through the use of "continuing characters" like the men and women who accompany Jesus from Galilee to Jerusalem and Herod (who ruled over Galilee, as Luke notes in 3:1). Darr explains, "Herod's presence has been felt in each phase of the unfolding divine plan from John's activities (3:1, 19–20) to Jesus' Galilean ministry (9:7–9) and the journey to Jerusalem (13:31–35). Herod also provides elements of conflict and suspense that maintain reader interest. It is only fitting then that the tetrarch play a role in the passion as well, for he is an important part of the dramatic connective tissue that binds the entire story together." See Darr, *Herod the Fox*, 191.

84. Walaskay offers five reasons scholars have proposed for why Pilate sent Jesus to Herod: (1) Pilate wanted to free himself of a difficult case; (2) Pilate wanted to appease Herod for having the Galileans massacred; (3) Luke had a special contact in Herod's house that provided him with this information; (4) a law of *forum domicilii* may have bound Pilate to send Jesus to Herod; and (5) Luke "worked up the story from Psalm 2:1-2." See Walaskay, *"And So We Came to Rome"*, 42–43.

85. Marshall adds that this transfer may also have been Pilate's attempt to pass off a difficult case to someone else or an attempt to solicit a Jewish opinion on the matter. See Marshall, *Gospel of Luke*, 855. Cf. Bovon, *Luke 3*, 259.

Pharisees had informed Jesus earlier in the narrative that Herod wanted to kill him (13:31). A threat from Herod would not have been taken lightly, of course, since Luke describes him as one who had done all sorts of evil things (3:19) like orchestrating John the Baptist's imprisonment (3:19–20) and beheading (9:9).[86] When Jesus receives the warning from the Pharisees, he insults Herod through the use of a rhetorical figure—a metaphor. He refers to Herod as a fox.[87] Furthermore, Jesus foreshadows his upcoming necessary (δεῖ)[88] death in Jerusalem (13:32–35), which the reader would likely recall when hearing 23:7–12.

And yet, despite his earlier threat to kill Jesus and his being called a fox by Jesus, Herod does not take advantage of the opportunity—finally at his fingertips—to kill Jesus. Although he and his soldiers do disdain and mock Jesus (23:11)—contributing to Luke's characterization of Herod as evil—they nonetheless send him back to Pilate where Pilate announces to the Jewish rulers and people that both he and Herod "found in this man no cause (for accusation)" (23:14). This announcement is Pilate's appeal to the previous judgment by a different ruler as a way of, yet again, refuting the charges against Jesus (cf. *Rhet. Her.* 2.13.19; Cicero, *Inv.* 1.42.79; Quintilian, *Inst.* 5.2.2). Ultimately, then, both Herod and Pilate examine Jesus (12:9, 14–15), and they find him innocent of the charges of perverting the nation. Thus, Luke places on the lips of Pilate the refutation that the charges are inadequate.

---

86. Darr argues that Luke primes his audience "to compare any interaction Jesus might have with Herod to what they know about John's interaction with the same ruler." See Darr, *Herod the Fox*, 173. Here Darr addresses the objection that the Pharisees were actually misrepresenting Herod for their own benefit (i.e., to get Jesus to leave their territory) and that Herod's interest in Jesus was only motivated by curiosity, not murderous intent. See ibid., 175–79.

87. Through the study of ancient physiognomy, Parsons shows that ancient people characterized foxes as reddish, of bad character, wily, deceitful, coy, evasive, rapacious, shrewd, and destructive. See Parsons, *Body and Character*, 69–71. Darr notes that given the way Luke has already characterized Herod in the narrative, ancient hearers of Luke would likely attribute the fox-like trait of destructiveness to Herod. See Darr, *Herod the Fox*, 182–83. Reich points out that the Pharisees are silenced by this attack against Herod; this is another instance of Jesus defeating his interlocutors through the use of figured speech. See Reich, *Figuring Jesus*, 84.

88. Fitzmyer notes that the purpose of this passage is "to stress the inevitability of Jesus' reaching a place of suffering (and of death). This is part of his destiny, and someone like Herod is not to stand in the way of it." See Fitzmyer, *Gospel according to Luke*, 1029. For more on δεῖ and divine necessity in Luke-Acts, see Cadbury, *Making of Luke-Acts*, 303–5; Cosgrove, "Divine ΔΕΙ," 168–90; Rothschild, *Luke-Acts*, 185–212.

Thus far, then, Luke has provided two different witnesses to Jesus' innocence—Pilate, twice, and Herod.[89] Marion Soards points out that because of his back story in Luke's Gospel, Herod is not an inconsequential witness: "If so wicked a man as Herod . . . is obliged to recognize his innocence, one cannot help but see the injustice of Jesus' execution."[90] Darr also points out that the Herod scene contains a reversal of expectations—the audience expects Herod to kill Jesus but he does not. This reversal "reinforces the major apologetic theme of 23:1–25: Jesus is innocent of all the charges brought against him by the rulers of the people. Even Jesus' enemy, the notorious Herod, agrees with Pilate that the accused is not guilty."[91]

Also significant about Jesus' appearance before Herod is that it parallels a portion of Paul's trial.[92] In Acts 26 Paul appears before Herod Agrippa at the initiation of the governor Festus, who declares, "This man is doing nothing to deserve death or imprisonment" (οὐδὲν θανάτου ἢ δεσμῶν ἄξιόν [τι] πράσσει ὁ ἄνθρωπος οὗτος; 26:31). While Herod Antipas has no direct discourse in Jesus' trial, as Agrippa does in Acts, Luke does tell us that Herod Antipas questions Jesus at length. Furthermore, although Herod never gives a verdict on the charges against Jesus, as Agrippa does in Acts, Pilate later reports on his behalf, "Neither has

---

89. See below for a fuller discussion of Herod as a second witness to fulfill the requirements of Deut 19:15. But also see Soards, who argues, "A look at the narrative reveals that it is not Herod's verdict or *testimony* for its own sake or as fulfillment of Deut 19, 15 that is of importance. Rather, this testimony functions most explicitly *to emphasize the innocence of Jesus.*" See Soards, "Tradition, Composition, and Theology in Luke's Account of Jesus," 363 (emphasis original).

90. Ibid., 361. Cf. Tyson, "Jesus and Herod Antipas," 239–46. Tyson points out that Herod perceived Jesus as part of the movement of John the Baptist (Luke 9:9). Herod had executed John out of fear of his political power, which suggests that "Herod Antipas was after a movement and not a man. The movement he was after was that which Herod thought had been begun by John and continued by Jesus" (240). Herod may have also felt threatened by members of his court (or their relatives) following Jesus (Joanna in Luke 8:3; Manaen in Acts 13:1).

91. Darr, *Herod the Fox*, 201. While Darr does not make this point, one could argue for a role reversal of Pilate, though one that is not nearly as drastic as Herod's. Besides Luke's note that Pilate was governor of Judea when John began his preaching (3:1–3), the only other time Luke mentions Pilate is in 13:1, where some people report to Jesus that Pilate had mixed some Galileans' blood with the blood of their sacrifices. Thus, prior to the passion narrative, the only mention of Pilate (outside of Luke's setting the stage in 3:1) is one that shows him as a sacrilegious murderous Gentile, though one not related to Jesus in any way.

92. Walaskay suggests that Luke has styled Jesus' trial after Paul's (not the other way around, as some suggest). See Walaskay, *"And So We Came to Rome"*, 43.

Herod [found Jesus guilty], for he sent him back to us. Indeed, he has done nothing to deserve death" (23:15). Thus, both Jesus and Paul appear before a Herod at the initiation of a Roman ruler, and both are proclaimed as undeserving of death.[93]

In Mark, Jesus does not appear before Herod, though some material in this pericope can be traced back to Mark. There are at least five connections between this pericope and Mark, four of which occur in a block in the middle of Luke's pericope. Table 5 shows these connections.

Table 5. Markan material in Luke 23:6–16

Mark 15:16–20	Luke 23:6–16
Jesus does not respond to the council (14:61) or Pilate (15:5)	Jesus does not respond to Herod (23:9)
The chief priests (οἱ ἀρχιερεῖς) accuse (κατηγορέω) Jesus of many things (15:5)	The chief priests (οἱ ἀρχιερεῖς) and scribes accuse (κατηγορέω) Jesus (23:10)
Roman soldiers clothe Jesus in purple, place a crown of thorns on him, hail him king of the Jews, strike him, spit on him, kneel before him, then redress him. (15:16–20)	Herod and his soldiers disdain Jesus, mock Jesus, and put shining clothes on him (23:11)
Allusion to Isa 42:2 (15:19)	Allusion to Isa 42:3 (23:9)
Reference to beating Jesus associated with Pilate (15:15)	Reference to beating Jesus associated with Pilate (23:16; cf. 23:22)

The first, discussed above, is Luke's rearrangement of Jesus' silence before his accusers to a place in the narrative where Jesus actually does not respond at all (in contrast to the cases in Mark 14 and 15, where Jesus does speak). If Luke wanted to preserve Jesus' words before the council and Pilate but wanted to mention Jesus' silence at some point, his appearance

93. Though he does not have a trial before Herod, Herod has James killed in Acts 12:1–2. Furthermore, he seizes and imprisons Peter, and, presumably, would have tried him had the angel not delivered him from prison (Acts 12:3–19).

before Herod would seem like a natural place. The second connection is the chief priests' accusations against Jesus. Luke elaborated on these accusations when Jesus was before Pilate (23:2, 5), but here he simply narrates that the chief priests, along with the scribes, accuse Jesus.

Luke maintains a third connection with Mark in his narration of Jesus' being mocked by soldiers, but there are significant differences between the two mockings. Mark's mocking by the soldiers occurs after Pilate hands Jesus over to be crucified and is done by Pilate's soldiers, whereas Luke's occurs before Pilate's sentencing and is done by Herod's soldiers. Furthermore, Mark's mocking scene is much more detailed than Luke's. Mark tells of the soldiers' taking Jesus into the palace courtyard and gives several specific examples of the mocking—clothing Jesus in purple, crowning him with a crown of thorns, saluting him with "Hail, king of the Jews," and kneeling to pay homage to him (15:17–19). Joel Marcus argues that these actions "reflect Roman triumphal processions," but since all of these actions are done in mockery, Mark actually depicts this as an "anti-triumph."[94] Mark also alludes to Isa 42:3 by describing Jesus being struck with a reed (κάλαμος).

While many agree that Luke is drawing on this scene from Mark for 23:11,[95] Luke does alter Mark significantly. Luke removes the beating with reeds, but he does not remove the allusion to Isa 42. By narrating Jesus' silence in this pericope instead of elsewhere, he maintains the allusion to Isa 42, only to v. 2 ("he will neither cry out nor lift up his voice nor let his voice be heard in the street") instead of v. 3 ("a bruised reed he will not break . . ."), the latter of which Mark chose. Whereas elsewhere Luke gives detail to some of Mark's summary statements, here Luke gives a summary statement of one of Mark's detailed descriptions. Luke removes Mark's purple clothing, crown of thorns, mocking hails, and kneeling and instead summarily explains that the soldiers disdain and mock him. This may be Luke's attempt to narrate only briefly "events that would distress the hearers" (Theon, *Prog.* 80 [Kennedy, 29]). He includes that Jesus was

---

94. Marcus, *Mark 8—16*, 1046–47. Marcus shows the similarities between Mark's portrayal of Jesus' mocking and Philo's description of the royal mockery of the lunatic Carabas, who was crowned with papyrus, given a royal robe, hailed as lord, and surrounded by a mock bodyguard (described in *Flacc.* 36–39).

95. Bovon lists several words that the passages have in common. See Bovon, *Luke 3*, 263, n. 16.

disdained and mocked, but he does not include details that may have unnecessarily upset his hearers.[96]

Another significant change that Luke makes to Mark's mocking account regards Jesus' clothing. In Mark, the soldiers dress Jesus in purple (ἐνδιδύσκουσιν αὐτὸν πορφύραν), mock him in several ways, then remove the purple clothing and put his own clothes back on him (15:17–20). As mentioned above, the purple clothing contributes toward the soldiers' mockery of Jesus' kingship, as purple signified royalty. Jesus' clothing in Luke has a different function, however. In Luke, Herod's soldiers put shining or bright clothing on Jesus (περιβαλὼν ἐσθῆτα λαμπρὰν) and send him back to Herod (23:11).[97] Darr notes that the scholar's natural inclination is to understand the shining clothing in terms of Mark's purple clothing and thus relate it to mockery of his supposed kingship.[98] Instead, he argues,[99] Luke's new terminology, along with his elimination of Mark's other kingly aspects like the crown and hailing him as king, symbolizes Jesus' innocence. Bright or gorgeous garments could indicate uprightness or innocence in antiquity;[100] when this connection is read in light of the verdict of innocence that Herod gives Pilate just a few verses later, we understand the clothing as Herod's way of communicating his conviction of Jesus' innocence to Pilate. Thus, Luke's substitution of shining clothes

---

96. Admittedly, Theon gives death as an example of an event that would distress hearers and that should thus be narrated briefly. The centrality of Jesus' death in early Christianity, would, of course, prevent Luke from narrating Jesus' death too briefly. Luke does, however, take care to remove portions of Mark that emphasize the suffering of Jesus (e.g., the flogging [Mark 15:15]; the crown of thorns [Mark 15:17]; the striking Jesus' head with a reed [Mark 15:19]).

97. Grammatically speaking, the clothing (περιβαλὼν) of Jesus seems to be linked with the sending (ἀνέπεμψεν) of Jesus back to Pilate. That is, περιβαλὼν is an attendant circumstance participle linked with ἀνέπεμψεν. Though they list other grammatical possibilities, Culy, Parsons, and Stigall support this understanding, as do Fitzmyer and Bock. See Culy, Parsons, and Stigall, *Luke: A Handbook*, 708–9; Fitzmyer, *Gospel according to Luke*, 1478; Bock, *Luke 9:51—24:53*, 1818. Bovon, too, connects περιβαλών with ἀνέπεμψεν. See Bovon, *Luke 3*, 269. Others, however, link περιβαλών with ἐμπαίξας. See, e.g., Johnson, *Gospel of Luke*, 364–66.

98. Bock, for example, interprets Herod's arraying Jesus in shining apparel as an attempt to mock Jesus. See Bock, *Luke*, 367. Others with this interpretation include Marshall, *Gospel of Luke*, 856; Schweizer, *Good News according to Luke*, 352; Johnson, *Gospel of Luke*, 366; Wolter, *Das Lukasevangelium*, 744; Bovon, *Luke 3*, 270.

99. Darr, *Herod the Fox*, 199–201. Brown and Müller argue for the same interpretation: Müller, "Jesus vor Herodes," 111–41; Brown, *Death of the Messiah*, 774–76; 866; Untergassmair, "Zur Problematik," 287.

100. Müller, "Jesus vor Herodes," 134–36. Cf. Rev 19:8; Josephus, *J. W.* 2.8.3.

for Mark's purple clothes is another editorial move that emphasizes his larger concern for Jesus' innocence.

Beyond these connections related to Herod, Luke also connects the larger scene (23:6–16) to Mark by introducing the "discipline" or "punishment" (παιδεύω) of Jesus in 23:16, something he mentions again in 23:22. The second reference appears to be Luke's redaction of Mark's flogging in 15:15. The first reference anticipates the second. In both of Luke's instances, Pilate's reference to the punishment immediately follows his declaration of Jesus' innocence and his proclamation that Jesus has done nothing to deserve death. Pilate presents the punishment as an alternative to issuing the death sentence, and his two-fold attempt to have Jesus punished (instead of crucified) functions as a further refutation of Jesus' guilt.

Luke's changing Mark's φραγελλόω to παιδεύω has at least two rhetorical effects. First, it is another example of Luke's tempering events that may have distressed his hearers. By changing Mark's φραγελλόω—a flogging or scourging of prisoners after the pronouncement of a death sentence—to παιδεύω—a less severe beating that would have been the extent of the punishment—he minimizes the physical abuse against Jesus.[101] Luke further tempers the events by never actually narrating the punishment. Whereas Mark explicitly states that Pilate flogged Jesus and handed him over for crucifixion (15:15), Luke keeps Pilate's punishment as a threat to happen in the future (παιδεύσας οὖν αὐτὸν ἀπολύσω; 23:16, 22). He never actually narrates that Pilate punishes Jesus physically. Second, Büchele notes that Luke's substitution of verbs from one that connotes a specific sentence with an official character (φραγελλόω) to one that connotes a general designation for a penalty (παιδεύω) is Luke's way of avoiding official confirmation of the guilt of Jesus. An official form of punishment, he argues, would have been viewed as an official confirmation of guilt.[102]

Beyond these five connections (Jesus' silence, the chief priests' accusations, the soldiers' mocking, the allusion to Isa 42, and the mention of punishment by Pilate), the rest of the material in 23:6–16 does not seem to stem from Mark's passion narrative—Pilate's transferring Jesus to

---

101. In addition to the standard lexica, see Brown, *Death of the Messiah*, 792–93; Green, *Death of Jesus*, 83–84, n. 277. Fitzmyer, *Gospel according to Luke*, 94–95, mentions other passages where Luke seems to temper violence in Mark. See, e.g., Mark 6:17–29//Luke 3:19–20 (John's death); Mark 11:15b–16//Luke 19:4 (the cleansing the temple); Mark 15:16–20//Luke 23:11 (Jesus' beating by soldiers). Cf. the discussion on Luke's softening of violence in Mark in Cadbury, *Style and Literary Method*, 92–94.

102. Büchele, *Der Tod Jesu*, 35, n. 77.

Herod (23:6–7); Herod's desire to see Jesus perform a sign (23:8); Herod's questioning Jesus then sending him back to Pilate (23:9a, 11c); Pilate and Herod's newfound friendship; Pilate reconvening the chief priests, rulers, and the people (23:13); Pilate's second declaration of Jesus' innocence (23:14); and Pilate's report that Herod found Jesus innocent (23:15). This large block of material that is unique to Luke raises the question of its origin. Did Luke create it himself (possibly drawing on other portions of Mark or on oral traditions), or did he derive it from a non-extant written source?[103]

Some scholars see enough Lukan features in these verses to be convinced that Luke wrote them himself—even some scholars who advocate for a special source for much of Luke's passion narrative. For example, Taylor, possibly the most renowned advocate for an additional source, concludes that "there is little to suggest the use of a source" for the Herod pericope in Luke 23:6–16 because it contains so many of Luke's own words and phrases.[104] It was most likely composed by Luke, Taylor believes, though "out of tradition contained in the non-Markan source."[105] In addition to Lukan vocabulary and phrases, Boismard also points to parallels with Acts as evidence that the scene originated with Luke, not

---

103. For the most thorough survey of source theories of the Herod pericope, see Harrington, *Lukan Passion Narrative*, 691–709. Harrington categorizes the theories into nine different groups: a continuous source or tradition; separate sources or traditions; unspecified sources independent of Mark; unspecified source(s) in conjunction with Mark; historical account with no reference to nature and extent of source; Lukan composition; inspired by Matthew; non-historical without further information; undetermined (provided no information on source of Herod pericope). These categories are far too detailed for our purposes here and can be grouped into the two we use here: written sources or Lukan composition, the latter of which was likely influenced by irrecoverable oral traditions in some cases.

104. Taylor, *Passion Narrative of St. Luke*, 87. Here Taylor relies on the distinctive word lists from Stanton and Rehkopf: Stanton, *Gospels as Historical Documents*; Rehkopf, *Die lukanische Sonderquelle*. Schweizer, *Good News according to Luke*, 351, makes a similar observation.

Scholars who generally argue against a special passion source also make this point. See, e.g., Büchele, *Der Tod Jesu*, 32; Müller, "Jesus vor Herodes," 114–16. Brown adds, "Writing and vocabulary heavily attested elsewhere in Luke-Acts are very much in evidence here, and there is virtually nothing in the episode that could be called nonLucan. Indeed, were this scene taken over as a whole by Luke from a special source, one would have to judge that the source had the same style as Luke!" See Brown, *Death of the Messiah*, 761 (see also 779).

105. Taylor, *Passion Narrative of St. Luke*, 89. This notion seems to contradict his comment from two pages prior that "there is little to suggest the use of a source."

another source.¹⁰⁶ Furthermore, Luke may have drawn on Mark's account of Herod killing John the Baptist (6:14–29), an account he omitted earlier in his Gospel.¹⁰⁷ Neyrey summarizes reasons to believe the Herod pericope originated with Luke: "[A]ll the materials in Lk 23:6–12 may be found either in the Markan source to the passion narrative (Mk 14:3–5, 16–20), in Lukan redactional additions to Mark's text (Lk 9:9 to Mk 6:14–16), or in Scriptural prophecies which are fulfilled (Acts 4:25–26). There is no need to demand a special source for 23:6–12."¹⁰⁸

Once these scholars argue that the pericope is from Luke's hand, they attempt to explain what prompted Luke to compose it. Some connect it to Deut 19:15, which requires that a matter be confirmed not by a single witness, but by two or three. In that case, Herod functions as the second witness, in addition to Pilate.¹⁰⁹ Others see it as a development of Ps 2, where Herod functions as the βασιλεύς and Pilate as the ἄρχων—the two characters who plot against the Lord's anointed one.¹¹⁰ This development of the psalm is consistent with Luke's connecting Herod and

---

106. Boismard, *Synopse des quatre Évangiles en français*, 418.

107. On the connections between Mark 6:14 ("King Herod heard of it"), Luke 9:9c ("And he sought to see him"—a comment not in Mark), and Luke 23:8 ("he [Herod] had been wanting to see him [Jesus] for a long time"), see Neyrey, *Passion according to Luke*, 78. Cf. Harrington, *Lukan Passion Narrative*, 717–21.

108. Neyrey, *Passion according to Luke*, 79. For responses to several of these points, see Fitzmyer, *Gospel according to Luke*, 1479.

109. See, e.g., Grundmann, *Das Evangelium nach Lukas*, 424. Grundmann explains, "Die eigentliche Bedeutung des Berichtes scheint jedoch in Folgendem zu liegen: Der Bericht läuft darauf hinaus, daß Herodes neben Pilatus zum Zeugen der Unschuld Jesu wird (V. 15), so daß entsprechend dem Grundsatz Deut. 19:15 „erst auf die Aussage zweier oder dreier Zeugen wird eine Sache bestätigt"–vgl. auch Deut 17,6; Joh 8, 17 u.a. - zwei Zeugen aufgeführt werden können. Zwei bezeugen am Eingang der Geschichte Jesu, daß er der verheißene Messias ist, Simeon und Hanna, zwei bezeugen am Ausgang seiner Geschichte, daß seine Messianität keine politische Herrschaft ist, Pilatus und Herodes."

Büchele goes even further and argues that Deut 19:15 influenced the way that Luke constructed his entire passion narrative. Each of the main sections of the passion narrative (23:1–25; 23:26–49; 23:50–56) contains at least three witnesses to the charge and thus meets the specifications of Deut 19:15. See Büchele, *Der Tod Jesu*, 70–75. Some see Büchele's understanding of the influence of Deut 19:15 on Luke as too rigid. For such a critique, see, e.g., Tyson, *Death of Jesus*, 116–17. Schweizer, *Good News according to Luke*, 353, also connects Herod as a second witness to Deut 19:15.

110. Those connecting Luke 23:6–16 to Ps 2 include Dibelius, "Herodes und Pilatus," 113–26; Cadbury, *Making of Luke-Acts*, 231; Schweizer, *Good News according to Luke*, 352. Marshall, *Gospel of Luke*, 855, exposes difficulties with the notion that Ps 2 gave rise to this pericope.

Pilate with Ps 2:1–2 in Acts 4:25–27: after citing Ps 2, Luke explains that Herod and Pilate gathered together with the Gentiles and people of Israel against God's holy servant Jesus, whom he anointed.[111] Still others argue that Paul's trial before Agrippa was the inspiration for the Herod story.[112] These possibilities, of course, are not mutually exclusive.[113]

Another camp, however, argues that Luke derived this material from a pre-Lukan source, be it L or a passion source.[114] Perry, for example argues that the seamless merging of the Herod scene with the Pilate scenes before and after it suggest that 23:1–16 derives from Luke's non-Markan source.[115] Both Tyson and Green find the thesis that Luke created the scene from Ps 2 unconvincing because Luke does not refer to the verse in the trial scene, because of the tensions between Luke 23 and Acts 4 (i.e., in the former, Pilate and Herod declare Jesus innocent; in the latter, they gather against him with the people), and because of the difficulty in seeing this psalm give rise to Luke 23:6–16 without some prior tradition.[116] These scholars handle the claim that this pericope is ripe with Lukan

---

111. See below for problems with this view.

112. Matera, "Luke 23, 1–25," 542–43.

113. E.g., Mattill thinks that Luke's knowledge of Paul's appearance before Herod, the early Christian community's interpretation of Ps. 2 as referring to Pilate and Herod, and Luke's desire to place Jesus and Paul in parallel prompted Luke to compose this scene. See Mattill, "Jesus-Paul Parallels," 39–40.

114. Easton argues for the former; Green argues for the latter ("an *alternative continuous narrative tradition*"), as does Grundmann. Easton, *Gospel according to St. Luke*, 343; Green, *Death of Jesus*, 82 (emphasis original); Grundmann, *Das Evangelium nach Lukas*, 14–17. In fact, Easton says that 21:10 through the end of the Gospel (sans 24:36–49) "is based chiefly on L, with free Markan contributions" (xxiv). He says that his conception of L is indebted to Weiss and Streeter (xxiii). For a fuller description of what constitutes L for Easton, see xxv–xxx. Grundmann believes this special passion tradition may have been associated with (but originally distinct from) Q.

115. For Perry, only v. 3 relies on Mark. See Perry, *Sources of Luke's Passion Narrative*, 45.

116. Tyson, "Lukan Version," 256; Green, *Death of Jesus*, 81–82. Brown adds that, save for the connection in Acts 4, Luke never refers to Herod Antipas as a βασιλεύς or to Pilate as an ἄρχων. See Brown, *Death of the Messiah*, 780–81, for more on Ps 2 as inspiration for Luke 23:6–16. I agree with Brown that the tradition about Jesus going before Herod likely did not arise from reading Ps 2 but rather "led to interpreting the psalm in the manner we see in Acts 4" (782).

vocabulary and phrases by either pointing to the problematic nature of word studies[117] or by positing continuity between Luke and his source.[118]

Regardless of on which side of the source issue scholars land, they agree on the function of the Herod scene—it provides another witness to Jesus' innocence. Fitzmyer even goes so far as to say that this scene is a "minor one" with "no significance for the understanding of Jesus' person or fate." Its sole importance lies "in the testimony that Herod brings to the story; he finds nothing worthy of punishment in Jesus and sends him back to Pilate. The scene enhances Jesus' innocence, because it discloses that *two* Palestinian authorities bear witness by their actions to this innocence."[119]

Ultimately, arguments against Luke's use of a source besides Mark for this pericope are stronger than those in support of it. First, Luke's reworking of Mark's Herod material elsewhere in his Gospel demonstrates that Luke felt free to rearrange and develop Mark's material about Herod.[120] Though some of the examples of paraphrase analyzed in the previous chapter show only slight revisions of the source, Theon's comments on advanced students' paraphrasing an entire speech (*Prog.* 110P) suggest that a reorganization and development of material like Luke does of Mark's Herod material was not unprecedented. That some of the material on Herod would show up in the passion narrative is natural in light of the judicial nature of Jesus' trials[121] and in light of Paul's appearance before Herod in Acts. Herod's return to the story in the passion narrative is a way of wrapping up the loose ends of a story Luke began earlier in the Gospel but did not bring to completion. Hearers may have wondered what resulted from Jesus' overt challenge to Herod ("Go tell that fox . . ."), and bringing resolution to that encounter in the passion narrative is fitting since Jesus mentions his own death in Jerusalem in his response to Herod (13:33). Furthermore, as described above, concluding the Herod material in the passion narrative is a way for Luke to achieve one of his

---

117. Green, *Death of Jesus*, 80–81. Green's point here is well taken, especially when those who argue against a special passion source often point to the problems with words studies.

118. Hoehner, *Herod Antipas*, 226.

119. Fitzmyer, *Gospel according to Luke*, 1480.

120. Though, of course, some attribute the differences between Luke and Mark's Herod material elsewhere in their works to Luke's having another source. See, e.g., Paffenroth, *Story of Jesus according to L*, 58.

121. I.e., a ruler from Galilee appearing as a judge fits naturally into the trial.

larger rhetorical goals—providing a high ranking and unexpected witness to Jesus' innocence, along with a second testimony from Pilate.

Second, Perry argues that the Herod pericope comes from a non-Markan source because it merges seamlessly with the Pilate scenes before and after it. This argument falters because it assumes that the Pilate scenes were also composed from the non-Markan source—a point that I refuted above (and will continue to refute below)[122] by showing that Luke likely composed 23:1-5 by reworking Mark. If his logic (that seamless merging of scenes implies that all the material in 23:1-25 is of the same origin) were applied to my findings (that 23:1-5, 13-25 are Luke's reworking of Mark), the seamless transitions between these scenes would actually suggest that Luke composed 23:6-12 out of Markan material.

Third, while relying almost exclusively on word lists to determine the origin of Luke's material is problematic,[123] the conclusion by Taylor—who generally assumes that differences from Mark suggests Luke's use of another source—that 23:6-16 was composed by Luke speaks to the extent of Luke's hand in the composition of the pericope. That so many other scholars arrive at the same conclusion as Taylor through means other than word frequency suggests that Taylor's conclusion is valid in this case.[124]

Could Luke have drawn this material from a separate written source? Of course, but recourse to such a source is unnecessary in light of the points just intimated. Rather, Luke likely pulls from material in Mark that he had not yet developed and develops it in a fitting place in the narrative—in the judicial proceedings. In addition to being fitting, this placement allows Luke to set up parallels between Jesus and Paul in Acts, and it gives Luke one more character through whom to develop his theme of innocence. The repetition of Jesus' innocence from Pilate (23:13-16) is little more than repetition of material Luke used in previous verses (and that he continues to develop in later verses)—he repeats the charge of misleading the people (23:14; cf. 23:2) and repeats almost verbatim his declaration of Jesus' innocence (23:14; cf. 23:4, 22).[125] The

---

122. See "Confirmation 2" and "Refutation 3" for my argument that Luke also composed 23:18-25 without the aid of an additional source.

123. On problems with using word lists to determine sources, see Green, *Death of Jesus*, 80-81. At the same time, however, Green relies on word statistics elsewhere to determine the likelihood of Luke relying on Mark. See, e.g., ibid., 83.

124. E.g., Matera, "Luke 23, 1-25"; Harrington, *Lukan Passion Narrative*, 711-12.

125. Compare 23:4 (οὐδὲν εὑρίσκω αἴτιον ἐν τῷ ἀνθρώπῳ τούτῳ) with 23:14 (οὐδὲν

theme of innocence is present in Mark, though subdued in comparison to Luke.[126] We could say that Luke begins to do something here akin to Quintilian's description of paraphrase: he "tak[es] up some thoughts and turn[s] them in as many ways as possible (*Inst.* 10.5.9). Luke takes this nascent theme of innocence from Mark and turns it on all sides by associating it with characters like Pilate and Herod, and several more to follow.

Confirmation 2: The Chief Priests, Rulers, and People (23:18–21)

The chief priests, rulers, and people[127] respond to Pilate's second declaration by demanding the release of Barabbas, thus voicing their continued support for the initial charges against Jesus. They cry out in unison (παμπληθεί), showing their unified support of Jesus' condemnation. They begin by shouting αἶρε τοῦτον (Luke 23:18), which parallels the cries of the crowd at Paul's arrest (αἶρε αὐτόν; Acts 21:36) and defense (αἶρε . . . τὸν τοιοῦτον; Acts 22:22).

Furthermore, the repetition of σταύρου in the crowd's cry in Luke—"Crucify, crucify him!"—draws the hearers' attention and "emphasiz[es] the vehemence of the cry, and the determination of the priest-led people."[128] They demand Jesus' crucifixion and ask for something advantageous for themselves instead. By demanding the release of Barabbas over Jesus (whom, Luke reminds his audience, "had been thrown in prison for a certain rebellion that happened in the city and for murder" [23:19]), they ultimately make Jesus out to be guiltier than a murderer. He deserves crucifixion more than this insurrectionist.

Luke's dependence on Mark in 23:18–21 (Mark 15:6–13) is more obvious than in the previous section. Though often worded differently, the content is similar. Both tell of the crowd's asking Pilate to release

εὗρον ἐν τῷ ἀνθρώπῳ τούτῳ αἴτιον ὧν κατηγορεῖτε κατ' αὐτοῦ). Luke reuses this material again in 23:22: οὐδὲν αἴτιον θανάτου εὗρον ἐν αὐτῷ.

126. For a less developed emphasis on Jesus' innocence, see, e.g., Mark 14:55 and 15:14.

127. Rau has argued that 23:13 should be read as ἄρχοντες τοῦ λαοῦ instead of τοὺς ἄρχοντας καὶ τὸν λαόν. His thesis, however, has several weaknesses, most notably the lack of any manuscript evidence for his conjecture. Few scholars have followed his proposal. See Rau, "Das Volk," 41–51. See Nolland, *Luke 18:35—24:53*, 1127, for a rebuttal of Rau.

128. Bullinger, *Figures of Speech*, 198. Bullinger notes that repetition "is a common and powerful way of emphasizing a particular word, by thus marking it and calling attention to it" (189).

Barabbas instead of Jesus. Both describe Barabbas' crimes as rebellion (στάσις) and murder (φόνος). Both tell of Pilate's desire to release Jesus and the crowd's subsequent demand for crucifixion.

Luke deletes several of Mark's details, however, and reworks some of this other material. He deletes Mark's description of the release of a prisoner for the people at the festival (15:6).[129] Though this deletion leads some commentators to judge Luke's mention of Barabbas in 23:13 as abrupt,[130] Fitzmyer is right that this evaluation is often a result of being influenced by Mark's form of the story.[131] Because Luke has already brought the crowd into the picture and announced his own and Herod's verdicts of innocence (23:13-16), mentioning the custom in the way that Mark does (as an introduction to the scene with Pilate and the crowd) would interrupt the flow of his narrative.

Much of Luke's editing of Mark's scene here entails reworking the discourse toward his own interest. Luke transforms Mark's "the crowd came up and began to ask [Pilate] to do as he had done for them [i.e., release a prisoner]" (15:8) into direct discourse: they shout together, "Away with this man! Release Barabbas for us!" (23:18). This change highlights the crowd's vehemence and their conviction of his guilt. Mark presents Pilate's response as direct discourse: "He answered them, 'Do you want me to release the king of the Jews for you?'" (15:9). Luke, instead, notes that Pilate "called out to them, wanting to release him" (23:20). This shift to indirect discourse gives the impression that Pilate cannot get a word in—their shouts overwhelm Pilate's desire to release him, and they cry out, "Crucify, crucify him!" This version stands in contrast to Mark, where the crowd's first demand for crucifixion is in response to Pilate's question: "'What do you want me to do with the one whom you call the King of the Jews?'" In Mark, their cry is prompted by a question; in Luke, the cry for crucifixion is unprompted, once more highlighting the intensity of the crowd's vehemence.

---

129. A variation of this verse does appear in some manuscripts of Luke but is missing in others. At least three things suggest it was not a part of the original: (1) early manuscript support for its absence (especially P^{75} A B it^a cop^{sa}), (2) the fact that that the verse appears in different places in different manuscripts (e.g., after v. 19 in D), and (3) the potential abruptness created by its removal that makes it the more difficult reading. Metzger, *Textual Commentary*, 179-80; Omanson, *Textual Guide*, 152.

130. E.g., Taylor, *Passion Narrative*, 88; Neyrey, *Passion according to Luke*, 82.

131. Fitzmyer, *Gospel according to Luke*, 1486.

Refutation 3: Pilate (23:22–25)

Pilate proceeds to refute the charges of Jesus' guilt once more, this time claiming that the basis of the charges is unclear: "What evil has this man done?" Pilate asks. "I have found in him no cause for death" (23:22). Thus far, then, Pilate has refuted the charges by highlighting their inadequacy (23:4, 14), by transferring the case to Herod (23:7), and by pointing out that the charges are unclear (23:22)—all of which were common topics of refutation in the rhetorical tradition. Even if the "trial" against Jesus lacks some formal characteristics of a trial, the topics proceeding from the lips of Pilate and the Jewish leaders to refute and confirm the charges highlight the juridical nature of the narrative.

As with the previous refutation and confirmation, this third refutation from Pilate is easily explicable through Luke's use of Mark. The first part of Pilate's response—his question about what Jesus has done—is material that Luke took from Mark 15:14 almost verbatim.[132] Luke found that Mark's material—an argument that an opponent's case was unclear—contributed to his larger rhetorical goals, so he retained it.

But Mark did not go far enough for Luke, so Luke supplements Mark's narrative with two more elements to emphasize the convictions of both sides of Jesus' innocence and guilt. First, Luke has Pilate explicitly proclaim Jesus' innocence for a third time: "I have found in him no cause for death" (23:22). Second, in 23:25 Luke mentions Barabbas' crimes for a second time—that he was a rebel and a murderer. Whereas Mark only mentions this once (15:7; which Luke follows in 23:19), Luke uses the repetition of Barabbas' crimes to emphasize the crowd's level of conviction of Jesus' guilt.[133] Luke highlights the contrast between Jesus and Barabbas as he closes out the scene in 23:25: instead of just saying that Pilate released Barabbas and handed over Jesus, as Mark does, Luke reminds the hearers that Pilate released Barabbas, "who had been thrown in prison for rebellion and murder."

When we step back and analyze Jesus' presence before Pilate as a whole (i.e., in 23:1–25), we see at least three additional rhetorical features that that were not visible on a micro level. First, Luke uses polyptoton—the

---

132. Compare Mark's τί γὰρ ἐποίησεν κακόν with Luke's τί γὰρ κακὸν ἐποίησεν οὗτος.

133. Neyrey proposes that the scene functions not only as a trial of Jesus (as argued here) but also as a trial of Israel. Their choosing Barabbas over Jesus signifies their rejection of God's prophet and ultimately brings judgment on them. See Neyrey, *Passion according to Luke*, 83–84.

use of the same proper noun in several cases[134]—to indicate that Pilate is the main character of this scene: whereas Jesus' name only occurs three times in these twenty-five verses, all in the accusative case, Pilate's name occurs nine times in three different cases (nominative, dative, and accusative). This draws attention to his role in the story—to declare Jesus innocent but to hand him over for crucifixion nonetheless. Although Pilate gives in to the demands of the Jewish crowd and rulers, Luke never says that Pilate agreed with the charges against Jesus. Rather, he "decided that their request be done" (ἐπέκρινεν γενέσθαι τὸ αἴτημα αὐτῶν [23:24]). Thus, although he hands Jesus over, it is not because he thinks Jesus is guilty, which his three-fold refutation made clear.

Second, when we analyze the scenes before Pilate, we see an increase in intensity from one to the next. In the first scene (25:3–5), Pilate makes a declaration of innocence only once (23:4) and the crowds and chief priests, though insistent (ἐπισχύω [23:5]), still only speak (λέγω) against Jesus. In the second scene, however, Pilate declares Jesus' innocence twice (23:14–15; 22). Furthermore, while Pilate continues to simply speak (λέγω [23:14, 22]; cf. προσφωνέω [23:20]), the voices of the crowd intensify to the point of shouting (ἀνακράζω [23:18]; ἐπιφωνέω [23:21]; φωναῖς μεγάλαις [23:23]). Furthermore, while Jesus speaks (albeit briefly) in the first scene (23:3), he is muted in the second scene. These shifts in intensity—the crowd becomes more demanding; Jesus becomes more muted; Pilate becomes more convinced of Jesus' innocence but relents despite his conviction—alert the hearers to the direction in which the narrative is headed. Despite some people's convictions of his innocence, the end of the trial may not fare well for Jesus.

---

134. *Rhetorica ad Herennium* describes polyptoton as a type of paronomasia (4.22.31). Luke uses grammar inflection elsewhere in his Gospel to emphasize his main point. For example, Parsons notes the use of inflection to emphasize the main point in Luke 15:11–32, the parable of the prodigal son. He explains, "We might reasonably expect that the subject of a parable or story would occur most frequently in the nominative case; however, if we take seriously the role of grammatical inflection in the educational system of late antiquity, then we might not be surprised to learn that not only does the word 'father' occur twelve times in the parable, it appears in all five cases at least once, and in four cases, including the vocative (a rarity in Luke) at least twice." Thus, an understanding of ancient rhetoric leads Parsons to posit that the father is the main character of the story. See Parsons, *Luke: Storyteller*, 29–30. Cf. Reich, *Figuring Jesus*, 40–41. Of course, others have argued that the parable ought to be called the parable of the father's love by means of a close reading of the parable (e.g., Jeremias, *Rediscovering the Parables*, 101), but this understanding of grammatical inflection in ancient education to which Parsons appeals provides ancient support for the argument.

Third, Pilate's three-fold declaration of Jesus' innocence parallels the three declarations of Paul's innocence by high-ranking rulers.[135] First, in his letter to Felix, the Roman commander Lysias contends that Paul "was charged with nothing deserving death or imprisonment" (23:29). Lysias eventually transfers Paul to Felix the governor, who leaves Paul in prison until he is succeeded by Festus as governor. When Festus hears the charges brought against Paul, he, too, "found that [Paul] had done nothing deserving death" (25:25). The story repeats itself with the Jewish king Herod Agrippa, who declares, "This man is doing nothing to deserve death or imprisonment." (26:31; mentioned above). These three declarations echo Pilate's third declaration regarding Jesus: whatever the one being charged has done, he does not deserve death or imprisonment.

Thus far Luke has alternated the refutations and confirmations of the charges against Jesus. After the initial charges, Pilate offered the first refutation (23:4). The Jewish leaders followed this with the first confirmation (23:5). Pilate again refuted the changes, this time with Herod on his side (23:6–16). The chief priests, rulers, and people then offered a second confirmation in 23:18–21, followed by a third and final refutation by Pilate in 23:22–25. This three-fold refutation by Pilate serves to emphasize the point that Jesus is innocent.[136] At this point the formal trial concludes, but an informal trial continues. After a transition to the cross—the place of the informal trial—the pattern of refutations and confirmations changes slightly but continues nonetheless. Instead of alternating back and forth, Luke provides three confirmations of the charges followed by three refutations of them—a closing argument of sorts. In the remainder of the passion narrative, Luke continues to adorn his text with figures, to create parallels with characters in Acts, and to use techniques related to paraphrase and narration. We now turn to scene two: the informal trial at the cross.

135. Bovon, *Luke 3*, 275, also notes that Pilate's three-fold declaration "momentarily compensates for Peter's threefold denial (22:54–62)." Meynet, *L'Évangile selon Saint Luc*, 228, makes a similar observation.

136. Marshall agrees that the repetition is emphatic, but because the three-fold declaration of Jesus' innocence is also present in John (18:38; 19:4, 6), he thinks the material is rooted in a common tradition and thus does not represent a special Lukan emphasis. See Marshall, *Gospel of Luke*, 853. This is a prime example of comparisons between the Gospels skewing the interpretation of one of the Gospels. Pilate's three-fold declaration being part of a common tradition (I agree with Marshall that its presence in John makes this likely) does not exclude it from representing a Lukan emphasis. What an author chooses to include is just as significant as what an author chooses to exclude. The inclusion of Pilate's three-fold declaration—particularly when read in light of the larger narrative which includes several more refutations and confirmations of the charges against Jesus—suggests that the truth of the charges against Jesus (i.e., whether he was guilty or innocent) was a primary concern for Luke.

4

Scene 2: Transition to the Cross (23:26–32) and the Informal Trial (23:33–39)

Transition: From the Trial to the Cross (23:26–32)

THOUGH THE REMAINDER OF the passion narrative is not a formal trial or interrogation scene, Jesus' innocence continues to be on trial by virtually everyone he encounters—those being crucified with him, the soldiers and passersby, the centurion, and even God. The two trial scenes—the formal trial (22:66—23:25) and the informal trial (23:33–49)—are separated by a transition scene. After Pilate hands Jesus over for crucifixion (23:25) but before Jesus is crucified (23:33), Jesus is led away to the place of the crucifixion. In this section, 23:26–32, Luke narrates Simon's carrying Jesus' cross and the great multitude of people (πολὺ πλῆθος τοῦ λαοῦ) following Jesus, including the wailing women. The heart of this section, however, is Jesus' words to the wailing women—Jesus' longest speaking part in Luke's passion narrative.

This section of the passion narrative overflows with rhetorical figures, all of which appear on the lips of Jesus. First is the antithesis[1] in v. 28, where Jesus instructs the women to weep not for him, but for themselves and their children (μὴ κλαίετε . . . κλαίετε . . .). Second is the assonance[2] in v. 29: μακάριαι αἱ στεῖραι καὶ αἱ κοιλίαι αἵ. . . . Third is the synecdoche[3] in v. 29 where the parts of the women (breasts and wombs) represent the entire woman. Fourth is the use of pleonasm in vv. 29 and 30. In v. 29 Jesus speaks of the barren and the wombs that did not bear. In v. 30 he speaks of telling the mountains to fall on us and the hills to cover us. In both these instances, Jesus "dwells on the same topic

---

1. Reich, *Figuring Jesus*, 8.
2. Described in chapter 3 under "Refutation 1."
3. Reich, *Figuring Jesus*, 18. Cf. *Rhet. Her.* 4.33.44; Quintilian, *Inst.* 8.6.19–22.

without saying something new."[4] Fifth is the isocolon[5] in v. 30 where both cola after λέγειν have ten syllables.[6] Sixth is that v. 30 is a proverb,[7] an exemplum,[8] or both. Seventh is the rhetorical question[9] in v. 31. Eighth is the paronomasia[10] in v. 31, with the change in letters from ξύλῳ to ξηρῷ.

Not all of these figures are significant independently, though some are. As discussed more thoroughly below, the antithesis functions to show where the true guilt lies. This antithesis sets up the point that Jesus develops in the verses that follow with the other figures: the guilty one is not Jesus, but Jerusalem who rejects him. The assonance that follows in 23:29 catches the hearers' attention and emphasizes how harsh the coming days will be for those guilty ones—they will be so harsh that the barren will consider themselves blessed. Furthermore, by concluding his words with a rhetorical question, Jesus offers a thought-provoking warning to those who reject him.

Perhaps more significant than the functions of the individual figures, however, is the rhetorical force of the whole passage, where so many figures are packed into so few verses. Earlier in the passion narrative (22:66–71), the presence of figures on Jesus' lips functioned to help Jesus defeat his opponents. While Jesus does not dialogue with people in these verses, his words still correct those with whom he has contact: Jesus' figured words combat the misunderstanding that the women ought to weep for him, and instead claim that the mourning ought to be for Jerusalem, whose fate will be far worse than his. These words, then, are not only a prophetic judgment on Jerusalem but also an implicit proclamation of Jesus' innocence. By adorning Jesus' words with rhetorical figures, Luke communicates to his audience that these verses are not merely a transition scene, but are instead words especially worthy of their attention.[11] As they did in 22:66–71, the presence of so many rhetorical figures here

---

4. Ibid., 16–17. Cf. *Rhet. Her.* 4.42.54; Quintilian, *Inst.* 4.53.66.

5. Described in chapter 3 under "Setting the Stage."

6. τοῖς ὄ-ρε-σιν· πέ-σε-τε ἐφ᾽ ἡ-μᾶς (10); καὶ τοῖς βου-νοῖς· κα-λύ-ψα-τε ἡ-μᾶς (10).

7. Bullinger, *Figures of Speech*, 765; Nolland, *Luke 18:35—24:53*, 1135. On the adaptation of v. 30 from the LXX of Hos 10:8, see ibid., 1137.

8. Reich, *Figuring Jesus*, 154. Cf. *Rhet. Her.* 4.49.62.

9. Described in chapter 3 under "Setting the Stage."

10. Reich, *Figuring Jesus*, 15. Cf. *Rhet. Her.* 4.21.29–23.32; Quintilian, *Inst.* 9.3.66–67.

11. Cf. Quintilian's note that ornamentation makes readers more attentive and ready to believe (*Inst.* 8.3.5).

continues to pull the hearers to Jesus' side, despite the opposition he faces in the narrative.[12]

In this short section of the narrative, Jesus speaks more extensively than he does in the preceding section of the narrative (23:1–25) and that which follows (23:33–49) combined.[13] These verses constitute not only Jesus' largest speaking part in the passion narrative, but also the longest piece of speech by anyone in the narrative. The length of the speaking and the large number of figures therein suggest that it plays an important role in the narrative.

Scholars have proposed various ideas regarding the function of this scene.[14] Some see Simon's character as an example for how the hearers should act as disciples.[15] Others say the encounter with the women demonstrates that early Christians believed Jesus fulfilled Old Testament prophecies.[16] Still others suggest that the women symbolize Jerusalem, whose fate Jesus interprets with his words.[17] Others argue that Jesus' words need to be understood in light of Jewish apocalyptic eschatology; in that context the words function as "an injunction against procreation."[18] Finally, still others focus on the type of speech Jesus makes—whether it

---

12. For a more detailed discussion of the function of rhetorical figures across Luke's passion narrative, see "Rhetorical Figures" in chapter 5.

13. In 23:1–25 Jesus says a mere two words (σὺ λέγεις; 23:3) before Pilate, Herod, and the Jewish leaders and people. In 23:32–49 Jesus speaks two to three more times (vv. 34 [albeit textually dubious], 43, 46)—twenty-six words if counting v. 34, eighteen if only counting vv. 43 and 46. Here in 23:28–31 he speaks sixty-two words. The closest comparable speech is Jesus' responses to the council in 22:67–70, which totals thirty-three words.

14. For a summary of the various views, see Soards, "Tradition, Composition, and Theology in Jesus' Speech," 222–24; Neyrey, *Passion according to Luke*, 108–28. These studies inform much of what follows in this section.

15. See, e.g., Büchele, *Der Tod Jesu*, 43, 67, 97. Cf. Marshall, *Gospel of Luke*, 863; Talbert, *Reading Luke*, 219; Schweizer, *Good News according to Luke*, 357; Tannehill, *Narrative Unity of Luke-Acts*, 273; Bovon, *Luke 3*, 301. This notion connects the phrasing of 23:26 (ἐπέθηκαν αὐτῷ τὸν σταυρὸν φέρειν ὄπισθεν τοῦ Ἰησοῦ) with 9:23 (ἀράτω τὸν σταυρὸν αὐτοῦ καθ' ἡμέραν καὶ ἀκολουθείτω μοι) and 14:27 (ὅστις οὐ βαστάζει τὸν σταυρὸν ἑαυτοῦ καὶ ἔρχεται ὀπίσω μου, οὐ δύναται εἶναί μου μαθητής). Loisy, however, argues against this connection since Simon does not carry the cross voluntarily and since the cross is not his own. See Loisy, *L'Evangile selon Luc*, 553. Cf. Bock, *Luke*, 371.

16. Soards, "Daughters of Jerusalem," 223.

17. Brown, *Death of the Messiah*, 921; Neyrey, *Passion according to Luke*, 108–28. This section of *Passion according to Luke* is a reprint and expansion of Neyrey's "Jesus' Address to the Women of Jerusalem (Lk 23:27–31)—A Prophetic Judgment Oracle."

18. Pitre, "Blessing the Barren," 60.

is a prophetic oracle of doom or judgment,[19] an invitation to repent,[20] or a warning motivated by compassion.[21] Here I am interested in how this pericope functions within the larger passion narrative,[22] and particularly with what it contributes to the refutation or confirmation of the charges against Jesus.

With the "do not weep . . . but weep . . ." antithesis, Jesus directs the attention off of the wrongful accusations against him and their resulting death sentence and directs the attention instead onto the fate of Jerusalem. His words for the Jerusalemites[23]—a prediction of the coming time when Jerusalem will be destroyed—suggest that *they* are the truly guilty ones, not him. The destruction of the temple to which these verses refer is a result of some Jews' rejection of Jesus and the church.[24] As he does here (ἔρχονται ἡμέραι in 23:29), Jesus elsewhere uses the phrase "the days are coming" to speak of wrath coming upon Jerusalem (see ἥξουσιν ἡμέραι in 19:43; ἐλεύσονται ἡμέραι in 21:6 [cf. 21:33f]).[25] The allusion to

19. Büchele, *Der Tod Jesu*, 43–44; Untergassmair, *Kreuzweg und Kreuzigung Jesu*, 38–39; Neyrey, *Passion according to Luke*, 108–9.

20. Schweizer, *Good News according to Luke*, 357; Grundmann, *Das Evangelium nach Lukas*, 430.

21. Fitzmyer, *Gospel according to Luke*, 1495; Marshall, *Gospel of Luke*, 862; Benoit, *Passion and Resurrection*, 167–68.

22. On Jesus' earlier words about and to Jerusalem (11:49–50; 13:34–35; 19:41–44; 21:20–24), see Brown, *Death of the Messiah*, 921–22.

23. Neyrey points to the important distinction in this passage between the people (πολὺ πλῆθος τοῦ λαοῦ) and the women who represent Jerusalem. The two groups are not synonymous. He explains, "As Luke tells the story, a distinction is ultimately made between 'the people' and Jerusalem. Many of the 'people' will repent and convert (Luke 23:48; Acts 2:41–42; 5:12–14); but Jerusalem is another matter. It is the daughters of Jerusalem—as distinguished from 'the people'—who are formally addressed in 23:27–31. They symbolize the element of Israel which continually rejected God's messengers. . . . In Luke the personified Jerusalem has twice earlier been addressed by Jesus in indictments of the city: 'Jerusalem, Jerusalem, killing the prophets . . .' (13:34) and 'he saw the city and said, "Would that even today you knew the things that make for peace"' (19:41). In light of the distinction noted above between 'the people' and Jerusalem, 'daughters of Jerusalem' should not simply be equated with Israel, but should be seen as identifying that element of Israel which consistently rejected God's messengers, i.e., the prophets, Jesus, and the apostolic preachers." See Neyrey, *Passion according to Luke*, 110–11.

24. Chance, *Jerusalem*, 116–18. Luke also makes this connection between the destruction of Jerusalem and Jewish rejection of Jesus in 13:34–35; 19:41–44; and 23:44–48.

25. Neyrey, *Passion according to Luke*, 112. While ἔρχομαι in 23:29 is in the present tense, the future tense verb that immediately follows (ἔρχονται ἡμέραι ἐν αἷς ἐροῦσιν)

Hos 10:8—a vivid picture of Israel's cry for relief from punishment for their idolatry and injustice—in 23:30 heightens the intensity of the guilt and resulting punishment of Jerusalem. Those days will be so awful that barren and childless women will be considered blessed.

The rhetorical question that concludes Jesus' words to the women—"If they do these things when the tree is green, what will be done when it is dry?"—is difficult to interpret because the subjects of the verbs are not stated. Brown summarizes four interpretive possibilities commonly offered by commentators: (1) The Romans are the subject throughout ("if the Romans so treat me whom they admit to be innocent, how will they treat those who revolt against them?"); (2) God is the subject throughout ("if God has not spared the beloved Jesus, how much the more will an impenitent Judaism receive the impact of divine judgment?"; (3) Humans are the subject throughout ("if people so behave before their cup of wickedness is filled, what will they do when it overflows?"); and (4) Jesus' opponents are the subject of the protasis, and God is the subject of the apodosis ("If they [the Jewish leaders and people] treat me like this in a favorable time [when they are not forced by the Romans], how much the worse will they be treated in an unfavorable time [when the Romans suppress them]?").[26] Regardless of which interpretive possibility is chosen,[27] Jesus' words in the prior verses suggest that the ones who will be treated more severely (i.e., the subject of γένηται) are those whom the daughters of Jerusalem symbolize, namely, Jerusalem, who is currently rejecting Jesus and who will later reject the apostles.[28] The contrast is stark: Jerusalem

---

suggests a future connotation.

26. Brown, *Death of the Messiah*, 926–27.

27. Brown notes that the εἰ plus the present indicative describes something that is happening in the present. I agree that this construction suggests that "they" refers to those who are killing Jesus. Furthermore, the use of a passive verb without a specified agent is often used to suggest action done by God. These factors (along with problems with options 1–3) make option 4 the most likely. See ibid., 925–26. Also supporting option 4 is the connection between this verse and Hos 9:16 (LXX). Pitre points out, "Hosea is using the imagery of dryness and infertility to depict the coming period of barrenness and judgment. Similarly, Jesus is contrasting the present age of fertility/peace ('green wood') with a coming period of barrenness/judgment ('dry wood')." See Pitre, "Blessing the Barren," 71.

28. Neyrey interprets these verses similarly. He sees the whole speech as a prophetic oracle of judgment against Jerusalem for rejecting God's prophets—it contains the formal elements of prophetic judgments in Jeremiah: identification of the city, a sentence of destruction, and the use of scripture as proof of God's condemnation. Luke 23:28–31, then, is "a *vaticinium ex eventu* . . . [that] interprets the fall of the city in 70

is guilty, while Jesus is innocent.[29] Ultimately, then, this transition scene functions to highlight who is truly at fault—those who have wrongfully convicted Jesus—and offers a dim preview of what awaits them.

But what is the origin of this pericope? Brown points out that Luke splits Mark 15:20b (καὶ ἐξάγουσιν αὐτὸν ἵνα σταυρώσωσιν αὐτόν) to produce a frame around this pericope. Like Mark, Luke begins by narrating that they led Jesus out, though Luke replaces Mark's ἐξάγω with ἀπάγω (23:26). Luke then places the idea of the second half of Mark 15:20b, that they crucified Jesus (σταυρόω), at the end his pericope: they led Jesus and the two criminals out to be put to death (ἀναιρέω; 23:32).[30] Both

---

AD as an act of divine retribution upon unbelieving Jews." Neyrey, *Passion according to Luke*, 121.

The potential guilt of the Jews (be it the Jewish leaders, Jerusalem, unbelieving Jews, or all Jews) for condemning Jesus to death has received ample scholarly attention. While I do think that Luke paints the Jewish leaders as the ones bearing primary responsibility for Jesus' death (in contrast to the Romans), I do not think that contrast is the primary purpose of his passion narrative and thus will not discuss it in depth here. For fuller treatments of the role of the Jews in Luke's passion narrative (including Luke's understanding of the destruction of the Jerusalem), see Conzelmann, *Theology of St. Luke*, 85–93; George, "Israël dans l'oeuvre de Luc," 481–525; Büchele, *Der Tod Jesu*, 105–10, 188; Bachmann, *Jerusalem und der Tempel*; Maddox, *Purpose of Luke-Acts*, 39–56; Giblin, *Destruction of Jerusalem*; Gaston, "Anti-Judaism," 127–54; Sanders, *Jews in Luke-Acts*; Brawley, *Luke-Acts and the Jews*; Chance, *Jerusalem*; Weatherly, *Jewish Responsibility*. See also Blinzler, *Trial of Jesus*, 10–21, who describes five different ways that scholars have interpreted the responsibility of Jesus' death.

While much of the scholarly attention has focused on the portrait of the Jews, Stenschke focuses on the Gentiles in the narrative. His work is an important reminder that Gentiles played a crucial role in Jesus' death—a role that ought not be downplayed. Key considerations include Jesus' third passion prediction of being handed over τοῖς ἔθνεσιν (18:32); the Roman soldiers' mocking of Jesus (23:36); Pilate's handing Jesus over for flogging and crucifixion despite knowledge of his innocence (in contrast to the Jews whom Acts 3:17 and 13:27 describe as acting out of ignorance); and accusations against the Gentiles in Acts 4:25–27. Stenschke concludes, "Luke is far from emphasing Pilate's or any other Gentile's innocence. *Had this been Luke's intention, he failed badly*" (125, emphasis original). And later: "Luke's passion account should only be called 'anti-Jewish', if one is to add that it is also 'anti-Gentile'" (143). For the full discussion, see Stenschke, *Luke's Portrait of Gentiles*, 113–44. Weatherly also argues that Luke implicates Gentiles in Jesus' crucifixion (especially Pilate), but adds that he "assigns the bulk of the blame to the Jews of Jerusalem." See Weatherly, *Jewish Responsibility*, 90–98 (quotation from 90). For more on the negative portrayal of Pilate, see Ahn, *Reign of God and Rome*, 183.

29. Marshall, *Gospel of Luke*, 862.

30. Brown, *Death of the Messiah*, 928, points out that Luke frames the episode by splitting Mark 15:20b. Büchele, *Der Tod Jesu*, 44, also sees Luke 23:32 as a redaction of Mark 15:20b. Taylor, *Passion Narrative*, 90, however, argues that v. 32 is non-Markan

Untergassmair and Soards add that Luke's use of two ἄγω-verbs in v. 26 (ἀπάγω) and v. 32 (ἄγω) creates an inclusio around the unit.³¹ The only other verse in this pericope that Luke derives from Mark is Mark 15:21—the narrative of Simon of Cyrene's carrying Jesus' cross. Though Luke alters it slightly, the two stories are so similar that commentators almost unanimously agree Luke derived it from Mark.³²

However, in between Luke's inclusio (23:26a; 23:32) and after his account of Simon carrying Jesus' cross (23:26b), stands vv. 27–31—a section unlike any other section of Luke's passion narrative because it has no visible connection to Mark's passion narrative or his Gospel. Some deny that Luke derived other sections of his passion narrative from Mark (e.g., the Herod pericope), but even in those instances, connections with Mark's passion narrative (e.g., a beating by soldiers) or Mark's larger Gospel (e.g., the mention of Herod) are visible, even if they do not convince scholars that the pericope originated with Mark. In Luke 23:27–31, however, no such connections are apparent. The crowd following Jesus to the cross, including the wailing women, and Jesus' words to the women are unique to Luke.

Because of the absence of a connection to Mark or any other canonical gospel,³³ many commentators argue that Luke derived these verses from a separate written source.³⁴ "The numerical argument alone

because it only shares three words with Mark 15:27, because it is in a different position than in Mark, and because it only has five characteristic Lukan expressions (ἄγω, δέ καί, ἕτερος, σύν, ἀναιρεῖν).

31. Untergassmair, *Kreuzweg und Kreuzigung Jesu*, 37–38; Soards, "Daughters of Jerusalem," 239.

32. E.g., Green, *Death of Jesus*, 87, states, "Luke's text is very close to Mark 15:20b–21, and there can be little doubt that he has simply rewritten the Second Gospel here." Taylor, *Passion Narrative*, 90, adds, "Verse 26 . . . is clearly derived from Mk. xv. 20b–21." Cf. Fitzmyer, *Gospel according to Luke*, 1494; Büchele, *Der Tod Jesu*, 43–44; Brown, *Death of the Messiah*, 929; Soards, "Daughters of Jerusalem," 226. One exception is Bovon, who thinks that Luke draws 23:6–43 from his special source instead of Mark, even though it resembles Mark. This fits his larger conception of Luke's use of sources—namely that Luke alternates between Mark and his special source, not favoring one, but also not interweaving them on a small scale. See Bovon, *Luke 3*, 294–95.

Because of the widespread agreement that Luke derived 23:26 from Mark 15:20b–21, I will not discuss Luke's alterations to Mark. Nolland and Marshall have concise explanations of many of these changes. See Marshall, *Gospel of Luke*, 863; Nolland, *Luke 18:35—24:53*, 1135–36.

33. See below on the connection between Luke and the *Gospel of Thomas*.

34. Besides Taylor and Green, discussed below, the following also attribute vv. 27–31 to a separate source: Perry, *Sources of Luke's Passion Narrative*, 47; Jeremias,

is conclusive," Taylor argues, pointing out that Luke only shares 14 of his 110 words with Mark (in vv. 26–32), eleven of which are in v. 26.[35] Taylor concludes that "Luke is editing a non-Markan source," not freely composing, because there are more pre-Lukan expressions than Lukan expressions.[36] Similarly, Green argues against Lukan composition of vv. 27–31 and instead for "a non-Markan source" that Luke edited.[37] The presence of characteristic Lukan vocabulary (e.g., λαός), constructions (e.g., κλαίω + ἐπί, a construction found in the NT only in Luke), and emphases (e.g., women) necessitates some degree of editing by Luke, but the presence of other elements (e.g., τότε instead of ἐν ἐκείναις ταῖς ἡμέραις, the latter of which is "a favorite Lukan redaction") and an inability to understand how this material could arise from material earlier in Luke's Gospel or from the LXX lead Green to posit a source behind this material.[38]

Appeals to Luke's vocabulary and style have led scholars to an impasse. For example, regarding the phrase "in which they will say" (ἐν αἷς ἐροῦσιν; 23:29), proponents of a special source argue that this is pre-Lukan style, while proponents of Lukan composition argue that the phrase is Septuagintal style—a style that Luke is often said to have employed—and thus recourse to a special source is unnecessary.[39] Furthermore, proponents of a special source emphasize word statistics as they relate to Mark (i.e., outside of v. 26, Luke has few words in common with Mark), while proponents of Lukan composition emphasize word statistics as they relate to the rest of Luke's Gospel and Acts (i.e., there is a relatively high presence of "typical Lukan vocabulary" in these verses).[40] The latter also point

---

"Perikopen-Umstellungen bei Lukas?," 115–19; Fitzmyer, *Gospel according to Luke*, 1494; Ernst, *Das Evangelium nach Lukas*, 481; Bovon, *Luke*, 295.

35. Taylor, *Passion Narrative of St. Luke*, 90.

36. As elsewhere, Taylor is relying on Rehkopf's word lists. Ibid. Elsewhere Taylor describes what Rehkopf means by "Pre-Lukan": "Rehkopf does not mean words and phrases used before Luke wrote, but expressions which normally Luke does not use of himself independently, but finds in sources, Q, L, Mk, and the Birth Stories." See Taylor, "Rehkopf's List," 62.

37. Green, *Death of Jesus*, 88.

38. Ibid., 88–89.

39. This example is described in Brown, *Death of the Messiah*, 923. On "Septuagintisms" in Luke, see Fitzmyer, *Gospel according to Luke*, 113–16.

40. E.g., Büchele, *Der Tod Jesu*, 43, n. 128; Brown, *Death of the Messiah*, 929. Of course, determining "typical Lukan vocabulary" is no easy task and commentators do not agree on what is typical. For example, Rehkopf (whom Taylor and Jeremias follow) says that Jesus' "turning" (στραφείς) in 23:28 is pre-Lukan. Soards and Nolland,

to the characteristics of these verses that the former often acknowledge (e.g., Green, above), such as how Luke's portrayal of the women in these verses is consistent with the larger picture of women in his Gospel.[41] But this point can be interpreted variously: is it consistent with Luke's larger picture of women because Luke composed it, did he borrow it from a source because it was consistent with his understanding of women, or did he edit a source to make it consistent with his own understanding? Since the possible source is not extant, it is impossible to say.[42]

Neyrey argues that these verses are consistent in theme and form with the other three warnings to Jerusalem in Luke: (1) 13:33–35; (2) 19:41–44; and (3) 21:20–24. In each of these cases, as well as in 23:27–31, there is a formal address to Jerusalem, the sentence of destruction is pronounced upon the city, and a scriptural tradition is used as proof of God's condemnation.[43] This consistency in theme and form suggest to Neyrey that Luke composed this fourth warning to Jerusalem in 23:27–31.[44] I will address these three warnings in order.

The first of these warnings to Jerusalem (13:33–35) Luke takes from Q or Matthew 23:37–39[45] and places right after Jesus' response to Herod's death threat (13:31–32). Thus, this first warning and the one in the passion narrative are both in close proximity to Luke's Herod material (cf. 23:6–12, in the scene prior to Jesus' words to the women). The second passage is distinct to Luke, and Luke may have drawn upon Hos 10:14

---

however, argue that στρέφω is characteristic Lukan vocabulary (they point to 7:9, 44; 9:55; 10:23; 14:25; 22:61; and three other instances in Acts), particularly since the only subject of this verb in Luke is Jesus. See Rehkopf, *Die lukanische Sonderquelle*, 97; Taylor, *Passion Narrative*, 90; Jeremias, *Die Sprache des Lukasevangelium*, 305; Soards, "Daughters of Jerusalem," 231; Nolland, *Luke 18:35—24:53*, 1137.

41. Soards, "Daughters of Jerusalem," 230.

42. Other examples of these differing interpretations of Luke 23:27–31 abound. Brown covers the differing views more thoroughly than most. See Brown, *Death of the Messiah*, 922–27.

43. Neyrey, *Passion according to Luke*, 119–20. In 23:27–31, the identification is "Daughters of Jerusalem" in v. 28; the sentence is "days are coming. . ." in v. 29; and the scripture cited is Hos 10:8 in v. 30. The saying in v. 31 functions as the crime that brings the judgment. All of these elements come together as a prophetic oracle of judgment against Jerusalem.

44. Ibid., 115–21.

45. Whether Luke used Q or Matthew is irrelevant here. Neyrey argues that Luke found the archetype of this form in Q and "appreciated it for what it was and consciously employed it again and again: in 19:41–44 . . . and in 23:27–31." See ibid., 121.

for 19:44.[46] If that were the case, the second warning and the one in the passion narrative are both connected to Hos 10. This is not problematic if one thinks that Luke composed both passages,[47] if one thinks that Luke composed one and drew on a source for the other, or if one thinks that Luke drew them from the same source. However, if Luke draws 23:30 from a special passion source and not one that was a source for other parts of his Gospel (i.e., 19:44), those who argue for a special passion source must concede that Luke drew from two different sources (the passion source and the source for 19:41–44) sayings of Jesus that connect Hos 10 with the judgment of Jerusalem. While this is not impossible, it is certainly not an easy solution. Finally, the third passage, though not directly addressed to Jerusalem like the other three passages, still contains "the same basic pattern of crime and punishment found in the formal oracles against the city."[48] Similar to 23:27–31, 21:20–24 is an insertion of non-Markan material into the middle of Markan material, though ch. 21 could be seen as a more natural insertion since Jesus is speaking in the surrounding verses in Mark, which is not the case in ch. 23. The lack of speaking roles given to Jesus in Mark's passion narrative,[49] however, would make a similar insertion in the passion narrative difficult. Furthermore, Luke 21:22 may also contain an allusion to Hosea (cf. αἱ ἡμέραι τῆς ἐκδικήσεως in Hos 9:7 and ἡμέραι ἐκδικήσεως in Luke 21:22), which presents a difficulty similar to the one described above with the use of Hos 10 in Luke 23:30 and 19:44.

One last piece of evidence must be considered before making a decision about the origin of Luke 23:27–31. While Luke 23:27–31 lacks a connection to any of the canonical gospels, it is connected to the *Gospel of Thomas*. What are two different logia in Luke 23:29 and Luke 11:27–28 is one logion in *Gos. Thom.* 79. See Table 6 for a comparison of the texts of Luke 23:39 and *Gos. Thom.* 79, divided by line by Soards:[50]

---

46. Ibid., 116; Schweizer, *Good News according to Luke*, 300; Fitzmyer, *Gospel according to Luke*, 1258.

47. However, Paffenroth's study argues against this possibility. See Paffenroth, *Story of Jesus*, 29, 150.

48. Neyrey, *Passion according to Luke*, 117.

49. On the silence of Jesus in Mark, see "Setting the Stage" in chapter 3.

50. Soards, "Daughters of Jerusalem," 234. Soards also compares Luke 11:27–28 with *Gos. Thom.* 79. Only a Coptic translation of this logion exists, available in Ehrman and Pleše, *Apocryphal Gospels*, 310–49 (logion 79 is on p. 328).

Table 6. Luke 23:39 and *Gospel of Thomas* 79

Reference	Saying
23:29a	For look! Days are coming in which they will say,
79f	For there will be days when you will say,
23:29b	'Blessed are the barren
23:29c	and the wombs that did not bear
79g	'Blessed is the womb which has not conceived
23:29d	and the breasts that did not feed'
79h	and the breasts that have not suckled'

Because of these similarities (and others), scholars debate the relationship between these works.[51] Goodacre, for instance, argues that Thomas used Luke 23:29 for logion 79 because "[t]he style, thought, and terminology are common elsewhere in Luke and are paralleled in agreed redactional reworkings of Mark and Matthew (or Q). . . . Since the same features are, on the whole, anomalous in *Thomas*, the conclusion from the data is that *Thomas* is indeed familiar with Luke's Gospel."[52] Soards, on the other hand, cautiously argues that the works are independent of one another but rely on similar tradition(s).[53] For him, the similarities between the two works are "insignificant" compared to the larger differences between

51. For a recent summary of the history of research and arguments regarding the relationship between the Synoptics and the *Gospel of Thomas*, see Goodacre, *Thomas and the Gospels*, 1–25. He says briefly, "These days, essays on the state of the question tend to represent the debate as a scholarly split, half on the side of *Thomas*'s independence, half on the side of its dependence on the Synoptics, though some claim that the scales are tipping in favor of Thomasine independence. . ." (5).

52. Ibid., 108. Goodacre lists the feminine imagery and the stress on hearing God's word and keeping it as examples of the distinctly Lukan style and thought of these verses. For Goodacre, the language, setting, imagery, and theology of *Gosp. Thom.* 79 are "so at home in Luke that the term 'diagnostic shards' risks understating the case for *Thomas*'s familiarity with Luke" (97). Other scholars who think Thomas had knowledge of Luke include Tuckett, "Thomas and the Synoptics," 132–57; Popkes, *Das Menschenbild*; Gathercole, *Composition of the Gospel of Thomas*.

53. His assessment on the composition of the work is as follows: "Luke 23,26–32 is a Lukan composition. Luke drew on Mark's Gospel in vv. 26a-d and 32a-b. Early Christian tradition, probably oral but possibly written, lies behind vv. 29a-d and 31a-b; Luke cites the LXX, perhaps from memory, in v. 30a-d. His own reflection and compositional effort explains vv. 26e-28c." Soards, "Daughters of Jerusalem," 240.

the two (e.g., the contexts of the sayings and elements from Luke that are lacking in Thomas).[54] While Soards does not discuss the similar traditions upon which Luke and the *Gospel of Thomas* may rely, Pitre's study shows that traditions containing blessings for the barren[55] were present before, during, and after Jesus' ministry. That Luke and the *Gospel of Thomas* could have independently drawn on such traditions is not hard to imagine, though one must ask if the strong verbal connections between the two works are best explained in this way since the verbal connections between Luke and the *Gospel of Thomas* are much stronger than between either of these works and the traditions described by Pitre.

The issue cannot be determined decisively. If Goodacre is correct that the *Gospel of Thomas* drew on Luke for his logion, then there are no known independent parallels to Luke 23:27–31. If Soards is correct that the *Gospel of Thomas* and Luke were independent of one another and simply drew on similar traditions, however, the presence of a known parallel to Luke 23:29 in *Gos. Thom.* 79 requires us to leave open the possibility that Luke may have drawn upon circulating oral or written traditions for these words of Jesus in his passion narrative.

Neither the case for or against Luke's use of a special passion source for 23:27–31 is airtight, of course, and our study of ancient rhetoric could support either the possibility that Luke is editing a source or the possibility that Luke composed the work on his own or from oral traditions and the LXX. If the former is the case, however, the presence of so many rhetorical figures on Jesus' lips[56] and an emphasis on Luke's key theme of Jesus' innocence[57] suggest that Luke edited the source in ways similar to

---

54. Ibid., 235. Patterson offers similar reasons for arguing that Luke and the *Gospel of Thomas* developed independently, even if they shared common oral or written sources. See Patterson, *Gospel of Thomas and Jesus*, 16–18. Others arguing that Luke and Thomas are independent of one another include Koester, *Introduction to the New Testament*, 154–58; Zöckler, *Jesu Lehren im Thomasevangelium*.

55. He provides ample evidence of blessings for infertile men and women and warnings against procreation due to upcoming tribulations. See, e.g., Isa 56:3–5; Wis 3:13–14; *2 Bar.* 10.3; Hos 9:11–16; 13:16; Jer 16:1–4, 9; *1 En.* 99.5; *Jub.* 23.24a; *4 Ezra* 5.1, 8; *Apoc. El.* (C) 2.35–36a, 37; *Sib. Or.* 2.190. Pitre, "Blessing the Barren," 64–78.

56. Reich has convincingly shown that one of Luke's rhetorical strategies entails placing figures on the lips of Jesus. The presence of so many rhetorical figures in vv. 27–31 is thus consistent with Luke's compositional and editorial activity elsewhere in his Gospel. See Reich, *Figuring Jesus*.

57. Neagoe argues that this multitude (particularly the women) function as witnesses to the injustice of Jesus' execution. They are the human witnesses while the future judgment of Jerusalem is the divine witness. See Neagoe, *The Trial of the Gospel*,

how he edited Mark.⁵⁸ That is, Luke has left his creative stamp on these verses, regardless of their origin.⁵⁹ The possibility of Luke having edited a source must remain on the table, but the fact that this passage is the only one in Luke's passion narrative that cannot be adequately explained by Luke's dependency on Mark,⁶⁰ along with plausible reasons why Luke could have composed the verses himself (especially in light of the many Jewish traditions about blessings for the barren), suggest that recourse to this potential source is unnecessary.

The Informal Trial—The Crucifixion Scene (23:33–49)

Confirmations 3, 4, 5: Rulers, Soldiers, and First Criminal (23:33–39)⁶¹

While Jesus is on the cross,⁶² three different groups or persons attempt to confirm the charges against him by offering him the same challenge:

---

94. I understand this passage less as the crowd's witness to the injustice and more as Jesus' explanation of where the true guilt lies. The two are not mutually exclusive, of course.

58. Nolland points out that weeping for a person as they go toward execution is a common motif in martyr texts. If one thinks that Luke is framing Jesus' passion as a martyrdom, this point would further support Luke's editorial work on these verses. Nolland, *Luke 18:35—24:53*, 1137. See chapter one for more on Jesus' passion in Luke as a martyrdom.

If one argues that Luke simply carried over from his source the martyrdom motif, the heavy use of rhetorical figures, and the strong emphasis on innocence, the question arises of how we can distinguish between Luke and his source if they are so similar.

59. Büchele, *Der Tod Jesu*, 43, n. 128, makes a similar point.

60. As argued in chapter 3 and in the remainder of this chapter.

61. Because these three refutations are similar and occur in such close proximity to one another, I am treating them together.

62. Some manuscripts of Luke contain one of Jesus' sayings from the cross at this point in Luke's narrative: "And Jesus said, 'Father, forgive them, for they do not know what they do'" (23:34). There is not universal agreement regarding whether this verse was original to Luke. The most early and diverse witnesses lack this verse (e.g., $\mathfrak{P}^{75}$ $\aleph^1$ B D* W Θ 070 579 597* 1241 it$^{a,\ d}$ syr^s cop$^{sa,\ bo\ mss}$), which, Metzger points out, makes the case for deliberate excision by copyists (who viewed the fall of Jerusalem as evidence that God had *not* forgiven the Jews) difficult. See Metzger, *Textual Commentary*, 154. The arguments on each side do not need to be rehearsed here. Generally speaking, arguments for the originality emphasize intrinsic probability, while arguments against originality emphasize external evidence. For a recent survey of the scholarly divide, see Eubank, "Disconcerting Prayer," 521–36. Cf. also Marshall, *Gospel of Luke*, 867–68.

I do not think these verses were originally part of Luke and so will not treat them as

save yourself! The rulers sneer, "He saved others; let him save himself if this man is the Messiah of God, the Chosen One" (23:35). The soldiers, too, mock him: "If you are the king of the Jews, save yourself!" (23:37). Finally, one of the criminals on the cross challenges Jesus, "Are you not the Messiah? Save yourself and us!" (23:39). All three of these instances are—on the surface—an attempt to refute Jesus' innocence, thus confirming the Jews' earlier charges (cf. the accusations regarding his being Messiah [22:67; 23:2] and king [23:2]). They attempt to do this on the basis that Jesus' actions are not consistent with his titles. His actions—namely, his inability to save himself or others—are at odds with his past actions of saving others and with his supposed identity as God's Messiah, the Chosen One, and the King of the Jews.[63] Here, then, we see the common topic of consistency being used in an attempt to confirm the charges. The charges must be correct since Jesus' titles are not consistent with his actions, they reason.

Information from elsewhere in Luke, however, suggests that these confirmations are actually ironic. Bock explains, "These taunts are ironic, unconscious testimonies. Though intended to make fun of Jesus, they speak truth about which the utterers are unaware."[64] The situation described in these verses aligns with Quintilian's description of the common rhetorical figure of irony. He explains that with irony, "we are asked to understand the opposite of what is said" (*Inst.* 9.2.44). He adds that "the whole context is generally straightforward" (*Inst.* 9.2.45). Thus, while the various groups mock Jesus at the cross, Luke's audience would hear the irony in their words because Luke has made Jesus' identity clear in the context of the earlier narrative. For example, although Jesus refused to confirm or deny his messiahship in 22:67–69 because he knew the leaders would not believe him, others in Luke's larger narrative testify to Jesus as Messiah, God's Chosen One, Savior, and King. At the transfiguration, for example, God provides testimony that Jesus is his Chosen One (ὁ ἐκλελεγμένος; 9:35)—the same title used to mock Jesus here by the rulers (ὁ ἐκλεκτός; 23:35).[65] Since divine testimony was viewed as one of the

---

part of my analysis. If anything, however, their inclusion would support my argument in that it would provide another refutation of the charges against Jesus (i.e., Jesus refutes the charges by saying that what they are doing is wrong and deserves forgiveness) and a parallel to Stephen in Acts (cf. Stephen's words in 7:60).

63. Carroll makes this point in his recent commentary: Carroll, *Luke*, 467.

64. Bock, *Luke*, 374.

65. There is only the minor shift from the participle of ἐκλέγω in 9:35 to the

most authoritative forms of testimony,⁶⁶ God's pronouncement of Jesus as the Chosen One in 9:35 would have enabled the hearers to recognize both the inadequacy of the rulers' attempt to confirm the charges and also the irony inherent in the mockery. The hearers would also remember the testimony of the angels to the shepherds at Jesus' birth—another example of authoritative testimony with divine origin. The angels identify Jesus as a savior, who is Christ the Lord (σωτὴρ ὅς ἐστιν χριστὸς κύριος; 2:11).⁶⁷ The angelic proclamation connects Jesus' messiahship (χριστός) with his being Savior (σωτήρ), which is the very same connection being made at the cross. Finally, Jesus' own teaching in 9:24—that those wanting to save their lives will lose them, and those who lose their lives will save them—flies in the face of the mockers' challenge to save himself by coming down from the cross. Thus, because the hearers are privy to these various pieces of information from earlier in the story—namely that Jesus is both Messiah and Savior—they can dismiss the accusers' mockery that if he is the Messiah he ought to be able to save himself, particularly since angelic testimony would have been more authoritative than the testimony of Jesus' opponents, whose motives Luke has shown to be malevolent throughout his larger narrative.

Finally, though nowhere else in Luke is Jesus identified specifically as the king of the Jews (save for the accusations against him in the passion narrative [23:2–3, 37–38]), he *is* identified as a king. In Luke 19:38, for example, in the midst of Jesus' triumphal entry into Jerusalem, a whole multitude of disciples quote Ps 118:26 and praise God saying, "Blessed is

---

adjective ἐκλεκτός in 23:35. In both instances Strauss sees Luke merging the Suffering Servant imagery with royal imagery because he sees ἐκλελεγμένος as an aullusion to Isa 42:1 (ὁ ἐκλεκτός). He explains, "Luke makes 'God's chosen Christ' a parallel for 'king of the Jews' (cf. 23:2–3) and so retains the royal-messianic sense present in Mark. Yet by adding what is probably an allusion to Isaiah 42.1 (ὁ ἐκλεκτός), Luke expands this royal designation with servant imagery.... The Jewish leaders cry out that if Jesus is God's chosen Christ (i.e., the royal messiah), he should save himself from death. Luke knows, however, that God's choice and anointing is for this very purpose: the messiah must first suffer and die (as servant) before entering his glory (Lk. 9.31–32; 24.26). It is likely, therefore, that both here and in the transfiguration, 'chosen one' contains royal significance, while at the same time alluding to Jesus' role as Isaianic servant." See Strauss, *Davidic Messiah*, 264–67 (quotation from 267). For more on Jesus as the Suffering Servant see 324–33.

66. McConnell, *Topos of Divine Testimony*, 47–50. Cf. Cicero, *Top.* 19.73; 20.76. See "Refutation 5" below for a fuller discussion.

67. Cf. other places in Luke where Jesus' identity as the messiah is confirmed: 2:26; 4:41; 9:20.

the king who comes in the name of the Lord." Thus, while the soldiers, rulers, and first criminal challenge Jesus' identity (and attempt to confirm the charges against him in doing so), the reader knows from information earlier in the narrative that these confirmations fall short.[68] Thus, their taunts ironically testify to his true identity.

Unlike most of the preceding pericope, it is easy to see that Luke is building his narrative here off of Mark's narrative. As he does in his reworking of Mark elsewhere, though, Luke adds to, subtracts from, and rearranges Mark's material. Both authors narrate the place (ἐπὶ τὸν τόπον) where Jesus is led, though Luke condenses Mark's Γολγοθᾶν . . . ὅ ἐστιν μεθερμηνευόμενον Κρανίου Τόπος (15:22) to τὸν καλούμενον Κρανίον (23:33). This extraction of the Aramaic "Golgotha" is easily explained by Luke's concern for clarity, as we remember that both Quintilian (*Inst.* 1.5.1–8) and Theon (*Prog.* 81) argue that foreign words decrease clarity. Luke edits Mark similarly in 22:39 where he replaces Mark's "Gethsemane" with "the Mount of Olives."[69]

After providing the place, Luke jumps over Mark 15:23 and picks up with 15:24 to state that they crucified Jesus. Here Luke adds the detail that they crucified Jesus with two criminals, one on his right and one on his left—a detail that Mark does not narrate until later in the scene (15:27). Thus Luke has taken Mark's two narrations that Jesus was crucified (15:24, 27) and combined them into one at the beginning of the scene (23:33). This combination creates a topic sentence that sets the scene (the hearers learn about the place, the characters,[70] and the event at once at the beginning of the scene) and deletes the redundancy in Mark. After

---

68. Though not discussed here because no one in this scene specifically mocks Jesus as a prophet (though, see 22:63–65), Carroll points out that this scene also confirms Jesus' identity as a prophet. Not only did he warn Jerusalem like a prophet in the preceding scene (23:27–31), but the rejection and death that he faces here confirms his role as prophet in light of his earlier announcements about the Son of Man's upcoming rejection and death (9:22, 44; 13:32–35; 17:25; 18:31–33). Carroll explains, "Because Jesus *is* Prophet, he inevitably encounters rejection and death. The cross, then, confirms rather than disconfirms Jesus' status as Prophet par excellence" (emphasis original). See Carroll, "Luke's Crucifixion Scene," 113–14. Cf., more recently, Carroll, *Luke*, 466–67.

69. Hoover says that the inclusion of "Golgotha" in Luke would have "create[d] a pointless problem for his readers." See Hoover, "Selected Special Lukan Material," 120.

70. Marshall also notes that Luke may have mentioned the criminals at the outset of the narrative in an attempt to "deliberately giv[e] notice of his intentions since he develops the story of the two criminals more thoroughly than Mark." See Marshall, *Gospel of Luke*, 866.

setting the scene, Luke tells how they cast lots for Jesus' clothes. Here he follows Mark's wording closely in an allusion to Ps 21:19:

Mark 15:24: καὶ <u>διαμερίζονται</u> <u>τὰ</u> <u>ἱμάτια</u> <u>αὐτοῦ</u>, <u>βάλλοντες</u> <u>κλῆρον</u> ἐπ' αὐτὰ τίς τί ἄρῃ

Luke 23:34: <u>διαμεριζόμενοι</u> δὲ <u>τὰ</u> <u>ἱμάτια</u> <u>αὐτοῦ</u> <u>ἔβαλον</u> <u>κλήρους</u>.

Luke provides one more detail before he turns to the specific confirmations of Jesus' guilt—he mentions that the people (ὁ λαός) stood by watching (23:35). If these people are the same as the great multitude (πολὺ πλῆθος τοῦ λαοῦ) and/or crowds (ὄχλοι) in the scenes that precede (23:4; 23:27) and follow (23:48) it—and I think that they are[71]—Luke adds this detail here to provide an intermediate step in the transformation of the people. Earlier they demanded his crucifixion; now they stand by as passive observers; in a short time they will mourn Jesus' death. If the people mocked Jesus at the crucifixion in Luke, as they do in Mark, their breast beating in 23:48 would have been too abrupt of a change. Their action here—passively watching while the leaders mock—suggests to the hearers that something has changed since the previous scene when they demanded his crucifixion along with the leaders. This gradual transformation from one scene to the next makes the change in the people seem more plausible.

When we compare the characters and their roles between Luke and Mark, we can see how Luke has rearranged and adapted Mark's material. See table 7, where italicized text signifies significant words in common that are spoken by different characters and underlined text signifies significant words in common that are spoken by the same characters.

---

71. See my justification in the discussion of 23:48 below.

Table 7. Responses to Jesus on the cross in Luke and Mark

Luke		Mark	
Character	Response to Jesus	Character	Response to Jesus
The people (ὁ λάος)	Stand by watching (23:35)	Passersby (οἱ παραπορευόμενοι)	Deride (βλασφημέω) and shake heads: "Aha! The one who is destroying the temple and rebuilding it in three days—save yourself by coming down from the cross." *οὐὰ ὁ καταλύων τὸν ναὸν καὶ οἰκοδομῶν ἐν τρισὶν ἡμέραις, σῶσον σεαυτὸν καταβὰς ἀπὸ τοῦ σταυροῦ.* (15:29–30)

SCENE 2: TRANSITION TO THE CROSS AND THE INFORMAL TRIAL

Luke		Mark	
Character	Response to Jesus	Character	Response to Jesus
The rulers (οἱ ἄρχοντες)	Sneer (ἐκμυκτηρίζω) and say: "He saved others. Let him save himself, if this one is the Messiah of God, the Chosen One."	Chief priests and scribes (οἱ ἀρχιερεῖς . . . μετὰ τῶν γραμματέων)	Mock (ἐμπαίζω) and say: "he saved others; he is not able to save himself. Let the Messiah, the king of Israel, come down from the cross now in order that we may see and believe."
	ἄλλους ἔσωσεν, σωσάτω ἑαυτόν, εἰ οὗτός ἐστιν ὁ χριστὸς τοῦ θεοῦ ὁ ἐκλεκτός. (23:35)		ἄλλους ἔσωσεν, ἑαυτὸν οὐ δύναται σῶσαι· ὁ χριστὸς ὁ βασιλεὺς Ἰσραὴλ καταβάτω νῦν ἀπὸ τοῦ σταυροῦ, ἵνα ἴδωμεν καὶ πιστεύσωμεν. (15:31–32)
Soldiers (οἱ στρατιῶται)	Mock (ἐμπαίζω) and say: "If you are the king of the Jews, save yourself!"	Soldiers (οἱ στρατιῶται)	Cf. 15:16–20, where the Roman soldiers mock him (ἐμπαίζω) and call him "King of the Jews." (βασιλεῦτῶν Ἰουδαίων)
	εἰ σὺ εἶ ὁ βασιλεὺς τῶν Ἰουδαίων, σῶσον σεαυτόν. (23:37)		

Luke		Mark	
Character	Response to Jesus	Character	Response to Jesus
Criminal 1 (κακοῦργος)	Derides (βλασφημέω) and says: "Are you not the Messiah? Save yourself and us!" οὐχὶ σὺ εἶ ὁ χριστός; σῶσον σεαυτὸν καὶ ἡμᾶς. (23:39)	Robbers (λῃστής)	Both taunt him (ὀνειδίζω) (15:32)

The material about Jesus' being mocked at his crucifixion is similar enough (in some cases verbatim) to conclude that Luke drew his material from Mark and not another source.[72] For instance Luke retains much of the content of the rulers' taunts[73]: both note that he saved others (ἄλλους ἔσωσεν), both employ a third-person imperative (σωσάτω in Luke; καταβάτω in Mark) in an attempt to chide Jesus into saving himself, and both refer to Jesus as ὁ χριστός. Both use the verbs ἐμπαίζω and βλασφημέω to describe the mocking, though Luke also uses ἐκμυκτηρίζω and Mark ὀνειδίζω. At times Luke retains Luke's vocabulary (e.g., οἱ στρατιῶται); at other times he substitutes synonyms for Mark's word

---

72. Contra Jeremias, "Perikopen-Umstellungen bei Lukas?," 115–19; Taylor, *Passion Narrative*, 92–99; Fitzmyer, *Gospel according to Luke*, 1500; Bovon, *Luke 3*, 296. These commentators disagree on whether Luke inserted his special material into Mark's narrative (Fitzmyer), whether Luke has inserted Markan material into the account in his special source (Taylor and Jeremias), or whether Luke alternated between sources (Bovon). Those who argue that the differences from Mark stem from Luke's hand and not a source include Brown, *Death of the Messiah*, 1002–3; Hoover, "Selected Special Lukan Material," 122–25. Both agree that 23:33–38 is Luke's redaction of Mark, but that Luke may be drawing on an independent tradition (one similar to that used for *Gos. Pet.* 4.13) for the material about Jesus' interaction with the criminals.

73. Though Luke simplifies Mark's "the chief priests with the scribes" into "the rulers."

choice (e.g., κακοῦργος for λῃστής; ἀριστερός for εὐώνυμος), but the overall meaning remains the same.⁷⁴

Some of Luke's larger divergences from Mark, however, warrant explanation. First, we note that Luke opens and closes the scene with people who do not mock Jesus—the people in 23:35 and the second criminal in 23:40–43.⁷⁵ This presentation stands in contrast to the characters in Mark, all of whom mock Jesus.⁷⁶ Luke's change suggests that he is concerned to show different responses to Jesus, which fits into his larger refutation-confirmation scheme. Brown also notes that this presentation "gives Luke a chance to have the mockery terminate with an act of salvation by Jesus, another instance of Luke's treating the suffering of Jesus as salvific."⁷⁷ But despite Luke's crafting his story in this way, Mark's influence is noteworthy. Not only are both of these sets of characters drawn from Mark (Luke's λαός = Mark's οἱ παραπορευόμενοι; Luke's κακοῦργος = Mark's λῃστής), but they are also the first and the last characters who mock Jesus in Mark (i.e., Luke maintains Mark's order). In the latter case, similar to how he does elsewhere in the passion narrative,⁷⁸ Luke takes the opportunity to flesh out a story that Mark chose to narrate only in passing. Whereas Mark says, "Those who were crucified with him also taunted him" (15:32), Luke gives words to both of those crucified with Jesus. The first criminal, like

---

74. I am not arguing that Luke's substitutions do not have rhetorical significance, but rather that the gist of the narrative is the same. As I noted in the preceding chapter, my argument does not require an explanation of every single change that Luke makes to Mark, especially minor adjustments in syntax, word substitutions, or minor additions or deletions. These may result from stylistic preferences, from a desire to rival or compete with Mark, or from other concerns not discernible to modern readers. For (often successful) attempts to explain some of these more minor changes, see the relevant sections in Büchele, *Der Tod Jesu*; Untergassmair, *Kreuzweg und Kreuzigung Jesu*; Neyrey, *Passion according to Luke*; Brown, *Death of the Messiah*. On Luke's replacing Mark's λῃστής with κακοῦργος, see Matera, *Passion Narratives*, 183–84.

Here Marshall falls into the trap of assuming that vocabulary substitutions necessarily mean that Luke was relying on a separate source. E.g., he says, "[T]here is no obvious reason for the change [to κακοῦργος] from λῃστής (other than use of a source), unless Luke is trying to avoid all association of Jesus with revolutionaries (but 23:19 is against this view)." See Marshall, *Gospel of Luke*, 866.

75. I do not include the second criminal in the chart since in Luke he does not mock Jesus and since I discuss him more fully under "Refutation 4."

76. Hoover, "Selected Special Lukan Material," 120.

77. Brown, *Death of the Messiah*, 984.

78. E.g., Mark says that the chief priests accused Jesus of many things (15:3), but Luke provides specific accusations (23:2, 5). Mark notes that the crowd asked Pilate to release Barabbas (15:8), but Luke provides the direct discourse (23:18).

the leaders and the soldiers, confirms Jesus' guilt. The second, which I discuss in "Refutation 4" below, refutes Jesus' guilt.

Second, showing a gradual change in the people's response to Jesus would have been difficult if the people mocked Jesus along with the leaders (as they do in Mark), so Luke moves the σῶσον σεαυτόν taunt from their lips (Mark 15:29–30) and places it instead on the lips of the soldiers (Luke 23:37). Luke may have been inspired to do this by the preceding scene in Mark, where the soldiers mock Jesus in the governor's palace (15:16–20). Since Luke transferred many elements of 15:16–20 to the scene where Jesus appears before Herod (23:6–12) and thus deleted Mark's scene in the governor's palace, he freed up the material of the Roman soldiers' mocking for the crucifixion scene. Neyrey points out that the soldiers' mockery here also sets up a contrast with the solider (centurion) who proclaims Jesus innocent after the crucifixion.[79] This is part of Luke's larger juxtaposition of negative and favorable reactions to Jesus. The mockery on the lips of the soldiers in 23:36–38 provides a direct contrast to the praise on the lips of the centurion—just one of many pairs that Luke contrasts in his Gospel.[80]

Third, besides moving the taunt from the passersby to the soldiers, Luke also substitutes some material for the remainder of the passersby's taunts in Mark. Because Luke removed the false accusation of Jesus' claim to destroy and rebuild the temple from earlier in Mark's narrative (14:58),[81] he removes it here as well. Instead, he prefixes the taunt with "if you are the king of the Jews"—information furnished by the inscription over Jesus' cross (23:38; Mark 15:26).

Finally, Luke synthesizes aspects of four different parts of Mark into one verse: (1) the mockery by the Roman soldiers (15:16–20, esp. 20), including a reference to Jesus as King of the Jews; (2) the offering of wine by the soldiers (15:23); (3) the offering of sour wine (15:36); and (4) the challenge to save himself, which in Mark appears on the lips of the passersby (15:30). Luke combines all these materials into the following sentence: "The soldiers also mocked him, coming up to him, offering him sour wine, and saying, 'If you are the king of the Jews, save yourself!'" (23:36). The first offering of the sweet wine may not have seemed necessary to

---

79. Neyrey, *Passion according to Luke*, 132.
80. See "Refutation 4" below on contrasting pairs in Luke.
81. See "Setting the Stage" in chapter 3.

Luke since, according to Mark, Jesus refused to take it.[82] Further, though Mark does not specifically say that the soldiers mocked Jesus by offering him wine, as Luke does, some commentators think that the act was still a mockery. Evans, for instance, argues that "the offer of fine wine to Jesus was in fact part of the ongoing mockery (cf. vv. 29–32). In effect, the soldiers were offering the finest wine to the 'king of the Jews.'"[83] Luke's connection between the Roman mockery and the offering of wine, then, could naturally arise from Mark's account. Since Luke removes Jesus' (Aramaic) dying words from the cross—words that made the bystanders think Jesus was calling Elijah—the offer of wine to prolong Jesus' life in an attempt to see if Elijah would come was no longer necessary. Ultimately, Luke's combination of these four elements from Mark into one verse results in a more streamlined,[84] clear,[85] and concise[86] narrative and explains why Luke's wording on the offering of wine to Jesus is different than Mark's.[87]

---

82. Büchele also notes that Luke may have removed this episode to avoid showing Jesus' weakness (i.e., accepting a pain-dulling substance). See Büchele, *Der Tod Jesu*, 45. Marshall entertains the possibility that Luke omitted this detail from Mark because it was a doublet, but ultimately decides that "it is more probable that it was missing from his non-Marcan source" since Luke generally retains features from Mark that would underline the martyr spirit of Jesus. See Marshall, *Gospel of Luke*, 867.

83. Evans, *Mark 8:27—16:20*, 501. For a survey of the various interpretive options, see Collins, *Mark*, 740–44.

84. He combines four elements from Mark into one verse.

85. He removes the Aramaic from Mark 15:34 (discussed more fully below). As noted above, both Quintilian (*Inst.* 1.5.1–8) and Theon (*Prog.* 81) argue that foreign words decrease clarity.

86. Luke condenses two wine offerings into one, omitting the one that Jesus refused.

87. Though both have the soldiers offer wine to Jesus, the two verses (Mark 15:23; Luke 23:36a) have only two words in common (καὶ and αὐτῷ). Luke's need to specify the subject (since he used the passive in 23:32 and did not state the subject in 23:33 or 23:34), his pulling ὄξος from 15:23 in place of οἶνος, and his goal of associating the mockery with the giving of wine justify how the two verses can be so different with regard to specific words even though Luke relied on Mark. This is a prime example of how word counts can be deceptive. Yes, the verses only have two words in common (and two rather insignificant ones at that), but they still mean virtually the same thing. This is a fitting example of paraphrase: changing the words without changing the meaning.

Refutation 4: Second Criminal (23:40–43)

As a Lukan hearer has come to expect, the tables turn once more and Jesus' trial continues. After the rulers, the soldiers, and the first criminal attempt to confirm the charges against Jesus, the second criminal, God, and the centurion defend Jesus. The second criminal rebukes the first criminal in two ways. First he asks his fellow criminal incredulously, "Do you not even fear God?" This question hints at the first criminal's godlessness. This accusation of not fearing God can be seen as the second criminal's attempt to discredit the first criminal's testimony, one way of refuting a charge according to Quintilian (*Inst.* 5.13.8). The second criminal follows this rhetorical question with a reminder that they have received the same sentence as Jesus. Like the crowd's insistence on the release of Barabbas over Jesus, which suggested that Jesus was more deserving of death than a murderer, this second criminal reminds the hearers that Jesus is receiving the same punishment as criminals—only he goes on to note how unjust this is. The second way the second criminal rebukes the first is by pointing out the inappropriateness of his claim: "Indeed, we (are condemned) justly, for we are receiving what is deserved for what we did, but this man has done nothing wrong" (23:41).[88] Yet again, then, Luke employs one of the common topics of refutation—inappropriateness—as a means of highlighting Jesus' innocence.

After the second criminal refutes the first, he requests that Jesus remember him when he comes into his kingdom.[89] This request suggests that the second criminal understands Jesus' true identity as King, despite his hanging on a cross. This stands in direct contrast to the refutations of the soldiers, for whom Jesus' being King and hanging on a cross were mutually exclusive. Jesus' response to the criminal—"Truly I say to you, today you will be with me in paradise"—also counters the refutations of Jesus' identity by the rulers, soldiers, and first criminal. They saw his hanging on the cross—his lack of saving himself—as proof that he was not Savior. Turning this notion on its head, Jesus offers salvation to this criminal who recognizes his innocence and his true identity. It is only

---

88. Brown, *Death of the Messiah*, 1004, notes the contrast between this criminal's words ("we are receiving what is worthy of what we did") and Pilate's words about Jesus in 23:15 ("There is nothing worthy of death that has been done by him"). Cf. Fitzmyer, *Gospel according to Luke*, 1508.

89. On the variant reading in 23:42 (ἐν τῇ βασιλείᾳ vs. εἰς τὴν βασιλείαν), see Marshall, *Gospel of Luke*, 872; Fitzmyer, *Gospel according to Luke*, 1510; Wolter, *Das Lukasevangelium*, 761.

by *not* saving himself that Jesus can offer salvation to this discerning criminal, another allusion back to Jesus' words in 9:24. In just a few short verses, then, Luke affirms Jesus' identity as both King and Savior.

Of the four canonical gospels,[90] only Luke places direct discourse on the lips of the criminals. As mentioned above, this discourse in Luke was likely prompted by Mark's statement, "Those who were crucified with him also taunted him" (15:32). As he did in 23:2 (Mark 15:3) and 23:18 (Mark 15:8), Luke takes something that Mark only narrates in passing and transforms it into a dialogue with more details. Luke does use some freedom in his composition, however, insomuch as Mark says that both the criminals taunt Jesus, while Luke has one taunt Jesus and one respond favorably to him.

Proponents of a special source behind Luke's passion narrative acknowledge "many signs of Luke's hand" in these verses but conclude that the presence of pre-Lukan vocabulary means that "Luke is editing a

---

90. In the *Gospel of Peter* one of the criminals (κακοῦργος) also speaks from the cross. One of the criminals reviles the executioners for casting lots for Jesus' clothing and says, "We have suffered like this for the evil things (τὰ κακά) we did; but this one, the Savior of the people—what wrong has he done you (τί ἠδίκησεν ὑμᾶς)?" (*Gos. Pet.* 13 [Ehrman & Pleše 380–81]). Beyond using κακοῦργος like Luke, the *Gospel of Peter* similarly emphasizes through the words of one of the criminals that Jesus did nothing wrong, in contrast to the criminals who deserved their fate. The differences are numerous, though: the criminal speaks to the soldiers instead of Jesus; only one criminal speaks (i.e., it lacks the contrasting responses that Luke has); Jesus does not converse with the criminal.

Scholars debate the relationship between the *Gospel of Peter* and the canonical gospels. Ehrman and Pleše hold that the author "constructed his Gospel on the basis of oral traditions and/or on recollections of accounts he had earlier read." See Ehrman and Pleše, *The Apocryphal Gospels*, 375. Similarly, Bovon thinks that the *Gospel of Peter* "was independent of the canonical Gospels but that it shares a tradition with Luke and his special source." See Bovon, *Luke 3*, 264–65. Brown finds it more likely that the *Gospel of Peter* drew upon the canonical gospels (though "not necessarily from their written texts but often from memories preserved through their having been heard and recounted orally"). See Brown, *Death of the Messiah*, 1001. When comparing the *Gospel of Peter* with the individual canonical gospels, Brown (1330) finds that "in content and sequence GPet's relationship to Luke is more distant than GPet's relationship to Matt."

I follow Ehrman and Pleše (375–76) and Brown (1341–42) in thinking that the *Gospel of Peter* most likely post-dates the canonical gospels, likely originating in the early to mid second century. Whether the *Gospel of Peter* relied on the canonical gospels, on similar traditions, or on both cannot be decided with certainty. Nonetheless, the similarities between Luke 23:40–41 and *Gos. Pet.* 13 demand that we leave open the possibility that Luke drew upon earlier traditions for these verses, though evidence for a written source containing this tradition is lacking.

pre-Lukan source."[91] As is often the case, some base this conclusion solely on vocabulary analysis with little concern for other factors.[92] Green is an exception, adding that Luke includes at least two elements that have no basis in Mark: a criminal who is positive toward Jesus and someone seeking salvation.[93] This point, however, suffers from the wrongful assumption that anything not found specifically in Mark must have arisen from a separate source. In at least two other places in his passion narrative Luke supplies detailed dialogue that Mark did not provide in a way similar to how he does here.[94] For example, Luke transforms Mark 15:3 ("And the chief priests accused him of many things") into three specific accusations, the content of which he drew from his earlier narrative.[95] He also transforms Mark 15:8 ("the crowd came up and began to ask [Pilate] to do as he had done for them") into direct discourse: "Away with this

---

91. Taylor, *Passion Narrative of St. Luke*, 95.

92. Taylor only considers Lukan or pre-Lukan words when making his decision (relying on the vocabulary studies of Stanton and Rehkopf, as he does elsewhere). Vocabulary is decisive for Nolland, too: "There is too little characteristically Lukan language here . . . for it to be likely that Luke has spun 23:39-43 entirely out of the brief Markan notice. . . ." For example, Nolland argues that καὶ ἔλεγεν in 23:42 is unlikely Lukan because Luke almost always edits this construction when he finds it in Mark (though 6:5 is an exception). Nolland, *Luke 18:35—24:53*, 1150-51 (quotation from 1150); Taylor, *Passion Narrative*, 1995.

93. Green, *Death of Jesus*, 95. Green also thinks that the second criminal's attitude is "consonant with the Jewish sentiment that to accept one's punishment as justified is an expression of penitence" and is thus pre-Lukan. Besides these two points, however, Green, like those mentioned in the previous note, bases most of his argument on Luke's vocabulary usage: (1) κρεμάννυμι is "pre-Lukan"—"There is no perceivable reason for Luke to have substituted this term for σταυρόω or συσταυρόω"; (2) κακοῦργος was present in Luke's source, he says, and "there is no basis for presupposing that Luke has deliberately chosen κακοῦργος over, says, ἄνομος"; (3) "Luke is hardly to be credited with introducing on his own accord the introductory ἀμὴν σοι λέγω."

94. This evidence goes against Green's claim that "[i]t is not like Luke to introduce direct speech where there was none in his source; indeed his tendency is to move away from direct discourse." Ibid., 64. Here Green relies on Sanders, *Tendencies of the Synoptic Tradition*, 261-62. Sanders gives several examples of this tendency in Luke, but there are enough instances where Luke edits in the opposite direction to make us hesitate in making too broad of a claim.

95. As detailed in "The Accusations" in chapter 3. Green considers these detailed accusations in 23:2-5 as "probable" redaction of his *Sonderquelle*, mostly based on vocabulary analysis but also because of a similar political emphasis in John's passion narrative which "points to a non-Markan tradition underlying the Johannine and Lukan texts." Green, *Death of Jesus*, 78, 324-27.

man! Release Barabbas for us!" (23:18). It is hardly a stretch to imagine that Luke might do this again just a few verses later.

Furthermore, these studies do not account for an important literary pattern in Luke's larger Gospel—Luke's interest in contrasting two figures (e.g., Zechariah and Mary, Mary and Martha, the rich man and Lazarus, the Pharisee and the publican).[96] It is impossible to tell if Luke borrowed these pairs from a source (e.g., "L") for his earlier narrative or if they stemmed from his own literary ingenuity, but, unless one thinks that Luke borrowed the material about the thieves from that same source,[97] then Luke would have found contrasting pairs in two separate sources— the one he used for his non-Passion material and the one he used for his passion material.[98] It seems more likely that Luke was accustomed to developing contrasting pairs earlier in his narrative (whether at his own initiation or prompted by his source), and when he saw a pair in Mark's narrative it inspired him to develop the two criminals as contrasting characters, even though in Mark both respond negatively to Jesus. This technique fits not only with his literary techniques earlier in his Gospel,[99] but also with the larger refutation and confirmation scheme of the passion narrative. In fact, Soards describes the passion narrative as "the culmination of the Lukan pattern of acceptance or rejection that has characterized the response of people to the earthly ministry of Jesus."[100] Since Lukan development of Mark 15:32 is plausible in light of rhetorical

---

96. These pairs are commonly noted. See, e.g., Brown, *Death of the Messiah*, 1002; Büchele, *Der Tod Jesu*, 49; Morgenthaler, *Lukas und Quintilian*, 301–2.

97. Fitzmyer argues that Luke probably derived this material in 23:39–4 from "L," the source that he thinks is behind Luke's special material outside of the passion narrative as well. This proposal eliminates the problem described above but is not without problems. See the arguments in Paffenroth's study of "L," which suggest that "L" did not contain a passion narrative. Fitzmyer, *Gospel according to Luke*, 1507; Paffenroth, *Story of Jesus*, 29, 150. See also Soards' study of the special material in Luke 22, where he concludes that "careful examination of the special Lukan material in Luke 22 supports neither the contention that Luke's Gospel is based upon a proto-Luke nor the claim that Luke had recourse to a written, integrated special Passion Narrative source that was itself an independent form of the Passion story." Soards, *Passion according to Luke*, 121.

98. This is the same situation described with reference to 23:26–32.

99. Neyrey explains, "Luke frequently presents in a narrative a 'division' in reactions to Jesus. He is, after all, 'set for the rise and fall of many' (2:34)." Neyrey, *Passion according to Luke*, 132. On 134–38, Neyrey explicates the various contrasts between the two criminals.

100. Soards, *Passion according to Luke*, 111.

techniques Luke uses elsewhere in his Gospel (e.g., creating dialogue out of a simple narration in Mark; employing pairs to contrast responses to Jesus), it is best to see these verses as Luke's development of Mark—possibly under the influence of oral tradition—and not his taking material from another source.[101]

Refutation 5: Darkness and Rending of the Veil (23:44-46)

In the remainder of the passion narrative, Luke continues to affirm Jesus' innocence, despite the apparent victory of Jesus' opponents through the crucifixion. Just prior to Jesus' death are two heavenly portents: the failing of the sun's light and the rending of the temple veil (23:44-46). McConnell points out that ancient people believed that the gods testified through utterances (be it direct speech or oracles), through visible heavenly emanations like fire, through the presence and flight patterns of birds, through portents on earth, and through dreams and visions. On this basis, he argues that the eclipse of the sun and the rending of the temple veil in Luke's passion narrative should be viewed as divine testimony expressing God's displeasure at Jesus' death.[102] Evidence of similar portents at Caesar's death (e.g., the eclipse of the sun) support this understanding. In the case of Caesar, McConnell explains, "the darkening of the sun was a testimony of the gods' displeasure over Caesar's death (thus portraying Caesar as being in favor with the gods), as well as

---

101. Other scholars arguing that Luke composed 23:39-43 *not* on the basis of a written source include Stanton, *Gospels as Historical Documents*, 2:308-10; Neyrey, *Passion according to Luke*, 124; Johnson, *Gospel of Luke*, 380; Hoover, "Selected Special Lukan Material," 123-24. Those arguing that Luke used a special source include Grundmann, *Das Evangelium nach Lukas*, 431; Taylor, *Passion Narrative*, 95; Fitzmyer, *Gospel according to Luke*, 1507; Nolland, *Luke 18:35—24:53*, 1150; Bovon, *Luke 3*, 294-95. Still others intentionally do not decide because of the complexity of the material. See, e.g., Büchele, *Der Tod Jesu*, 51; Marshall, *Gospel of Luke*, 871.

102. McConnell, *Topos of Divine Testimony*, 1-2, 230-31. Though discussed in much less detail, Bock, too, sees the darkness and the tearing of the temple curtain as "the heavens ... issuing their own commentary on events." As it does in Joel 2:10, 20-31; Amos 8:9, the midday darkness "suggests the presence of judgment." See Bock, *Luke*, 376.

a condemnation of his murderers."[103] A similar function appears to be at work in Luke's passion narrative.[104]

Through the darkness in the sky and the tearing of the curtain at the temple—both places associated with the divine—God offers testimony that shows his displeasure at Jesus' death. Thus, not only have Pilate, Herod, and the second criminal refuted the charges against Jesus, but so has God. We remember from chapter 2 that ancient people viewed the gods as the most authoritative type of witness because of their outstanding virtue.[105] Thus, God's testimony at Jesus' death increases not only the quantity of witnesses who refute the charges against Jesus but also the quality of the witnesses.

Luke sets up a parallel to this divine testimony in his account of Paul's trial in Acts.[106] As Paul is transferred to Rome to appear before Caesar his ship encounters a storm, and those on board eventually wash ashore at Malta where Paul survives a snake bite. Both shipwrecks and snakes were associated with the hand of the gods in the Greco-Roman world.[107] Paul's shipwreck story is similar to many others in the Greco-Roman world where a storm is the result of natural causes, but the outcome (in Paul's

---

103. McConnell, *Topos of Divine Testimony*, 230. Cf. a similar assessment in Fitzmyer, *Gospel according to Luke*, 1518.

104. Of course, divine testimony does not exhaust the meaning of the darkness and the rending of the curtain. The darkness also represents "the central role in this death of the satanic forces who operate in conjunction with the Jewish leaders" (cf. 22:53). See Chance, *Jerusalem*, 119. Cf. the survey of primary source evidence in antiquity that relates the rending of the curtain to the destruction of the temple in Allison, *End of the Ages*, 31–32. The darkness may also signal the inauguration of the "last days," described more fully in Peter's Pentecost sermon with the reference to Joel—the last days are accompanied by heavenly and earthly portents, including the darkening of the sun. Fitzmyer adds that "[t]he darkness and the rending of the Temple veil may have an apocalyptic and cosmic dimension; but they should rather be related to the Lucan idea of evil's 'hour' and 'the power of darkness' (22:53), which reigns as Jesus dies." Fitzmyer, *Gospel according to Luke*, 1519.

105. McConnell, *Topos of Divine Testimony*, 49–50. McConnell cites Cicero, *Top.* 19.73, as evidence here.

106. Chance also sees a parallel between the rending of the temple curtain in Luke 23:45 and the shutting of the temple gates when Paul was seized in Acts 21:30. For him, both events represented the destruction of the temple for Luke. See Chance, *Jerusalem*, 121–22.

107. For a sizeable list of sea storm type-scenes in Greco-Roman literature (where a storm is either caused by the gods, overcome by the gods, or both), see Talbert, *Reading Acts*, 212–13. For the connection between snakes and the divine, see McConnell, *Topos of Divine Testimony*, 221–22.

case, deliverance) is the result of the divine will.[108] Luke makes it clear that the shipwreck results from natural causes, but that the outcome is a result of God's will. Luke mentions that they are sailing in a dangerous time of year (27:9) and that they must search for a suitable harbor since winter is approaching (27:12). When things begin to look grim, however, Paul announces that they will all survive, which he knows because an angel of God told him (27:23). Thus, God's hand is behind their safety and the shipwreck ought not be viewed as a judgment against Paul.

In the scene at Malta, Luke further mitigates against the notion that the storm and shipwreck are the result of God's judgment against a potentially guilty Paul. Upon their landing, a snake bites Paul (28:3). McConnell convincingly demonstrates that the appearance of snakes was generally understood as "the gods' condemnation of a character."[109] This is certainly how the native Maltans understand the situation. In response to the snakebite they say, "This man must be a murderer; though he has escaped from the sea, justice has not allowed him to live" (28:4). However, in an unexpected twist, the snakebite does not harm Paul, which leads them to reverse their earlier evaluation and instead proclaim Paul to be a god (28:6). Even though the natives still make an inaccurate judgment about Paul (i.e., that he is a god), the scene nonetheless demonstrates that an ancient audience would have viewed the survival of the shipwreck and snakebite as divine portents affirming Paul's innocence.[110] Thus, the stories of both Jesus and Paul include divine testimony affirming their innocence—for Jesus, God speaks through darkness[111] and the rending of the temple curtain; for Paul, God speaks through deliverance from a shipwreck and deliverance from a snake bite.[112]

---

108. Talbert, *Reading Acts*, 215.

109. McConnell, *Topos of Divine Testimony*, 221. See his examples from Plutarch and Livy, which lead him to conclude that "divine testimony through signs and portents in creation [e.g., snakes] can be a display of the anger of the gods, but can also demonstrate their favor" (223).

110. Cf. ibid., 241–42.

111. One could argue that darkness is also a divine portent in Paul's narrative. When the storm is underway, Luke narrates that "neither the sun nor the stars shone for many days" (27:20). However, this could also simply be viewed as the natural conditions during a storm. Since it was daytime during Jesus' crucifixion, however, the darkness is more obviously from the hand of God.

112. The divine deliverance from the shipwreck and snakebite have led some to view Paul's journey to Rome as a parallel to Jesus' death and resurrection. See, e.g., Radl, *Paulus und Jesus*, 222–51; Goulder, *Type and History*, 34–39.

Beyond the portents, Jesus' crucifixion narrative contains another parallel with Luke's story of the church in Acts. Jesus' final words from the cross in Luke are a trusting prayer to God: "Father, into your hands I commit my spirit" (23:46). These words are echoed in Stephen's prayer at his death, only addressed to the Lord Jesus instead of the Father: "Lord Jesus, receive my spirit" (Acts 7:59). Both Jesus and Stephen place their trust in God as they face death.

Both Luke and Mark set off these final events of the crucifixion from the earlier mockery with a time reference. Mark notes that it was the sixth hour (ὥρας ἕκτης; 15:33), and Luke that it was about the sixth hour (ὡσεὶ ὥρα ἕκτη; 23:44). Luke then follows Mark verbatim in setting the scene: σκότος ἐγένετο ἐφ' ὅλην τὴν γῆν ἕως ὥρας ἐνάτης (Mark 15:33; Luke 23:44). Luke, however, provides an explanation for the darkness—the sun's light failed (τοῦ ἡλίου ἐκλιπόντος)[113]—and omits Mark's second reference to the ninth hour in the following verse (15:34). Matera attributes the omission to Luke's style, whereas Mark marks off the crucifixion in three hour periods (15:25, 33, 34), Luke suppresses two of these (15:25, 34) and prefers the indeterminate participle ὡσεί, a word he frequently uses to introduce age, number, time, or distance.[114] Matera also adds that the reference to the sun makes the connection to Joel 2:28–32 (3:1–5 LXX) stronger.[115]

After describing the time and the cosmic details, Luke jumps over the last words of Jesus and the calling of Elijah in Mark and moves forward the tearing of the sanctuary curtain (Luke 23:45b; Mark 15:38). Besides the fronting of the verb, Luke follows Mark almost verbatim in the first part of the verse.[116] In the second part of the verse, however, Luke replaces Mark's εἰς δύο ἀπ' ἄνωθεν ἕως κάτω ("in two from top to bottom")

---

113. Commentators agree that this is a causal genitive absolute. See, e.g., Fitzmyer, *Gospel according to Luke*, 1517; Culy, Parsons, and Stigall, *Luke*, 727. Green, *Death of Jesus*, 96, calls the genitive absolute "not surprising in Lukan editorializing."

114. Matera, "The Death of Jesus according to Luke," 472. Matera provides references for Luke's use of ὡσεί. Green, too, calls ὡσεί "a characteristic addition in Lukan redaction." Green, *Death of Jesus*, 96. See also Jeremias, *Die Sprache*, 307.

115. Joel 2:31 (3:4 LXX) explicitly connects the sun to the darkness (ὁ ἥλιος μεταστραφήσεται εἰς σκότος) as Luke does here with the addition to Mark. See Matera, "Death of Jesus," 473.

116. Compare Mark's καὶ τὸ καταπέτασμα τοῦ ναοῦ ἐσχίσθη εἰς δύο ἀπ' ἄνωθεν ἕως κάτω with Luke's ἐσχίσθη δὲ τὸ καταπέτασμα τοῦ ναοῦ μέσον.

with μέσον ("down the middle"), which may be nothing more than an attempt to be concise (cf. Theon, *Prog.* 83; Quintilian, *Inst.* 4.2.40–43).[117]

This rearrangement of the tearing from after Jesus' death in Mark to before it in Luke has significant implications for the interpretation of the tearing. In Mark, the tearing immediately follows Jesus' last breath (15:37) and thus appears to be a result of the death and "gives the impression of some sort of judgment against the temple."[118] Luke's placement of the tearing before Jesus' death removes the immediate judgment against the temple by not making it a result of Jesus' death. It helps "avoid the impression that the death of Jesus is the end of the temple and its cult."[119] This shift in meaning is consistent with Luke's posture toward the temple elsewhere in his Gospel and Acts—a posture that is much more positive than Mark's.[120] Keeping Mark's less positive view toward the temple here

---

117. Green explains that this substitution "corresponds to classical usage and is consistent with Luke's terminological preferences." See Green, *Death of Jesus*, 96.

118. Matera, "Death of Jesus," 473–74. Of course, this is not the only way to interpret the rending of the veil in Mark. Geddert, for example, lists thirty-five ways of interpreting the rending of the veil (many of which are not mutually exclusive). Several of these interpretations do not relate specifically to the temple. Those interpretations that do think the rending relates specifically to the temple, however, see these implications as negative (e.g., "the abolition of the cult"; "the loss of significance for the temple itself"; the destruction of the whole temple is being presaged"; "the temple is rending its garments to mourn its impending doom." See Geddert, *Watchwords*, 141–43.

119. Matera, "Death of Jesus," 475. Green contends with Matera's notion that Luke's rearrangement attempts to avoid the impression of Jesus as the end of the temple and its cult. He asks, "If, as Matera insists, Luke wanted to avoid the impression that Jesus' death is the end of the temple, then why include this detail at all," especially since he removes Mark's material on the temple elsewhere? While Green agrees with Matera that Luke does not "harshly reject" the temple, he does see Luke's retention of the temple reference in 23:45 as signifying that the temple is giving way or being displaced by Jesus. See Green, *Death of Jesus*, 97.

While Green is right that at times Luke simply deletes (or moves elsewhere) material in Mark that does not support or that goes against his themes or emphases, Luke very well may have felt bound to keep this dramatic divine portent either because of its importance in the tradition or because he felt like it would go beyond the bounds of proper editing of Mark.

120. Maddox explains, "Elsewhere . . . Luke emphasizes the destruction of the Temple as punishment for the failure of Israel to produce the fruits of God's covenant with his people, but without any hint that the Temple is intrinsically an evil institution." See Maddox, *Purpose of Luke-Acts*, 53 (cited in Matera, "Death of Jesus," 474). Matera (474–75) discusses other ways in which Luke edits Mark to remove negative attitudes toward the temple (e.g., eliminating Mark 11:16; not bracketing the temple cleansing with the cursing of the fig tree, which "for Mark probably symbolizes the end of the temple cult"). As noted above, Luke also removed the charge that Jesus would

would have resulted in an inconsistent narrative, particularly when looking ahead to the role that the temple plays for the early Christians in Acts. Additionally, Luke's rearrangement of the tearing of the curtain links it more closely with the darkness and thus connects the two portents[121] to form one testimony from God. Carroll also points out that this rearrangement results in only positive responses after Jesus' death.[122]

If it does not suggest immediate judgment against the temple itself, what does the tearing of the curtain mean in Luke? Several possibilities have been proposed, with varying degrees of merit:

1. It forewarns the destruction of the temple if the people continue to reject Jesus.[123]

2. It symbolizes a portent of the last days prophesied by Joel (the darkness is the sign in the heavens; the rending of the veil is the sign on earth).[124]

3. It is a sign that Jesus' death tore down the barrier between God and humans.[125]

4. It represents Jesus' communion with God in the temple immediately preceding his death.[126]

---

destroy the temple (Mark 14:58) and the mockery that he would destroy the temple (Mark 15:28). This benevolent posture continues in Acts, where church life is related to the temple (2:46; 3:1; 5:20, 21, 42), where Paul fulfills his vow in the temple (21:26; 24:18), and where Paul specifically says that he does not act against the temple (25:8). Brown also adds that since Luke removed the prediction that Jesus would destroy the temple from Mark's Sanhedrin trial, "at the cross there was no need to portray a fulfillment of that prediction after Jesus' death." See Brown, *Death of the Messiah*, 1103.

121. Marshall, *Gospel of Luke*, 874; Brown, *Death of the Messiah*, 1033.

122. Carroll, *Luke*, 470.

123. Büchele, *Der Tod Jesu*, 52; Marshall, *Gospel of Luke*, 875; Brown, *Death of the Messiah*, 1104. Green's position is similar: "Luke portrays the rending of the temple veil as symbolic of the destruction of the symbolic world surrounding and emanating from the temple, and not as symbolic of the destruction of the temple itself." See Green, "Demise of the Temple," 514.

124. Matera, "Death of Jesus," 475.

125. Harrington, *Gospel according to St. Luke*, 267–68.

126. Sylva, "Temple Curtain and Jesus' Death," 243. This interpretation requires Sylva to repunctuate the verses as follows: "It was now about the sixth hour and there was darkness over the whole land until the ninth hour: the sun having failed. Then, the curtain of the temple tore down the middle, and Jesus, crying with a loud voice said, 'Father, into Your hands I commit my spirit.'"

5. It is a symbolic act in which God legitimates Jesus' temple ministry and confirms that it was designed to be a "house of prayer" (as evinced by Jesus' prayer immediately following the rending).[127]

Though the options are not mutually exclusive in all cases, its coupling with the darkness makes the first option the strongest of the possibilities proposed. This maintains a degree of continuity with Mark's interpretation (not surprising since they are narrating the same event) without as much negativity toward the temple (making it consistent with Luke's larger portrayal of the temple). As a warning, it also hints at the dire consequences of a continued rejection of Jesus.

Though he pulls some of the material from later in Mark's account, Luke stays fairly close to Mark's words in 23:44-45.[128] Besides removing two redundancies in Mark—the second reference to the ninth hour (15:34; discussed above) and the second reference to a "great cry" (15:37)—Luke retains much of Mark. He keeps Mark's wording that Jesus let out a great cry (Mark 14:34; Luke 23:46),[129] and he retains Mark's δὲ . . . ἐξέπνευσεν (Mark 14:37; Luke 23:46).

The key difference between the two accounts, however, is the second part of v. 46, where Luke replaces Mark's ελωι ελωι λεμα σαβαχθανι; ὅ ἐστιν μεθερμηνευόμενον· ὁ θεός μου ὁ θεός μου, εἰς τί ἐγκατέλιπές με; (15:34) with πάτερ, εἰς χεῖράς σου παρατίθεμαι τὸ πνεῦμά μου (23:46). As mentioned in "Confirmation 4" earlier in the chapter, Luke may have replaced Mark's words here for two reasons: (1) for the sake of clarity, he wanted to remove the Aramaic in Mark (as he does elsewhere)[130]; (2) Mark's words did not align with Luke's larger portrait of Jesus' death. The first reason is not enough in itself. If his concern was simply to increase the clarity by removing the foreign language (cf. Quintilian, *Inst.* 1.5.1-8; Theon, *Prog.* 81), Luke could have simply removed the Aramaic and left Mark's translation of the same words.[131] Instead he quotes a different psalm to fit the different way he has portrayed Jesus' death. Rather than following the abandonment theme in Mark (for which Ps 22:1 [21:2

---

127. Neagoe, *Trial of the Gospel*, 101.

128. Of the twenty-six words in Luke 23:44-45, seventeen are in Mark.

129. Though Luke replaces Mark's βοάω with φωνέω.

130. Of course, Jesus' final (Aramaic) words in Mark would have been particularly poignant, regardless of whether the audience knew Aramaic. On the rhetorical effect of Jesus' speaking in Aramaic, see Brown, *Death of the Messiah*, 1046, 1061-62.

131. On the Hebrew and Aramaic of Ps 22, along with Mark and Matthew's transliterations, see ibid., 1051-54.

LXX] provides the perfect climax), Luke downplays that theme[132] and instead brings to completion a theme he developed throughout his Gospel: Jesus' compulsion (δεῖ) to do his Father's will (e.g., 2:49; 4:43; 9:22; 13:33; 17:25; 22:37).

The substitution of Ps 31:5 (30:6 LXX) for Ps 22:1, then, is the culmination[133] of Jesus' trust in his Father and his determination to his do will: "Father, into your hands I commit my spirit."[134] Matera explains:

> In Luke, therefore, the task of Jesus is to trust in his Father and to accomplish the Father's will. Given such an agenda, it is clear that the cry of dereliction, as recorded by Mark, would have militated against Luke's carefully constructed story line. By contrast, Ps 31:5(6) is the perfect completion of a narrative in which Jesus has continually sought to do his Father's will. Jesus' words show that he is one with the Father not only in life but also in death.[135]

Ultimately, these words on Jesus' lips verify that, despite what appearances may suggest, Jesus is God's Son who remains in communion with him until the end.[136]

This substitution of Jesus' final words required Luke to remove the crowd's suspicion that Jesus was calling Elijah (as well as the redundant second offering of wine). Without the cry (*elōi*) that resembled the name Elijah,[137] the crowd's response would be inexplicable. Thus, Luke removed

---

132. E.g., Jesus notes that despite his denials, Peter's faith will not fail (22:32); his disciples tried to prevent his arrest (22:49–50); Luke does not mention the disciples' fleeing (cp. Mark 14:50); Jesus' acquaintances (πάντες οἱ γνωστοὶ αὐτῷ) and the women from Galilee were present at the cross (23:49). Matera, "Death of Jesus according to Luke," 476.

133. Brown points out that a character's last words in a drama are especially significant. See Brown, *Death of the Messiah*, 1045.

134. Luke slightly alters the psalm by adding πάτηρ and by shifting from the future παραθήσομαι to the present παρατίθεμαι. The psalmist expresses confidence in God to deliver him from his enemies.

135. Matera, "Death of Jesus," 476.

136. Carroll, "Luke's Crucifixion Scene," 116. Cf. Schweizer, *Good News*, 362.

137. On whether Mark's readers knew the Semitic languages and whether Semitic speakers would mistake Mark's *Elōi* for the name Elijah, see Brown, *Death of the Messiah*, 1061–62. Because Mark regularly translates Aramaic words for his audience and explains Jewish customs, Brown contends that Mark's readers probably did not know Semitic. After hearing the "exotic" Aramaic words and being told that the Jewish bystanders at the cross understood it as an appeal to Elijah, Mark's readers "would have assumed that the Semitic underlying the Greek form of the prophet's name was

this incident from his account and moved straight from the portents to Jesus' final words.

The differences between Mark's account and Luke's account (the rearrangement of material, the different last words, the absence of the Elijah incident) lead some to posit that Luke relied not upon Mark for his rendering of the events but on a special source.[138] Luke's concern for consistency and clarity in his narrative, however, can explain these differences. These concerns, along with Luke's positive view of the temple elsewhere in Luke and Acts, the similarities between Jesus' last words and Stephen's prayer in Acts, the connection to Luke's larger theme of Jesus' trust in God's will, and close connections with Mark in neighboring verses suggest instead that Luke 23:44–46 was inspired by Mark 15:33–38.[139]

Refutation 6: The Centurion (23:47–49)

The final declaration of Jesus' innocence—the final refutation of his guilt—immediately follows Jesus' death. After the divine portents (23:44–45) and after Jesus' final words (23:46), Jesus breathes his last. Luke then narrates, "Now the centurion, seeing what happened, began praising God[140] and said, 'Certainly this man was δίκαιος'" (23:47). In her study on praise responses in Luke and Acts, Kindalee Pfremmer De Long points out that the centurion's praise is not simply in response to the things that had happened (τὸ γενόμενον)[141] but also to what those things

---

close to the transliterated Aramaic *Elōi* that Jesus used. That is what hearers of Mark's Gospel who know no Aramaic have been doing ever since."

138. E.g., Jeremias, "Perikopen-Umstellungen bei Lukas?," 118–19; Taylor, *Passion Narrative*, 95–96; Green, *Death of Jesus*, 97–98. All three see a number of Lukan words and Markan influence. For example, Green thinks that Luke edits Mark for vv. 44–45, but draws v. 46 from his *Sonderquelle*. Even strong advocates of a separate passion source agree that the case for a separate passion source is weakest at this point in the narrative. See, e.g., Marshall, *Gospel of Luke*, 874; Green, *Death of Jesus*, 99; Nolland, *Luke 18:35—24:53*, 1155.

139. Those following this line of reasoning include Marshall, *Gospel of Luke*, 874; Matera, "Death of Jesus," 472; Brown, *Death of the Messiah*, 1067, 1099.

140. On ἐδόξαζεν as an ingressive imperfect, see Culy, Parsons, and Stigall, *Luke*, 728 (cf. 50). Cf. Carroll, *Luke*, 471.

141. This could simply refer to Jesus' final prayer and death, or it could include the divine portents and Jesus' dialogue with the criminal. Nolland believes it refers to Jesus' commitment to God through his sufferings, but also the darkness (pointing to the evil of what was happening) and possibly the promise of paradise to the criminal and the forgiveness of his executioners. See Nolland, *Luke 18:35—24:53*, 1159. Cf.

reveal.¹⁴² God has revealed Jesus' innocence to the centurion, certainly, and possibly also Jesus' connection with God.¹⁴³

De Long's observation about what God reveals at the cross—Jesus' innocence and possibly his connection with God—touches on one of the interpretive cruxes of Luke's passion narrative: what does Luke mean by δίκαιος? Scholars have long debated the meaning of δίκαιος in this passage. As discussed in chapter 1, scholars generally fall into one of three camps.¹⁴⁴ One camp argues that it should be translated as "righteous" or "just," arguing that (1) δίκαιος and its cognates elsewhere in Luke and Acts are never restricted to the meaning "innocent"¹⁴⁵; (2) the centurion's

---

Fitzmyer, *Gospel according to Luke*, 1519.

142. De Long's study revealed that "praise appears as a distinctive phenomenon in ancient texts, described with a particular set of vocabulary and recognizable independent of the form in which it appears" (14). She explains, "[T]he praise motif creates and resolves narrative tensions, functions symbolically, marks key moments in the plots, and clusters around three primary contexts: divine revelation, healing, and conversion" (15). The praise by the centurion at Jesus' death is a case of divine revelation. See De Long, *Surprised by God*, 13–16, 239–42.

143. Ibid., 240. Fitzmyer argues that Luke's Gospel was written in stages: "Stage I of the gospel tradition is concerned with what the historical Jesus of Nazareth did and said; Stage II with what was preached and proclaimed about him after the resurrection; and Stage III with what NT writers decided to put in writing concerning him. What immediately confronts the reader of the Lucan Gospel is a form of Stage III of that tradition" (viii). Regarding the understanding of δίκαιος, he argues that "on the lips of the historical centurion [presumably stage I], *dikaios* would have meant 'innocent,'" but that at stage III, Luke may have meant more, "since Jesus is at times called the 'Righteous One' in Luke's writings (Acts 3:14; 7:52; 22:14)." See Fitzmyer, *Gospel according to Luke*, 1520.

I agree that on the lips of a "historical centurion," δίκαιος would likely have connoted political innocence. However, I am less interested in the "historical centurion" and more in the way that Luke's hearers would have understood the words on the centurion's lips in light of Luke's larger narrative (i.e., Fitzmyer's Stage III). While Luke's presentation of Jesus as the "righteous one" in Acts is important (though, of course, δίκαιος requires interpretation there, too!), placing believable speech on the lips of the centurion would have also been important to Luke in crafting his narrative. Would hearers have found it plausible (one of the virtues of narration) for a centurion to declare Jesus righteous—with all of the connotations that held for early Christians? Of course, Luke could be working with a two-level meaning here, which I think is most likely. But the most obvious meaning of the centurion's praise in the immediate narrative (where Jesus' innocence has been proclaimed by several other characters in the narrative) is that it signifies political innocence.

144. For a more detailed discussion and interaction with the scholars mentioned here, see "The Translation of δίκαιος" in chapter 1.

145. E.g., the δικαι-roots in 23:41 and 23:50 mean "justly" and "righteous."

praise for God earlier in the verse implies a theological interpretation rather than a juridical one; and (3) Jesus' recitation of Ps 31 (a psalm of the righteous suffering one), which Luke develops in Acts through the proclamation of Jesus as ὁ δίκαιος, suggests that δίκαιος here would also connote righteousness.[146] The second camp argues for the translation of "innocent" because (1) this translation accords with Luke's larger theme of innocence in the passion narrative; (2) a proclamation of "righteous" would not be fitting speech for a centurion; (3) it aligns with Luke's apologetic motive, which stresses that Jesus was not politically subversive; and (4) it is consistent with other elements of Luke's passion narrative that align with the ancient noble death and martyr traditions.[147] A third camp, which manifests itself in a variety of ways, adopts the both-and approach, stressing that "just" and "innocent" are related ideas and acknowledging that Luke could intend a double-meaning, even if he emphasized one over the other.[148]

My aim here is not to analyze the merits of each side of the issue, as both sides have legitimate points.[149] Rather, taking into consideration my analysis thus far, which demonstrates that Luke has constructed his passion narrative as alternating refutations and confirmations of the charges against Jesus, I argue that the structure of Luke's narrative strongly suggests that δίκαιος connotes political innocence. A similar emphasis on Paul's innocence in the many parallels in Acts further supports this claim, as does the strategic placement of figures of speech throughout his passion narrative to emphasize the testimony to Jesus' innocence.[150] Such a claim does not deny that δίκαιος also connotes justness or righteousness,

---

146. See Schweizer, *Good News according to Luke*, 362; Karris, "Luke 23:47," 66–67; Nolland, *Luke 18:35—24:53*, 1155, 1159; Doble, *Paradox of Salvation*, 25–183.

147. See Kilpatrick, "Theme of the Lucan Passion Story," 34–36; Cassidy, *Jesus, Politics, and Society*, 72; Talbert, "Martyrdom in Luke-Acts," 99; Schmidt, "Luke's 'Innocent' Jesus," 117–18.

On similarities to the martyr and noble death traditions, see Dibelius, *From Tradition to Gospel*, 201; Talbert, "Martyrdom in Luke-Acts," 118–19; Kloppenborg, "*Exitus Clari Viri*," 106–20; Collins, "From Noble Death," 481–503; Sterling, "*Mors Philosophi*," 383–402; Scaer, *Lukan Passion*.

148. See Büchele, *Der Tod Jesu*, 54, n. 233; Beck, "*Imitatio Christi*," 42–43; Matera, "Death of Jesus," 479; Green, *Death of Jesus*, 99; Brown, *Death of the Messiah*, 1163; Bock, *Luke*, 377; Marguerat, *First Christian Historian*, 69–70; Neagoe, *Trial of the Gospel*, 102–3; Easter, "'Certainly This Man Was Righteous,'" 35–51.

149. See Brown, *Death of the Messiah*, 1160–67, for an assessment of many of these arguments.

150. I discuss these points more fully in chapter 5.

but it suggests that any interpretation that does not include political innocence misses a large part of what Luke is attempting to do in his passion narrative.[151]

This final refutation of Jesus' guilt by the centurion is particularly forceful for a few reasons. First, the centurion's proclamation is the last instance of direct discourse until the two men speak to the women at the tomb; it thus comprises the final verdict on the charges brought against Jesus—the final word at the cross is that Jesus is innocent. Thus, while readers wait in anticipation for the resurrection—Jesus' ultimate vindication—they can rest assured on the testimony of many witnesses that Jesus was indeed innocent.

Second, the centurion's proclamation is forceful because of who makes the proclamation. The Roman centurion's role was to oversee Jesus' death—he "represents the occupying power of Rome at the execution."[152] By proclaiming Jesus innocent, this Roman official essentially admits that he just oversaw the death of an innocent man.[153] Jesus received a punishment he did not deserve, and for that the centurion is guilty. Both the first and the last refutations of the charges against Jesus are made by Gentile Roman officials—Pilate and the centurion. As De Long points out, this hearkens back to Simeon's anticipation of a revelation to the Gentiles in Luke 2:32 and foreshadows the positive response that the gospel will receive from Gentiles in Acts.[154]

Finally, the centurion's proclamation has a parallel in the narrative of Paul. After Paul's near-death experience with a snake bite, the locals declare that he is in fact a god (in contrast to their earlier declaration that he was a murderer). While their declaration is misinformed, it nonetheless functions to show that they viewed Paul as innocent rather than guilty. Thus, both Jesus (by the centurion) and Paul (by the natives of Malta) have a favorable declaration after their death or near-death.[155]

---

151. See chapter 5 for the larger implications of this understanding.

152. Fitzmyer, *Gospel according to Luke*, 1519.

153. The risk involved in this admission fights against the comments of Beck and Easter that the centurion's proclamation of Jesus' innocence is anticlimactic. See Beck, "'Imitatio Christi' and the Lucan Passion Narrative," 42; Easter, "'Certainly This Man Was Righteous,'" 41. Cassidy agrees that the centurion's proclamation is all the more dramatic since he was likely in charge of the execution. See Cassidy, *Jesus, Politics, and Society*, 72.

154. De Long, *Surprised by God*, 241. Wolter, *Das Lukasevangelium*, 759, makes a similar observation about the divided response of the two criminals.

155. Talbert, *Literary Patterns*, 18, sees the centurion's favorable opinion of Jesus in

Although the centurion's response is the last discourse before the resurrection, it is not the only response to Jesus' death that Luke narrates. In addition to the centurion's response, Luke also tells about the response of the crowds: "And all the crowds (ὄχλοι) who had come together for this spectacle (θεωρίαν), when they saw what happened (τὰ γενόμενα), returned, beating their breasts (τύπτοντες τὰ στήθη)" (23:48). The only other use of ὄχλοι in the passion narrative refers to the crowd whom Pilate addresses along with the chief priests in 23:4.[156] This crowd at 23:48 is likely equivalent to the people (ὁ λαός) who stood by watching while the rulers sneered in 23:35[157] and thus also the great number of people (πολὺ πλῆθος τοῦ λαοῦ) of whom the wailing women were a part that followed Jesus to the crucifixion (23:27).[158] The use of the term λαός along with their connection with the rulers (23:35) suggests that these people who beat their breasts at Jesus' death are some of the same group that demanded his crucifixion just verses earlier (23:13–23), as does the fact that they follow Jesus from the place where he was sentenced.

Thus, while the ὄχλοι (23:4–5) and λαός (23:13, 18, 23–25) joined forces with the leaders during the trial before Pilate, they do not remain joined with them until the end.[159] When the rulers mock Jesus at the crucifixion, the people simply watch (23:35) and eventually beat their breasts in remorse for their wrongful condemnation.[160] First they demanded

---

23:47 as parallel to the centurion who is favorable to Paul in 27:3, 43. Luke may have conceived of his parallels as working on multiple levels.

156. If one includes the arrest scene in the passion narrative, an ὄχλοι is present there and led by Judas (22:47). Besides Judas and the crowd, the only other persons or groups named in the scene are the chief priests, the temple officers, and the elders (22:52). It is unclear whether these latter groups make up the crowd in its entirety or if they should be understood as separate groups. Weatherly, *Jewish Responsibility*, 64, n.1, argues for the former. Brown, *Death of the Messiah*, 741, on the other hand, hesitates to connect the crowd with this group of leaders since Luke differentiates between the chief priests and the crowd in 23:4.

157. Luke uses θεωρέω in both 23:35 and 23:48 to describe these groups.

158. Tannehill makes these connections between the people and the crowds in *Narrative Unity*, 165–66.

159. Carroll, "Luke's Crucifixion Scene," 111–12.

160. This is the same phrase that Luke uses in 18:13 in the parable of the Pharisee and tax collector. The contrite tax collector beat his breast (ἔτυπτεν τὸ στῆθος αὐτοῦ) and pleaded for mercy: "God, be merciful to me, a sinner." His beating his breast expressed his remorse for his sin. Grundmann understands the crowd's response as a sign of repentance. Fitzmyer and Marshall propose that the beating could also connote mourning for the death of Jesus. The former interpretation, however, would connote

Jesus' crucifixion, willingly participating in bringing out the demise of Jesus; then they stood by watching, unwilling to participate in the rulers' sneering, and thus signaling a shift in their thought; finally, after seeing what took place, they beat their breasts and returned, remorseful of their wrongdoing. This shift from bold conviction of Jesus' guilt—Jesus was so guilty that he deserved crucifixion more than Barabbas—to bitter remorse at the crucifixion of Jesus suggests that even some who were so convinced of his guilt earlier ultimately recognized his innocence.

There are several close connections between Mark and Luke regarding the events following the crucifixion, but Luke also adds some material to Mark. The centurion's confession in Luke is different from his confession in Mark by only a few words, but the import is significant. Mark's centurion (κεντυρίων) says, "ἀληθῶς οὗτος ὁ ἄνθρωπος υἱὸς θεοῦ ἦν," while Luke's centurion (ἑκατοντάρχης[161]) says, "ὄντως ὁ ἄνθρωπος οὗτος δίκαιος ἦν." The word order varies slightly—of little concern here[162]—but of major concern is Luke's substitution of δίκαιος for Mark's υἱὸς θεοῦ.

Some proponents of Luke's use of a written source in addition to Mark view this difference as evidence for their case. For example, Taylor sees this difference as one piece among many pieces of evidence that Luke used a pre-Lukan source for 23:44–49. Since "it is very improbable that δίκαιος in the centurion's confession (v. 47) is a modification of υἱός θεοῦ in Mk. xv. 39," Luke must have been relying on a written source.[163]

---

some sense of responsibility for what happened. See Grundmann, *Das Evangelium nach Lukas*, 435–36; Fitzmyer, *Gospel according to Luke*, 1520; Marshall, *Gospel of Luke*, 877. Carroll and Brown both warn against reading too much into this phrase. The people are remorseful, but not yet repentant. Their repentance does not come until later in Acts 2:37–41. See Carroll, "Luke's Crucifixion Scene," 112; Brown, *Death of the Messiah*, 1168.

161. Here Luke replaces Mark's Latin loan-word (used by him alone in the NT) with the term Luke commonly uses in both his works (seventeen times). Green, *Death of Jesus*, 99.

162. These minor rearrangements and substitutions (e.g., ὄντως for ἀληθῶς) require neither explanation nor recourse to another source. As discussed previously, Luke would have been familiar with the practice of changing words in his source while maintaining its meaning—precisely what occurs here.

163. Taylor, *Passion Narrative*, 96. Here and elsewhere, Taylor often simply states conclusions rather than arguing for them. Cf. his discussion on Luke's inversions of Mark's order on 123. On the larger unit of 23:44–49, Taylor points to stylistic phenomena like the genitive absolute (τοῦ ἡλίου ἐκλιπόντος; 23:45), the use of μέσος (23:45), and the plethora of participles as signs of embellishment of sources (96).

Brown counters the notion that δίκαιος could not be a modification of υἱός θεοῦ. He points to Wis 2:12—3:1 (a passage probably widely known to early Christians), where

Grundmann, too, unable to find a reason why Luke would replace Mark's "Son of God," finds Luke's special source (SLk) to be the best explanation for the difference.[164] Thus, deviation from Mark implies reliance upon another written source.

Others, however, argue that Luke did not use another written source in addition to Mark and instead attribute Luke's differences from Mark to Luke's larger theological or rhetorical goals. Matera relates Luke's change here to his unique Christology: "... [Luke] has the centurion pronounce that Jesus is righteous in the sense of the OT. This interpretation ... places the centurion's cry more squarely within the main lines of Luke's christology, thereby suggesting that Luke rather than another Passion source is responsible for the cry."[165] Others propose the possibility that

---

the wicked plot to destroy the δίκαιος one who calls God his father and where "the souls of the δίκαιος are in the hand of God." These verses have connections with Luke's passion narrative (δίκαιος in 23:47; calling God father in 23:46; and a connection with God's hands in 23:46). Brown explains, "The combined ideas that the just entrusted himself to God's hand (as Jesus did in the prayer at his death) and that the just one was God's son may explain why Luke could regard *dikaios* as an interchangeable alternative for Mark's *huios theou* in the centurion's reaction to Jesus' prayer." The early church's use of *dikaios* as a christological title (e.g., Acts 3:14; 7:52; 22:14; Jas 5:6; 1 Pet 3:18; 1 John 2:1) may have provided further prompting for Luke. See Brown, *Death of the Messiah*, 1165–66. For more on Wisdom in the background of Luke's passion narrative see Doble, *Paradox of Salvation*, 187–225.

Of course, Brown's argument assumes that the centurion's words in Mark 15:39 are to be taken at face value—an honest confession that Jesus is the Son of God. This understanding aligns with the common interpretation that the centurion's confession is the climax of Mark's Gospel. Several scholars challenge this notion, however, arguing instead that the centurion's confession is meant as ironic, a mockery, and/or a continuation of Mark's secrecy theme. See, e.g., Johnson, "Is Mark 15:39 the Key," 14–17; Myers, *Binding the Strong Man*, 393–94; Shiner, "The Ambiguous Pronouncement of the Centurion and the Shrouding of Meaning in Mark," 19. If Luke understood Mark's centurion in this way, he does something altogether different, both in the content of the confession but in its larger function in the narrative. Johnson reflects on the differences between Luke and Mark, noting how Luke provides a more favorable attitude toward centurions (e.g., the centurion with great faith in Luke 7; the centurion protecting and helping Paul in Acts 22–27), the former example of which prepares the readers for the centurion's acceptance and proclamation of Jesus at the cross.

164. Grundmann, *Das Evangelium nach Lukas*, 435.

165. Matera, "Death of Jesus," 479. He arrives at this conclusion by looking at the function of *doxazein* in Luke and Acts (Luke uses it when people glorify God as a response to God's manifestation of his salvific work in Jesus), the sense of *dikaios* in Luke and Acts (it is a Messianic title related to the righteous and innocent sufferer), and the meaning of the centurion's praise (it functions not as a confession but as a statement glorifying God for what he did in Jesus). In the remainder of the article, he

Luke thought "Son of God" might be misunderstood by his readers when coming from the mouth of a Gentile centurion.¹⁶⁶ Even Green—who advocates for a special passion source in addition to Mark—is convinced that the δίκαιος substitution derived from Luke's hand rather than a special source because it "continues the theme of Jesus' innocence, points to Jesus' death as the fate of the Suffering Righteous, and alludes to his fate as the Suffering Servant of Yahweh (as in Acts 3:13–14)."¹⁶⁷

Besides the substitution in the centurion's confession, Luke's primary addition to Mark is the response of the crowds (23:48) and the presence of Jesus' acquaintances (23:49a). The motivation for Luke's addition of the crowds is discussed above; the presence of the acquaintances (like that of the women) may be a simple way of preparing for the presence of Joseph in the next scene, as Marshall suggests, and those (besides the eleven) to whom the women proclaim the resurrection in 24:9, as Brown suggests.¹⁶⁸

Finally, Luke concludes the scene with information from Mark 15:40–41—the presence of the women who had journeyed with Jesus from Galilee (v. 49b). Mark provides the women's names and describes their provisions for Jesus, details that Luke does not need to include here since he introduced the women in 8:1–3.¹⁶⁹ In both Mark and Luke the presence of these women anticipates their role in the resurrection narrative that follows.¹⁷⁰ Luke follows Mark in describing their place at the crucifixion as ἀπὸ μακρόθεν. Thus, the two accounts differ in some details and are the same in some details, but Luke retains Mark's meaning.

---

does similar analyses (and comes to similar conclusions) on the sun's failure and the temple curtain, Jesus' final words from the cross, the Elijah incident, and the repentance of the crowd.

166. E.g., Goulder, *Luke*, 770. Fitzmyer, who does not come down on the source issue on these verses, suggests this possibility as well. See Fitzmyer, *Gospel according to Luke*, 1515.

167. Green, *Death of Jesus*, 99. In addition to Matera, Goulder, and Green, both Kilpatrick and Marshall (the latter of whom usually advocates for a special source) argue that the differences in the centurion's confession between Mark and Luke do not derive from a separate source. See Kilpatrick, "Theme of the Lucan Passion Story," 36; Marshall, *Gospel of Luke*, 874.

168. Marshall, *Gospel of Luke*, 877; Brown, *Death of the Messiah*, 1173.

169. Worth noting is that Luke uses the same imperfect verb (διηκόνουν) in 8:3 to describe the women's activity as Mark uses in 15:41, testifying to Luke's willingness to transfer elements of Mark to different points in his own narrative.

170. Büchele notes that it is as witnesses of Jesus' death that the women become reliable witnesses to the empty tomb. Büchele, *Der Tod Jesu*, 56.

The Big Picture

When we step back and look at the passion narrative as a whole, a picture of Jesus emerges that is characterized by composure and control. Save for his correction of the reason for the women's weeping (which implicitly contains a defense of his innocence), Jesus does not spend time defending himself. Because he knows that his suffering and death must happen, he spends little time refuting his accusers (22:67b–69) and instead offers short (22:70; 23:3) or no (23:9) responses. Neither does he respond to those who demand that he save himself from the cross (23:35, 37, 39). Instead, a host of others defend Jesus.

The times that Jesus does speak (besides those just mentioned) are significant. As described above, the second criminal defends Jesus from the rebukes of the first criminal. He claims that Jesus did nothing wrong and asks Jesus to remember him when he comes into his kingdom, which prompts Jesus to extend to him an offer of salvation. While Luke does not state it explicitly, it seems as if the manner in which Jesus handles his (wrongful) execution is what prompts this criminal's conversion. Besides his words to the second criminal, Jesus' other words from the cross are his final prayer, "Father, into your hands I commit my spirit" (23:46). Here he expresses his ultimate trust in God. This composure at his death—offering up his spirit in a prayer to God—along with the other events at the crucifixion prompt the centurion to glorify God and proclaim his innocence. As with the criminal, here, too, Jesus' innocence and his manner of facing death are related to the centurion's positive response toward God.

The formal rhetorical analysis of Luke's passion narrative is now complete. We have seen Luke compose his narrative by using Mark in ways consistent with how the rhetorical tradition describes paraphrase—substitutions, rearrangements, additions, and subtractions. Many of these alterations are in the direction of clarity, conciseness, and plausibility—the three virtues of narration. Some of the alterations set up parallels with characters in Luke's second volume. Furthermore, Luke has adorned his narrative with rhetorical figures, particularly on the lips of Jesus to highlight his innocence, and he frames the entire narrative as a trial about Jesus' innocence, complete with common topics of refutation and confirmation. In the final chapter, I will summarily highlight those specific rhetorical techniques at work in Luke's narrative—refutation and confirmation, rhetorical figures, synkrisis, paraphrase, and narration—and discuss how those observations speak to the unresolved interpretive issues related to Luke's passion narrative outlined in chapter 1.

5

Synthesis and Conclusions

A Return to the Exercises and Techniques

HAVING COMPLETED THE RHETORICAL analysis of the Luke's passion narrative, I now want to highlight those specific rhetorical techniques at work in the narrative. Following that section, I will conclude the study by returning to the interpretive issues described in chapter 1 and discussing how my analysis informs those issues.

Refutation and Confirmation

The preceding chapters demonstrated that Luke uses the common topics associated with refutation and confirmation as a structural device for his passion narrative. The first scene alternates between refutations and confirmations of the charges against Jesus, and the second scene opens with three confirmations and concludes with three refutations.

The headings or topics that were commonly used in preliminary exercises on refutation and confirmation or in forensic discourse appear in several places throughout Luke's passion narrative (Cf. Theon, *Prog.* 76, 95, 121; Ps.-Hermogenes, *Prog.* 11; Aphthonius, *Prog.* 27–28, 30; Nicolaus, *Prog.* 30–33). Twice Pilate refers to the inadequacy of the Jewish leaders' charges by pointing out the lack of basis for their accusations (23:4, 14). Elsewhere he shows that the charges are unclear by asking for reasons he should crucify Jesus: "Why [should I have him crucified]? What evil has this man done?" (23:22). The lack of clarification from those demanding Jesus' death suggests that Pilate's refutation is legitimate. Furthermore, in response to the first criminal's derision of Jesus, the second criminal appeals to the common topic of justice. He points out the just (δικαίως) nature of their condemnation on the basis that their condemnation is worthy (ἄξιος) of their deeds. Jesus, on the other hand, did nothing wrong, so his condemnation is, by extension, unjust.

The defense, however, is not the only side to use the topics in an attempt to forward their case. The Jewish leaders emphasize the geographical extent of the accusations against Jesus by telling Pilate that Jesus "stirs up the people by teaching throughout all Judea starting from Galilee [and coming] as far as this place" (23:5). These words are an attempt to confirm their accusation by emphasizing the extensive geographical impact of Jesus' teaching. This concern with the place is one of the elements that several ancient rhetoricians recommended using when refuting or confirming a narrative (Theon, *Prog.* 94; Nicolaus, *Prog.* 30; Quintilian, *Inst.* 5.10.37–42). This concern varied from case to case. Theon, for example, shows that one might argue from the place of the crime (e.g., that Medea would not have killed her children in Corinth because their father lived there) to contribute to the prosecution's narrative seeming incredible (*Prog.* 94). Quintilian, on the other hand, points out that one might intensify the nature of a crime by focusing on the place: if a theft takes place in a temple, it is not only theft, but sacrilege (*Inst.* 5.10.39). Similarly, the leaders use the place of Jesus' "crime" (not only in Judea, but also in Galilee and Jerusalem) to intensify the nature of what he did. Later in the narrative, the rulers, soldiers, and first criminal use the topic of consistency to try to confirm Jesus' guilt. They use the fact that Jesus does not save himself or the criminals from the cross to argue against his identity as God's Messiah, Chosen One, and King of the Jews. In their eyes, the inconsistency between Jesus' titles and his actions confirms the charges against him. The audience, of course, recognizes the irony inherent in the mockery and knows that Jesus' position on the cross is not inconsistent with his identity. In fact, Luke has notified them several times that Jesus' suffering is, in fact, a necessary component of his identity and mission (e.g., Luke 2:49; 4:43; 9:22; 13:33; 17:25; 22:37), and thus, despite his opponents' attempts, they do not successfully confirm the charges against him.

In addition to the common topics that he places throughout the passion narrative, the characters in Luke's passion narrative also refute the charges against Jesus in other ways. Pilate seeks to transfer Jesus' case and then appeals to the judgment of Herod on the issue, both of which were ways that the ancient rhetorical tradition recommended countering a charge (Quintilian, *Inst.* 5.2.2; 5.13.3; *Rhet. Her.* 2.13.19; Cicero, *Inv.* 1.42.79). Furthermore, the second criminal attempts to discredit the first one by asking him incredulously if he does not even fear God—an accusation that, if true, would have made the first criminal's testimony against Jesus even less credible. According to Quintilian, discrediting a witness was yet another way of refuting a charge (*Inst.* 5.13.8).

Finally, Luke makes use of a wide cast of characters—both in terms of quantity and quality—for their testimony about Jesus. The following persons or groups of persons refute or confirm the charges against Jesus in some capacity: the Jewish assembly (23:1); Pilate (23:4, 14–16, 22); Herod (23:15); the chief priests, rulers, and the people (23:18–25; cf. 23:13, 35); the soldiers (23:36–37); the first criminal (23:39); the second criminal (23:40–41); God (23:44–45); and the centurion (23:47).

The sheer number of witnesses is impressive, but the quality of those witnesses who testify on Jesus' behalf is even more impressive. Cicero notes that those who hold public office are generally considered virtuous witnesses (*Top.* 20.78), which might give credence to the testimonies of Pilate and Herod had Luke not previously given his readers information about their malevolent character (i.e., that Herod killed John the Baptist [9:9] and that Pilate had shed the blood of the Galileans [13:1]). This malevolent character, however, ends up adding weight to their testimony because of the unlikelihood that such characters (at least one of whom wanted to kill Jesus earlier in the narrative) would find Jesus innocent. The centurion's testimony is particularly valuable as well, since his proclamation was ultimately an admission that he oversaw the death of an innocent man. Aristotle points out that those who share the risk of the trial are not valuable for evaluating the quality of an act (as the centurion does here) but only if something happened (*Rhet.* 1.15.16). This advice would make us suspicious if the centurion proclaimed Jesus guilty because such a proclamation would be lowering his risk of involvement. His proclamation of Jesus' innocence, however, actually increases his risk since it makes him liable for overseeing an undeserved crucifixion. Of course, the most valuable testimony on Jesus' behalf is that of God through the divine portents. Since the gods were considered the most authoritative witnesses based on their virtue (Cicero, *Top.* 19.73; 20.76), the star witness in the whole trial is on Jesus' side proclaiming him innocent.

All of these elements—the underlying structure of the narrative, the use of several topics commonly employed in refutation and confirmation exercises or in forensic discourse, and the concern with both quality and quantity of witnesses—highlight both the judicial nature of Luke's passion narrative and Luke's concern with Jesus' innocence. Furthermore, the sheer amount of narrative that Luke devotes to these refutations and confirmations shows that a primary concern of his narrative is how people respond to Jesus.[1]

Rhetorical Figures

Rhetorical figures are present throughout Luke's passion narrative, but they are dominant in a few specific places. Luke places them most frequently on Jesus' lips—Jesus uses figures at least twelve times in the passion narrative, more than all the other characters combined. Here we will discuss the placement and function of the figures in the passion narrative noted above.

The first cluster of figures is at the beginning of the passion narrative during the council and accusations. Of the five figures observed in 22:66—23:3, four are on the lips of Jesus: repeated negation (22:67), isocolon (23:68), epanaphora (22:67-68), and antonomasia (22:69). These four figures unite to make Jesus' response to the council pleasing to the ear and to make the audience disposed to his side of the case. They also draw attention to the content of his words, namely, that his accusers will find him guilty regardless of what he says. Their response—highlighted by the rhetorical question on the lips of the accusers (22:71)—proves Jesus right: despite Jesus' somewhat evasive answers to their questions, they still hear what they want to hear and insist on accusing him before Pilate. Ultimately, then, the rhetorical figures used in this exchange between Jesus and his accusers are a means for Jesus to defeat his interlocutors and bring the audience to his side—an important move at the beginning of a trial. This function is consistent with Luke's use of rhetorical figures elsewhere in his Gospel, as Reich has shown that Luke frequently places figures on Jesus' lips as a means of defeating his narrative interlocutors and pulling the audience to his side.[2] Finally, the rhetorical question in

---

1. For instance, in 23:32-49, Jesus' crucifixion and death, Luke tells us surprisingly little about Jesus himself: he says that they crucified him at the Skull and cast lots for his clothing (23:33-34); he tells of Jesus responding to the second criminal (23:43); and he narrates Jesus' dying words and death (23:46). All of the other verses tell about other people's response to Jesus (people watching the crucifixion; rulers and soldiers mocking Jesus; criminal one deriding Jesus; criminal two defending Jesus; the centurion glorifying God; the crowds beating their breasts; the acquaintances and women watching) and narrative details (criminals crucified on his right and left; inscription over the cross; the supernatural events).

2. Reich, *Figuring Jesus*, 20-21, 67-86. See, e.g., Luke 13:15-16; 14:3-5; 20:4-7, 17-18, 22-26, 41-44. In contrast to several of these examples where Luke tells us that

22:71 highlights the theme of testimony, a theme which Luke develops throughout the rest of his passion narrative in conjunction with the alternating refutations and confirmations.

In the next scene the rhetorical figures are less frequent and less condensed, with only three figures spanning twenty-five verses (23:1–25). An analysis of the grammatical cases of the various characters' names in this scene reveals that Luke used polyptoton to draw attention to Pilate's role in the story. Pilate's role is to proclaim Jesus' innocence to a group insistent upon his guilt. Three times Pilate makes this declaration (23:4, 14–15, 22), the first of which Luke highlights through the use of assonance. In contrast to Pilate's deep conviction of Jesus' innocence, Jesus' enemies are equally convicted of his guilt, which they emphasize with repetition in their shout, "Crucify, crucify him!" (23:21). As the placement of figures in the pre-trial scene suggested, Luke continues to highlight the theme of testimony with his placement of rhetorical figures. Whether Jesus is guilty or innocent, whether he is worthy of death or not, occupies a prominent role in Luke's passion narrative.

The next cluster of rhetorical figures in Luke's passion narrative is the most concentrated of all. In Jesus' words to the wailing women at least eight figures are present in only four verses: antithesis, assonance, synecdoche, pleonasm, isocolon, a proverb, a rhetorical question, and paronomasia. Jesus' first words are a command formed as an antithesis: the women are to weep not for him but for themselves and their children. This antithesis establishes a key point that Jesus develops through the use of more figures in the verses that follow—he is not the guilty one; Jerusalem is, and its fate will be far worse than his. The assonance catches the hearers' attention to emphasize the harsh days that await the guilty ones, and the rhetorical question functions as a thought-provoking warning to those who reject him. Ultimately, though, the number of rhetorical figures in so few verses is where the real force lies. Their cumulative effect emphasizes Jesus' prophetic judgment on Jerusalem and draws attention to another, albeit implicit, declaration of Jesus' innocence.

Jesus silenced or shamed his interlocutors (13:17; 14:5; 20:26), in this scene in the passion narrative, Jesus does not silence his interlocutors. Instead they vehemently go forward with their plan. Their actions, however, do not mean that Jesus did not defeat them or that the audience was not brought over to his side. Rather, it underscores the inevitability of what is about to happen to Jesus but assures the audience that Jesus is in the right.

Finally, Luke uses a rhetorical question and irony in the crucifixion scene to highlight Jesus' true identity and to show that the mockers' attempts to confirm Jesus' guilt are inadequate. The taunts and rhetorical question ("Are you not the Messiah?") of the leaders, the soldiers, and the first criminal challenge Jesus' identity on the surface, but a closer look reveals that Luke uses these testimonies ironically (cf. Quintilian, *Inst.* 9.2.44–45). Because Luke affirmed Jesus' identity as King, Messiah, and Savior throughout his narrative, his hearers would realize that the mockers—despite their ignorance—were actually making accurate claims about Jesus' identity—he is King, Messiah, and Savior, just not in the way that they expect. Luke's audience, however, knows that saving one's life looks like losing it (9:24), so the irony functions to validate their beliefs that Jesus is innocent and that he is the King, Messiah, and Savior.

In sum, Luke uses rhetorical figures in several sections of his passion narrative for various purposes. Frequently the figures do not have their own individual function, but rather work together to draw attention to important parts of the narrative. The figures make the audience disposed to Jesus' side of the case, they underscore the fact that his accusers will find him guilty regardless of what he says, they help Jesus defeat his interlocutors and bring the audience to his side of the case, and, in several instances, they draw attention to the important theme of testimony in Luke's passion narrative as it relates to Jesus' innocence.[3] They also function to highlight Jesus' identity as King, Messiah, and Savior. Luke may have strategically placed the figures throughout his narrative not only to help his readers remain attentive, but also to make them "readier to believe" his argument (Quintilian, *Inst.* 8.3.5).

Synkrisis

The parallels between Jesus and Paul are numerous,[4] particularly with regard to their trials.[5] The Jewish leaders charge both Jesus and Paul

---

3. These purposes align with those functions outlined by Reich on the basis of the handbooks' instructions: emphasis, making the narrative pleasing to the ear, making it memorable or powerful, and inviting audience participation. See ibid., 19–20.

4. On the parallels between Jesus and Paul outside of the trials, see Radl, *Paulus und Jesus*, 68–220; Moessner, "Christ Must Suffer," 247–56; Mattill, "Jesus-Paul Parallels," 22–30.

5. Scholars organize or categorize these parallels in different ways, but they generally agree upon the content of the parallels. For example, Heusler categorizes them

with perverting the Jewish nation, opposing Caesar's decrees, claiming the sovereignty of Christ over Caesar, and having a wide geographical influence. Luke provides a host of declarations of innocence in support of both Jesus and Paul. Prominent rulers (Pilate, Herod Antipas, Lysias, Festus, Herod Agrippa) pronounce both men innocent and suggest that the accusations against them are untenable (or at least unworthy of imprisonment and death). Characters without as much political clout also proclaim the innocence of Jesus and Paul: a criminal, a centurion, the native Maltans, and Paul himself. Finally, even God—the most authoritative of witnesses—provides his verdict on both characters' innocence through divine portents of darkness, the rending of the temple veil, deliverance from a shipwreck, and healing from a snakebite. Both Jesus and Paul are exonerated in situations that ancients typically viewed as a curse or judgment from the gods: crucifixion, shipwrecks, and snakebites.[6] While the characters refute the charges in a variety of ways, all make the same declaration: the one being charged is innocent and undeserving of death or imprisonment.

In addition to these parallel declarations, still other parallels exist between the trials of Jesus and Paul. They both appear before both Roman and Jewish rulers (and both before one named Herod in the latter case). Both go before a ruler who hopes to receive something from the accused. Luke tells us that Herod Antipas was glad to see Jesus "because . . . he was hoping to see some sign performed by him" (23:8). Similarly, Felix sent for Paul often when he was in his custody because "he hoped that money would be given him by Paul" (24:26).[7] Another parallel between the trials of Jesus and Paul is that they are both transferred from ruler to ruler (Jesus from Pilate to Herod Antipas to Pilate; Paul from Lysias to Felix to Festus to Herod Agrippa). No one ruler handles their entire case. Additionally, the crowds turn on both Jesus and Paul, shouting strikingly similar phrases: αἶρε τοῦτον (Luke 23:18), αἶρε αὐτόν (Acts 21:36), and αἶρε . . . τὸν τοιοῦτον (Acts 22:22). Furthermore, both

---

as an interrogation by the Jewish council (Luke 22:61–71; Acts 22:30—23:10), a hearing before a Roman governor (Luke 23:1–7; Acts 24:1–22), a meeting before a Jewish king (Luke 23:13–25; Acts 25:1–12), and a follow-up meeting before a governor (Luke 23:13–25; Acts 25:1–12). See Heusler, *Kapitalprozesse im lukanischen Doppelwerk*.

6. At least the ancient Jews viewed crucifixion as a curse by God (Deut 21:22–23). On the connection between storms, snakebites, and the divine, see Talbert, *Reading Acts*, 212–13; McConnell, *Topos of Divine Testimony*, 221–23.

7. Mattill, "Jesus-Paul Parallels," 33–34.

men have the potential of being released, but this release does not come to fruition. Twice Pilate states that he will release Jesus (23:16, 22), but eventually he concedes to the crowds; Agrippa tells Festus that Paul could have been released had he not appealed to the emperor (26:32).

Finally, Luke constructs at least two parallels between Jesus and Stephen. First, both are brought before the council (συνέδριον; Luke 22:66; Acts 6:12). Second, they speak similar dying words: "Father, into your hands I commit my spirit" (Luke 23:46) and "Lord Jesus, receive my spirit" (Acts 7:59). That Luke has deliberately designed the parallels between these characters is generally accepted by scholars.

When we recall the instructions about synkrisis from the rhetorical tradition, some aspects of Luke's passion narrative become clearer. First, it is not surprising that these comparisons or parallels appear in a narrative context, since the exercises in synkrisis were designed to be adapted to different contexts or literary genres (Theon, *Prog.* 61). Second, by setting Jesus in parallel with Paul, and to a lesser extent Stephen, Luke is not necessarily attempting to cast one as better than the other. Since each of the characters is shown in a positive light (e.g., they are innocent, they face death courageously), it is safe to assume that Luke is emphasizing the equality or similarity between them (cf. Ps.-Hermogenes, *Prog.* 19; Nicolaus, *Prog.* 60), one type of synkrisis.

When we analyze these sections of Luke and Acts in relation to the topics commonly used in an encomion[8]—goods of the body, goods of the mind, and external goods—we see at least two different goods emphasized. First is the topic of virtue—the virtue here being innocence—which was considered a good of the mind. Over and over Luke has characters proclaim the innocence of Jesus and Paul in the face of wrongful accusations. They are declared innocent by Roman rulers, by Jewish rulers, by people they had previously never met, and by God. This innocence, however, does not result in release from death or imprisonment for either character.

The second topic commonly used in an encomion that Luke employs in these narratives is the manner of death, an external good. Though not explored extensively in this study, many see Luke's portrait of Jesus' death

---

8. See Ps.-Hermogenes, *Prog.* 19, who recommends that students use the encomiastic topics when composing a synkrisis. Cf. Quintilian, *Inst.* 2.4.21; Aphthonius, *Prog.* 31R; Nicolaus, *Prog.* 59–60. On the goods of the mind, goods of the body, and external goods, see Theon, *Prog.* 109; cf. Ps.-Hermogenes, *Prog.* 15–16; Aristotle, *Rhet.* 1.5.4; *Rhet. Her.* 3.6.10; Cicero, *De or.* 3.29.115.

fitting within the noble death or martyr traditions.⁹ The emphasis on innocence, Jesus' composure or courage facing his death, the presence of friends in the narrative, and Jesus' confidence in God are only a few of the characteristics that lead some to place Luke in this same tradition. Similar to Jesus, Stephen also faces death with courage and composure, praying for his accusers (7:60) and giving up his spirit as Jesus did (7:59). Though some of these elements are lacking in Paul's trial narrative (not surprisingly, though, since Luke is not presenting the narrative of Paul's death), Paul nonetheless faces his charges, accusers, arrest, and near-death in a noble way.¹⁰ Jesus, then, and his parallel characters in Acts are virtuous in their innocence and in the manner in which they face death.

While these virtues are significant in and of themselves, what is also significant, according to Theon, is the actions that result from their virtue (*Prog.* 110). In the narratives of Jesus, Stephen, and Paul, their virtue results in the conversion of others or the spread of the gospel. In Luke, the second criminal is granted salvation because of his recognition of Jesus' true identity, and the centurion praises God when he recognizes Jesus' innocence—a praise that has led some to conclude that the centurion was converted.¹¹ In Acts, Stephen's death initiates a persecution and scattering of Christians, but this ultimately advances the gospel. Luke explains that "those who were scattered went out proclaiming the word" (Acts 8:4). Additionally, once Paul lands in Rome he has the opportunity to speak with some Jewish leaders. A significant portion of his words to them is a defense of his innocence—he tells them that he was arrested despite the fact that he had done nothing against their nation or customs (28:17) and explains that the Romans wanted to release him since there was no basis for giving him the death penalty (28:18). Paul's story prompts them to want to hear more from him (28:22) and ultimately leads to his preaching the gospel in Rome "with all boldness and without hindrance" (28:31), where some were persuaded by his message (28:24). For Jesus, Stephen, and Paul, then,

---

9. See "Translation of δίκαιος" in chapter one.

10. This is especially highlighted through the primacy of the innocence motif, since the theme of innocence was a crucial part of the noble death tradition. Kloppenborg points to the reflections on Socrates' innocence in Plato, *Phaed.* 118A, and Xenophon, *Apol.* 28. See Kloppenborg, "*Exitus Clari Viri,*" 113.

11. E.g., Beck, "*Imitatio Christi,*" 46: "As the verb ἐδόξαζεν shows, [the centurion] is converted by Jesus' behaviour in his last hours, and makes a positive, Christian comment upon it."

their virtue—in particular their innocence—and their manners of death lead to the conversion of others and the glorification of God.

We now return to the function of synkrisis, discussed in chapter 2, in an attempt to discover Luke's aim in creating these parallels between Jesus, Stephen, and Paul.[12] Aphthonius notes that authors would place the virtues of characters side by side because "when measured against each other they become more worthy of imitation" (*Prog.* 43 [Kennedy, 114]). Plutarch's *Parallel Lives* provides a specific example roughly contemporaneous with Luke and Acts of an author deliberately drawing parallels between two characters with the aim of producing virtue in his readers, which is consistent with Aphthonius' description of the function of synkrisis. Luke's parallels between the characters in his books—particularly as they relate to the characters' innocence (good of the mind) and manner of death (external good)[13]—suggest that Luke may be doing something similar in his accounts of these characters.

A passage from earlier in Luke's Gospel clarifies why Luke might want to emphasize these particular goods to his readers. In Luke 21:12–19 Jesus foretells the persecution that his disciples will face:

> But before all of these things, they will lay their hands on you and persecute you, handing you over to the synagogues and prisons—you who are brought before kings and governors on account of my name. This will lead to an opportunity for you for testimony. Therefore, decide in your hearts not to prepare beforehand to defend yourselves. For I will give you words and wisdom that none of your opponents will be able to resist or deny. And you will be betrayed even by parents, siblings, relatives, and friends, and they will put some of you to death. And you will be hated by all because of my name, but not even a hair

---

12. Even though written at different times, I assume a narrative unity across Luke and Acts. While I agree with Parsons and Pervo that "[e]ach work can stand on its own and has long done so," I nonetheless maintain that Luke had conceived of the parallels between Jesus and Paul when he wrote Luke, perhaps anticipating what he would write in Acts and perhaps letting his understanding of Paul influence his construction of the Third Gospel, even though he had not yet written Acts when he wrote Luke. See Parsons and Pervo, *Rethinking the Unity*, 122.

13. Similar to Luke's use of rhetorical figures, the significance of Luke's construction of parallels between Jesus, Stephen, and Paul is less in the details of the parallels (e.g., both Jesus and Paul appeared before a Herod) and more in the overall portrayal of Stephen's and Paul's trials and/or death aligning with Jesus' in many ways. Because many of the parallels are so striking, readers could not help but notice the similarities between the characters' situations.

from your head will perish. By your endurance you will gain your souls. (cf. 6:40; 12:8–12)

Andrew Clark points out the indefinite audience of Jesus' eschatological discourse here (e.g., "his disciples" in 20:34; "some spoke" in 21:5; "they asked him" in 21:7; cp. Mark's "Peter and James and John and Andrew" in 13:3). This indefiniteness, he suggests, makes Jesus' words in Luke "more appropriate for a figure such as Paul, in addition to the apostles, to be portrayed as fulfilling the prophecies given."[14] Clark is correct that this passage sounds much like what happens to Paul,[15] but Luke also may have envisaged (or known from experience) that this same thing might happen (or was happening) to the readers of his Gospel (i.e., Jesus' "indefinite" disciples were now present in Luke's community). If that were the case, Jesus and Paul (and to a lesser degree, Stephen)—similar to one another in so many ways in Luke's portrayal—serve as exemplars of innocence, or, as Plutarch puts it, as "the fairest of . . . examples" whose virtues are worth emulating.

The parallels between the stories would also accentuate the potentially grim reality of being a disciple of Jesus: innocence does not necessarily imply escape from death or imprisonment, but will guarantee that they will gain their souls. If the readers are persecuted, imprisoned, or handed over to the authorities, they, like Jesus, Stephen, and Paul, might face death or imprisonment. For followers of Jesus, innocence does not imply release. Nonetheless, despite death and imprisonment, the stories of Jesus and Paul communicate hope: resurrection (Luke 24:1–12), the conversion of others (Luke 23:43, 47), and the spread of the gospel (Acts 8:4; 28:23–30).

Finally, the extensive use of parallels in Luke's passion narrative highlights Luke's willingness to alter his source's chronology for the sake of rhetorical effectiveness. It is no coincidence that those places where Jesus is parallel to Stephen or Paul are almost exclusively where Luke

14. Clark, *Parallel Lives*, 188. Johnson, *Gospel of Luke*, 325. Johnson adds that Luke "first eliminates much of the explicitly 'eschatological' language from the first part of the discourse, leaving out Mark's language about the 'birth pangs' and the 'abomination of desolation,' and certainly not heightening this element as Matthew does by referring to the time 'of your *parousia* (coming).'" He then carefully shades the language he does take over from Mark in the direction of specific historical incidents rather than the end-time." Cf. Carroll, "Luke's Crucifixion Scene," 118–20; Neyrey, *Passion according to Luke*, 85–88.

15. For specific examples of these verses playing out in Acts, see Johnson, *Gospel of Luke*, 322.

alters Mark.[16] Thus, as might be expected from our study of synkrisis, when creating parallels between Jesus and other characters Luke may be more willing to sacrifice the chronology of his source for the sake of displaying the virtue of the characters. That is, his larger goal of presenting Jesus, Stephen, and Paul as characters worth emulating overrides strict chronological concerns.

Narration

The virtues of narration in the *progymnasmata* and handbooks help us understand how and why Luke reworked Mark in the way that he did. Both similarities and differences between Mark and Luke are often explicable in light of ancient understandings of what constituted a clear, concise, and plausible narrative. Here we will organize Luke's editing of Mark according to those narrative virtues, noticing that there is often overlap between them.[17]

Many times when Luke reworks Mark, he does so in service of clarity, which stemmed from the order of the events and the language that the author used (Theon, *Prog.* 80–81). One achieved narrative clarity by keeping related things together, not narrating the same thing twice, being concerned with logical order rather than chronological order, and avoiding foreign words (Theon, *Prog.* 80–81; Quintilian, *Inst.* 1.5.1–8; 4.2.83).

These concerns explain several instances where Luke reworks Mark. First, Luke rearranges Mark's material to keep related events together. We see this, for example, when he moves Peter's denial to before the pre-trial hearing, which results in a narrative that focuses on Jesus without interruption from the pre-trial hearing. Second, Luke removes portions of Mark's narrative that narrate the same thing twice. For example, Luke has only one council meeting (22:66–71) instead of Mark's two (14:53–65; 15:1); he has fewer references to Jesus' silence (Luke 23:9; cp. Mark 14:60–61; 15:4–5); he only narrates the offering of wine once (23:36), in contrast to Mark's two times (15:23, 36); and Luke only includes one of Jesus' two "great cries" at the cross that are present in Mark (Luke 23:46; cp. Mark 15:34, 37). Since the narrative virtues often have related concerns, it would not be surprising if Luke's removal of Mark's doublets

---

16. As detailed in previous chapters. See Mattill, "Jesus-Paul Parallels," 22.

17. The examples provided are meant to be representative, not exhaustive.

also stemmed from a concern for brevity—he "prune[s] away everything which can be removed without in any way damaging either the process of judgment or our own interest" (Quintilian, *Inst.* 4.2.20).

Third, Luke often reworks Mark in ways that stem from a concern for logical (and at times theological) order. For example, Luke does not include Mark's description about the custom of releasing a prisoner (15:6)—an introductory description that sets off a new scene in Mark—because he has already introduced the scene in 23:13-16. Including Mark's description (as some manuscripts do in an attempt to harmonize the two) interrupts the flow of the scene by breaking up the dialogue (23:16, 18) with a narrative aside. Since including that piece of information would have disrupted the orderliness of his narrative, Luke does not include it. Elsewhere, in order to remain consistent with his larger concerns, Luke rearranges Mark's order. For example, he alters Mark's mockery scene at the cross (both through additions and rearrangements) in order to provide a positive frame around the scene (it begins and ends with positive responses toward Jesus) (cp. Mark 15:25-32 and Luke 23:32-43). This change is consistent with his larger refutation-confirmation schema that includes both positive and negative responses to Jesus. Additionally, he rearranges the order of the divine portents at the cross, moving the rending of the temple veil to before Jesus' death in order to maintain consistency in his posture toward the temple (Mark 15:33, 38; Luke 23:44-45). He is generally benevolent toward the temple in Luke and Acts, but presenting the tearing as a result of Jesus' death as Mark does could have given the readers the wrong impression that Jesus' death was the end of the temple and its cult. By coupling the rending with the darkness, he forms one testimony from God and removes this potential inconsistency. A final way that Luke attempts to maintain clarity in his narrative is by removing foreign words from Mark (e.g., "Golgotha" from 15:22; the cry of dereliction in 15:34).

Closely related to clarity is conciseness, which was concerned to include only the most important things, "not adding what is not necessary nor omitting what is necessary to the subject and the style" (Theon, *Prog.* 83 [Kennedy, 32]). Doing this entailed anticipating the effect that the narration would have on hearers. An author should strive to be brief when narrating events that would distress hearers but not when narrating events that were pleasant to the hearers (Theon, *Prog.* 80). In addition to removing Mark's doublets, which showed a concern both for clarity and conciseness, Luke condenses or deletes material from Mark in several places, which seems to express a concern to avoid those topics that would distress hearers. Obviously the nature of a passion narrative does not allow for the removal of all material that would distress hearers, but Luke does prune away some of the more distressing material. For example, he removes Mark's details about the crown of thorns, the purple clothing for mockery, the mocking hails, and the soldiers' kneeling to Jesus (15:17–19) and instead narrates only briefly that the soldiers disdained and mocked him (23:11). Luke is also attentive to material that might distress his readers when he changes Mark's severe beating of Jesus (φραγελλόω; 15:15) to a less severe one (παιδεύω; 23:16, 22) that remains a future threat. In other places Luke's concern for brevity is manifest in Luke's word substitutions (e.g., replacing Mark's εἰς δύο ἀπ' ἄνωθεν ἕως κάτω [15:38] with μέσον [23:45]), and in still other places where he combines several elements of Mark into once sentence (e.g., Mark 15:24, 27 into Luke 23:33; cf., Mark 15:16–20, 23, 36, 30 into Luke 23:36).

Finally, Luke's editing of Mark is also explicable in terms of Luke's concern for plausibility. Key to a plausible narrative was consistency in the times and order of events (Theon, *Prog.* 80), providing reasons for events (Quintilian, *Inst.* 4.2.52), and specifying the place, time, and other important facets of the narrative (Quintilian, *Inst.* 4.2.52). These concerns manifest themselves in Luke's narrative in several places. For example, Luke removes references to Jesus' silence from a place in Mark where Jesus speaks (Mark 14:58, 60–62) and instead places that reference in his narrative where Jesus is actually silent (Luke 23:9). Luke also sets the pre-trial hearing in the morning (22:66) instead of the evening (14:53–64), possibly concerned that a nighttime meeting would sound suspicious or implausible. He also removes the presence of false witnesses at that hearing (Mark 14:55–56) and instead has the council members make the charges against Jesus, not wanting this portion of the trial to be discredited. Further, Luke's addition to Mark 15:33—that darkness came over the land *because the sun was darkened* (Luke 23:44)—can be understood as his explanation for the darkness (i.e., providing the reason for the event, as Quintilian suggests). Throughout his narrative, then, Luke demonstrates concerns for clarity, conciseness, and plausibility in the ways that he incorporates Mark into his own narrative.

Paraphrase

Finally, an understanding of those techniques associated with ancient paraphrase helps us understand the extent to which an ancient writer like Luke could adapt source material. We return to Theon's description of paraphrase—"changing the form of expression while keeping the thoughts" via addition, subtraction, and rearrangement of words or thoughts, via alteration of syntax, or via a combination of these techniques (*Prog.* 107P [Kennedy, 70]). Quintilian, too, describes the exercise as "abbreviat[ing] and embellish[ing] some parts, so long as the poet's meaning is preserved" (*Inst.* 1.9.2). A student accomplished this by adding force to the original's thoughts, supplying information that was left out, and deleting redundancies (*Inst.* 10.5.4). The *Bodleian Greek Inscription* 3019, an ancient example of paraphrase discussed in chapter 2, also provides evidence that students were taught to elaborate on the original stylistically through the addition of rhetorical figures and parallelism. Morgan describes it as walking the line between "an act of creative composition and an elementary exercise . . . [which] does not seek to keep slavishly close to the original."[18] This aligns with other ancient writers' conceptions of paraphrase, who liken it to a competition—the one who paraphrases "rival[s] and vie[s] with the original in expressing the same thoughts" (Quintilian, *Inst.* 10.5.5; cf. Pliny, *Ep.* 7.9.4).

The goal here is not to recount every instance in which Luke adds to, subtracts from, or rearranges Mark's narrative, as these edits were detailed thoroughly in the preceding chapters. Nor is the goal to argue that Luke's passion narrative ought to be described as a paraphrase of Mark's—applying new titles to techniques already long observed by scholars is not helpful in itself. At this point in the analysis, we are less interested in the details previously described and more interested in the larger practice and what that teaches us about how ancient authors and orators worked with sources.

This study has argued that the similarities and differences between the passion narratives of Mark and Luke are best understood as Luke's creative reworking of Mark for his larger rhetorical purposes with the incorporation of some of his own traditions. As discussed in chapter 2, even someone with a basic primer in paraphrase[19] was familiar with

---

18. Morgan, *Literate Education*, 208.

19. We remember that Theon recommends introducing paraphrase at the beginning of a student's training (*Prog.* 65).

the process of reworking a source in a variety of ways—some big and some small—to improve the original while preserving its meaning. The previous chapters demonstrated that Luke's redaction of Mark fits within the parameters of ancient paraphrase. Exercises in paraphrase taught students that not everything in their source needed to be changed, and thus the similarities between Luke and Mark are best viewed as Luke's retention of material that fit his larger purposes. The differences between the two passion narratives—which is where the heart of the debate lies— should be viewed as Luke's attempt to improve on Mark's original. This understanding aligns well with Luke's stated purpose in his prologue and is consistent with how ancient authors and rhetors were taught to work with sources. Even those places where Luke diverges from Mark in substantive ways (e.g., the addition of the Herod pericope) fit within the parameters of how an ancient author might transform another's work,[20] either as a rhetorical exercise or in an attempt to rival the original in some way. I agree with Soards' conclusion that "the greatest differences between Luke and Mark may be the result of Luke's strongest motive(s) for writing his gospel."[21] Thus, since Luke's editing fits within the parameters of how ancient authors worked with sources and since evidence for a separate passion source for Luke's passion narrative is lacking,[22] the best solution to the source problem of Luke's passion narrative—discussed more fully below—is that Luke used Mark as his sole *written* source.

Summary

Through this rhetorical analysis, we have seen that Luke organizes his passion narrative as an alternation between refutations and confirmations of the charges against Jesus, and he employs common topics from the rhetorical tradition to do so. The quality and quantity of witnesses ultimately support the characterization of Jesus as innocent. The placement of rhetorical figures throughout the narrative also contributes to Luke's characterization of Jesus as innocent. Furthermore, by setting up parallels between Jesus and Stephen and between Jesus and Paul, Luke

---

20. The paraphrase of the *Iliad* in the *Bodleian Greek Inscription* 3019 was three times longer than the original, which is evidence that authors were at liberty to add significant amounts of their own material to their paraphrase.

21. See Soards, *Passion according to Luke*, 123.

22. And, I would argue, the impetus to search for one is decreased in light of this understanding of paraphrase.

presents the characters as models whose innocence and manner of death are to be imitated, should his readers be put in situations similar to those of the characters, which Luke may anticipate. When it comes to the composition of Luke's passion narrative, the exercises and techniques associated with narration and paraphrase suggest that Luke did not use a non-canonical written source as a basis for his passion narrative and that he edited Mark toward clarity, conciseness, and plausibility through addition, subtraction, rearrangement, and the alteration of syntax.

Implications for Interpreting Luke

In chapter 1, I intimated three areas of debate in current scholarship on Luke's passion narrative: (1) the sources Luke used for his passion narrative; (2) the best translation for the centurion's confession in 23:47; and (3) the purpose of the parallels between Jesus and characters in Acts. It is now time to return to those questions and bring the findings of the rhetorical analysis to bear on them.

The Sources of Luke's Passion Narrative

Put briefly, scholars are divided into two main camps regarding the sources of Luke's passion narrative: those who think Luke used a non-canonical written source in addition to Mark for his passion narrative and those who think he did not.[23] The former tend to base their argument on three things: (1) word statistics; (2) verbatim agreement in terminology and order; and (3) correspondences between Luke and John. They often assume that content and order different from Mark are best explained by Luke's reliance on another source, which, in its extreme form, results in a picture of Luke as primarily an editor or compiler of previous traditions. The latter base their argument primarily on two things: (1) the theological continuity between Luke's passion narrative and the rest of his Gospel and Acts; and (2) Luke's stylistic and compositional tendencies. They view Luke as a creative and capable author and theologian, not merely piecing together sources.

This rhetorical analysis supports the latter position—that Luke did not use a non-canonical written source in addition to Mark. The

---

23. See chapter 1 for an explanation of why I do not treat Luke's potential use of Matthew and John here.

techniques associated with paraphrase and narration teach us how, to what extent, and why ancient authors would edit sources and compose narratives in certain ways. An understanding of these rhetorical techniques suggests that recourse to multiple sources to explain the differences between Luke and Mark is not the best explanation. It ought to be the last resort rather than the first, especially when other viable options exist. Since these differences between the passion narratives of Luke and Mark fit within the parameters of editing and composing taught in ancient education, and since those differences can often be understood in terms of Luke's larger theological goals, it is unnecessary to posit a hypothetical source that lacks hard evidence. Thus, this study critiques the tendency amongst some scholars to attribute to another source nearly all of Luke's divergences from Mark.[24]

The Translation of δίκαιος

Scholars are divided into three camps regarding the translations of δίκαιος in the centurion's confession in Luke 23:37: (1) those who think it means "righteous"; (2) those who think it means "innocent"; and (3) those who advocate a dual or overlapping meaning. Though with different emphases, all three camps take into account the context of the narrative (camp 1 emphasizing the translation of cognates as "justly" and "righteous" in nearby verses; camp 2 emphasizing the proclamations of innocence by Pilate, Herod, and the second criminal; camp 3 noting both). The first camp also sees their translation accounting for Luke's theological thrust (describing the centurion's words as δοξάζω and having Jesus recite Ps 31). The second camp sees their translation accounting for Luke's political thrust (aligning with Luke's larger theme of innocence, his aim to show that Jesus was not politically subversive, and his potential framing of his narrative in line with the noble death/martyrdom tradition). The third camp insists that both meanings ought to be acknowledged.

This study ultimately challenges the first view, which does not account for Luke's larger emphasis on Jesus' political innocence. The preceding rhetorical analysis has shown that Luke's concern for Jesus' innocence goes beyond those explicit proclamations of his innocence to

---

24. Though he swings the pendulum too far in the other direction, positing Lukan creativity where there is sometimes no basis to do so, Goulder is nonetheless right in posing the following question: "Why then should we limit this creative activity to the passages where the relationship is so close as to be undeniable?" See Goulder, *Luke*, 75.

which advocates of the second view point. Luke weaves that concern into the very structure of his narrative by casting the entire passion narrative as a series of refutations and confirmations of Jesus' guilt. Further, Luke employs a host of topics common in the ancient rhetorical tradition to show the varying responses to accusations against Jesus, and he shows concern for both the quantity and quality of those witnesses. The strategic placement of rhetorical figures in Luke's passion narrative also underscores Luke's emphasis on Jesus' innocence. Finally, Luke's parallel concern with Paul's innocence in Acts further highlights the political dimensions of Luke's passion narrative. These rhetorical elements of Luke's narrative—not just the blatant proclamations of Jesus' innocence—show that Luke is deeply invested in portraying Jesus as politically innocent,[25] and thus any translation and resulting interpretation of the centurion's confession must acknowledge its political dimensions.

Luke's Passion Narrative, Parallels, and the Purpose of Luke-Acts

Finally, scholars are divided over how to interpret the parallels between Jesus in his passion narrative and characters in Acts. While the parallels are interesting on an aesthetic level, their presence demands exegetical explanation. Did Luke align these characters for an apologetic purpose (to defend Christians to the Romans, to defend the Romans to Christians, or to defend Paul's sufferings), for a pastoral purpose (to provide models for his readers or to show continuity between Jesus and the church), for a theological purpose (to show that Peter, Stephen, and Paul must suffer like prophets as Jesus did), or for some combination of these purposes?[26] While each of these proposals has merits, a successful proposal must account for at least two things: (1) Luke's emphasis on the characters' innocence, which is a dominant element not only of Luke's entire passion narrative, but also of the parallels between Jesus and Paul; (2) the rhetorical tradition's understanding of synkrisis. The latter both instructs (in the *progymnasmata*) and models (in Plutarch's *Parallel Lives*) that one ought to compare characters' goods of the body, goods of the mind (e.g., the virtue of innocence), and/or external goods (e.g., the manner and

---

25. It is worth noting that Luke's presentation of Jesus as politically *innocent* does not necessarily mean that Luke also saw or presented Jesus as politically *innocuous*.

26. For the scholars who advocate these various proposals, see "Luke's Passion Narrative, Parallels, and the Purpose of Luke-Acts" in chapter 1.

results of a person's death) as a way of producing virtue in the readers by providing them with models for imitation.

Though there are significant differences between Plutarch's comparisons and Luke's, it does seem that Luke has in mind both goods of the mind (e.g., the virtue of innocence) and external goods (e.g., the composed manner of dying; the conversions resulting from death) as he constructs these parallels between Jesus, Stephen, and Paul.[27] But is the fact that Plutarch employed synkrisis for the purpose of moral formation enough evidence to argue that Luke had similar intentions? If Luke had made no indication that he had similar motivations for his larger work, it would not. But, as detailed above, Luke's comments in 6:40, 12:8–12, and especially 21:12–19 suggest that he thought his readers might face trials and/or deaths similar to Jesus, Stephen, and Paul. Thus, he had an impetus for providing models on how to conduct themselves in trying times. Furthermore, Luke's synkrisis does not seem designed to present one character as better than another, as some synkreses did. This sense of equality may be Luke's attempt to clarify the continuity between Jesus, the church, and his own readers, not unlike how Plutarch's synkrisis portrayed the Roman Empire as a continuation of Hellenism.[28]

Which of the views described above best accounts for Luke's emphasis on innocence and the rhetorical tradition's understanding of synkrisis—one of the apologetic motivations, one of the pastoral motivations, or a theological motivation? The best proposal seems to be a combination of the two pastoral proposals. The first pastoral proposal, which sees the parallels as Luke's attempt to provide models for his hearers, accounts both for Luke's emphasis on innocence in the parallels (i.e., his hearers are to exemplify this virtue as their models did) and for his concern that his hearers may face situations similar to that of the models (e.g., 6:40; 12:8–12; 21:12–19). It also accounts for Luke's highlighting the manner of the characters' death, particularly its potential for the conversion of others. These parallels suggest that, though Luke's hearers may not be spared from imprisonment or death, they will experience vindication in the end and their difficult circumstances serve a purpose larger than themselves. The second proposal, which sees the parallels as Luke's attempt to show continuity between Jesus and the church, does not account for the innocence motif and does not necessarily extend the continuity to

---

27. And Michael Martin has shown Luke's concern for other encomiastic topics in the rest of Luke's Gospel. See Martin, "Progymnasmatic Topic Lists," 18–41.

28. Radl, *Paulus und Jesus*, 374–77.

Luke's hearers, but it does account for the type of synkrisis Luke employs (i.e., using the comparison to show similarities and equality, not differences and superiority).

What do we make of the theological and apologetic proposals? The theological proposal articulated by Moessner,[29] while different from the pastoral proposal, does not contradict it in any way, and thus can be seen as a supplement to the pastoral proposal advocated here. The strength of the various political apologetic proposals described above is that they account for the political tenor of the comparisons between Luke, Stephen, and Paul (including a translation of δίκαιος that connotes political innocence). However, insomuch as these apologetic purposes do not consider ancient examples of synkrisis (and thus at times come to interpretations that directly oppose one another[30]), this motivation ought to be seen as secondary to the pastoral concern. Luke was certainly not bound to a singular purpose in his construction of these parallels, not least since Luke and Acts could be read either separately or together. Thus, while Luke may have had political aims in constructing these parallels, these aims ought to be viewed as secondary to his pastoral concerns since the latter account for both the specifics of the parallels and the larger rhetorical purpose of synkrisis. Of course, this proposal needs to be evaluated in light of the parallels outside of the passion narrative, but it nonetheless provides some important methodological considerations and one key part of that larger study.

Conclusion

This study proposed a new method for approaching old problems. With a compositional-rhetorical method, I analyzed Luke's passion narrative in an attempt to understand his sources, his presentation of Jesus as δίκαιος, and the purpose of the parallels he constructs between Jesus, Stephen, and Paul. The ancient rhetorical techniques of refutation and confirmation, rhetorical figures, synkrisis, narration, and paraphrase illuminated Luke's compositional habits, his characterization of Jesus as δίκαιος, and the structure of his narrative. Ultimately this study answered the three interpretive issues as follows. (1) Luke did not use a non-canonical written

---

29. Moessner, "Christ Must Suffer."

30. For critiques of the apologetic proposals, see Maddox, *Purpose of Luke-Acts*, 20–21, 91–99.

source for his passion narrative. Differences between the two passion narratives derive either from Luke's hand (mostly) and oral traditions (in some cases) and were motivated by his larger theological goals of presenting Jesus as politically innocent and showing diverse responses to Jesus. This study did not explore Luke's potential use of Matthew or John as sources for his passion narrative, and it neither supports nor denies those hypotheses. My hope is that this study and the methodology employed here can serve as a basis for those discussions, both of which deserve scholarly attention informed by an understanding of ancient rhetoric. (2) Any translation and interpretation of the centurion's confession in Luke 23:47 must acknowledge its political dimensions—Luke strongly emphasizes that Jesus was *politically innocent*. This study does not deny that Luke was concerned to portray Jesus as the righteous sufferer of Ps 31, but it argues, at a minimum, for a both-and interpretation. (3) Luke constructed the parallels between Jesus, Stephen, and Paul—in their trails and deaths, in particular—primarily with pastoral concerns in mind, though he may have had secondary theological and/or apologetic motivations. Anticipating that his hearers might face situations of trial, imprisonment, and death, Luke sets up Jesus, Stephen, and Paul as models who exemplify innocence, a worthy manner of death, and sufferings which result in the spread of the gospel. Thus, there is continuity not only between Jesus and his immediate successors, Stephen and Paul, but also with the church of later generations, Luke's hearers included.

Bibliography

Ahn, Yong-Sung. *The Reign of God and Rome in Luke's Passion Narrative: An East Asian Global Perspective*. Biblical Interpretation Series 80. Leiden: Brill, 2006.
Allison, Dale C. *The End of the Ages Has Come: An Early Interpretation of the Passion and Resurrection of Jesus*. Philadelphia: Fortress, 1985.
Aristotle. *Rhetorica*. Translated by John Henry Freese. Loeb Classical Library. Cambridge: Harvard University Press, 1926.
[Aristotle]. *Rhetorica ad Alexandrum*. Translated by H. Rackham. Loeb Classical Library. Cambridge: Harvard University Press, 1957.
Aune, David E. *The Westminster Dictionary of New Testament and Early Christian Literature and Rhetoric*. Louisville: Westminster, 2003.
Bachmann, Michael. *Jerusalem und der Tempel: Die geographisch-theologischen Elemente in der lukanischen Sicht des jüdischen Kultzentrums*. Beiträge zur Wissenschaft vom Alten (und Neuen) Testament 9. Stuttgart: Kohlhammer, 1980.
Barrett, C. K. *Luke the Historian in Recent Study*. Facet Books, Biblical Series 24. Philadelphia: Fortress, 1970.
Beck, Brian E. "'*Imitatio Christi*' and the Lucan Passion Narrative." In *Suffering and Martyrdom in the New Testament: Studies Presented to G. M. Styler by the Cambridge New Testament Seminar*, edited by William Horburg and Brian McNeil, 28–47. Cambridge: Cambridge University Press, 1981.
Benoit, Pierre. *The Passion and Resurrection of Jesus Christ*. Translated by Benet Weatherhead. New York: Herder & Herder, 1969.
Blinzler, Josef. *The Trial of Jesus: The Jewish and Roman Proceedings against Jesus Christ Described and Assessed from the Oldest Accounts*. Translated by Isabel McHugh and Florence McHugh. Cork: Mercier, 1959.
Bock, Darrell L. *Luke*. The IVP New Testament Commentary Series 3. Downers Grove, IL: InterVarsity, 1994.
———. *Luke 9:51—24:53*. Baker Exegetical Commentary on the New Testament. Grand Rapids: Baker, 1994.
Boismard, M. E. *Synopse des quatre Évangiles en français*. Vol. 2. Paris: Éditions du Cerf, 1965.
Booth, Alan D. "Elementary and Secondary Education in the Roman Empire." *Florilegium* 1 (1979) 1–14.
Bovon, François. "The Lukan Story of the Passion of Jesus (Luke 22–23)." In *Studies in Early Christianity*, 74–105. Grand Rapids: Baker Academic, 2005.

———. *Luke 1: A Commentary on the Gospel of Luke 1:1—9:50*. Translated by Christine M. Thomas. Hermeneia. Minneapolis: Fortress, 2002.

———. *Luke 3: A Commentary on the Gospel of Luke 19:28—24:53*. Translated by James E. Crouch. Hermeneia. Minneapolis: Fortress, 2012.

Brawley, Robert L. *Luke-Acts and the Jews: Conflict, Apology, and Conciliation*. Society of Biblical Literature Monograph Series 33. Atlanta: Scholars, 1987.

Brookins, Timothy A. "Luke's Use of Mark as Παράφρασις: Its Effects on Characterization in the 'Healing of Blind Bartimaeus' Pericope (Mark 10.46–52/Luke 18.35–43)." *Journal for the Study of the New Testament* 34 (2011) 70–89.

Brown, Raymond E. *The Death of the Messiah: From Gethsemane to the Grave: A Commentary on the Passion Narratives in the Four Gospels*. 2 vols. New York: Doubleday, 1994.

Büchele, Anton. *Der Tod Jesu im Lukasevangelium: Eine redaktionsgeschichtliche Untersuchung zu Lk 23*. Frankfurter Theologische Studien 26. Frankfurt am Main: Josef Knecht, 1978.

Bullinger, Ethelbert W. *Figures of Speech Used in the Bible, Explained and Illustrated*. Grand Rapids: Baker, 1968.

Bundy, Walter E. *Jesus and the First Three Gospels: An Introduction to the Synoptic Tradition*. Cambridge: Harvard University Press, 1955.

Burkitt, F. Crawford. *The Gospel History and Its Transmission*. Edinburgh: T. & T. Clark, 1906.

Butts, James. R. "The 'Progymnasmata' of Theon: A New Text with Translation and Commentary." PhD diss., Claremont Graduate School, 1986.

Cadbury, Henry J. "Four Features of Lucan Style." In *Studies in Luke-Acts: Essays Presented in Honor of Paul Schubert*, edited by Leander E. Keck and J. Louis Martyn, 87–102. London: SPCK, 1968.

———. *The Making of Luke-Acts*. London: SPCK, 1958.

———. *The Style and Literary Method of Luke*. Harvard Theological Studies 6. Cambridge: Harvard University Press, 1920.

Carroll, John T. *Luke: A Commentary*. New Testament Library. Louisville: Westminster John Knox, 2012.

———. "Luke's Crucifixion Scene." In *Reimaging the Death of the Lukan Jesus*, edited by Dennis D. Sylva, 108–24. Frankfurt am Main: Hain, 1990.

Cassidy, Richard J. *Jesus, Politics, and Society: A Study of Luke's Gospel*. Maryknoll, NY: Orbis, 1978.

Chance, J. Bradley. *Jerusalem, the Temple, and the New Age in Luke-Acts*. Macon, GA: Mercer, 1988.

Cicero. *Brutus*. Translated by G. L. Hendrickson. Loeb Classical Library. Cambridge: Harvard University Press, 1939.

———. *De inventione rhetorica*. Translated by H. M. Hubbell. Loeb Classical Library. Cambridge: Harvard University Press, 1949.

———. *De oratore*. Translated by E. W. Sutton and H. Rackham. 2 vols. Loeb Classical Library. Cambridge: Harvard University Press, 1942.

———. *Partitiones oratoriae*. Translated by H. Rackham. Loeb Classical Library. Cambridge: Harvard University Press, 1942.

———. *Topica*. Translated by H. M. Hubbell. Loeb Classical Library. Cambridge: Harvard University Press, 1949.

[Cicero]. *Rhetorical ad Herennium*. Translated by Harry Caplan. Loeb Classical Library. Cambridge: Harvard University Press, 1954.

Clark, Andrew C. *Parallel Lives: The Relation of Paul to the Apostles in the Lucan Perspective*. Paternoster Biblical and Theological Monographs. Carlisle, UK: Paternoster, 2001.

Collins, Adela Yarbro. "From Noble Death to Crucified Messiah." *New Testament Studies* 40 (1994) 481–503.

———. *Mark: A Commentary*. Hermeneia. Minneapolis: Fortress, 2007.

Connolly-Weinert, Frank. "Assessing Omissions as Redaction: Luke's Handling of the Charge against Jesus as Detractor of the Temple." In *To Touch the Text: Biblical and Related Studies in Honor of Joseph A. Fitzmyer, SJ*, edited by Maurya P. Horgan and Paul J. Kobelski, 358–68. New York: Crossroad, 1989.

Conzelmann, Hans. *The Theology of St. Luke*. Translated by Geoffrey Buswell. New York: Harper, 1961.

Cosgrove, Charles H. "The Divine ΔΕΙ in Luke-Acts: Investigations into the Lukan Understanding of God's Providence." *Novum Testamentum* 26 (1984) 168–90.

Cribiore, Raffaella. *Gymnastics of the Mind: Greek Education in Hellenistic and Roman Egypt*. Princeton, NJ: Princeton University Press, 2001.

———. *Writing, Teachers, and Students in Graeco-Roman Egypt*. American Studies in Papyrology 36. Atlanta: Scholars, 1996.

Culy, Martin M., Mikeal C. Parsons, and Joshua J. Stigall. *Luke: A Handbook on the Greek Text*. Baylor Handbook on the Greek New Testament. Waco, TX: Baylor University Press, 2010.

Darr, John A. *Herod the Fox: Audience Criticism and Lukan Characterization*. Journal for the Study of the New Testament: Supplement Series 163. Sheffield: Sheffield Academic, 1998.

De Long, Kindalee Pfremmer. *Surprised by God: Praise Responses in the Narrative of Luke-Acts*. Beihefte zur Zeitschrift für die neutestamentliche Wissenschaft 166. Berlin: Walter de Gruyter, 2009.

Dibelius, Martin. *From Tradition to Gospel*. Translated by Bertram Lee Woolf. New York: Scribner, 1935.

———. "Herodes und Pilatus." *Zeitschrift für die neutestamentliche Wissenschaft und die Kunde der Älteren Kirche* 16 (1915) 113–26.

Dionysius of Halicarnassus. *De Thucydide*. Translated by Stephen Usher. Loeb Classical Library. Cambridge: Harvard University Press, 1974.

Doble, Peter. *The Paradox of Salvation: Luke's Theology of the Cross*. Cambridge: Cambridge University Press, 1996.

Donahue, John R. "Introduction: From Passion Traditions to Passion Narrative." In *The Passion in Mark: Studies on Mark 14–16*, edited by Werner H. Kelber, 1–20. Philadelphia: Fortress, 1976.

Duff, Tim. *Plutarch's Lives: Exploring Virtue and Vice*. Oxford: Clarendon, 1999.

Easter, Matthew C. "'Certainly This Man Was Righteous': Highlighting a Messianic Reading of the Centurion's Confession in Luke 23:47." *Tyndale Bulletin* 63 (2012) 35–51.

Easton, Burton Scott. *The Gospel according to St. Luke: A Critical and Exegetical Commentary*. Edinburgh: T. & T. Clark, 1926.

Ehrman, Bart D., and Zlatko Pleše. *The Apocryphal Gospels: Texts and Translations*. New York: Oxford University Press, 2011.

Eisenhut, Werner. *Einführung in die antik Rhetorik und ihre Geschichte.* 4th ed. Darmstadt: Wissenschaftliche Buchgesellschaft, 1990.
Ernst, Josef. *Das Evangelium nach Lukas.* Regensburger Neues Testament. Regensburg: Friedrich Pustet, 1993.
Eubank, Nathan. "A Disconcerting Prayer: On the Originality of Luke 23:34a." *Journal of Biblical Literature* 129 (2010) 521–36.
Evans, Craig A. *Mark 8:27—16:20.* Word Biblical Commentary 34B. Nashville: Thomas Nelson, 2001.
Farrer, Austin. "On Dispensing with Q." In *Studies in the Gospels: Essays in Memory of R. H. Lightfoot,* edited by Dennis Eric Nineham, 55–88. Oxford: Blackwell, 1955.
Fitzmyer, Joseph A. *The Gospel according to Luke: Introduction, Translation, and Notes.* 2 vols. Anchor Bible 28. Garden City, NY: Doubleday, 1981.
Focke, Friedrich. "Synkrisis." *Hermes* 58 (1923) 327–68.
Foerster, Richard, and Karl Münscher, "Libanios." In *Paulys Realencyclopädie der classischen Altertumswissenschaft.* Edited by G. Wissowa. New edition. Vol. 12. Munich: A. Druckenmüller, 1980.
Frazier, Françoise. *Histoire et morale dans les* Vies Parallèles *de Plutarque.* Collection d'études anciennes 124. Paris: Les Belles Lettres, 1996.
Fuchs, Albert. *Sprachliche Untersuchungen au Matthäus und Lukas. Ein Beitrag zur Quellenkritik.* Analecta biblica 49. Rome: Biblical Institute, 1971.
Fuhrmann, Manfred. *Das systematische Lehrbuch: Ein Beitrag zur Geschichte der Wissenschaften in der Antike.* Göttingen: Vandenhoeck & Ruprecht, 1960.
———. *Die antike Rhetorik: Eine Einführung.* Munich: Artemis, 1984.
Gaines, Robert N. "Roman Rhetorical Handbooks." In *A Companion to Roman Rhetoric,* edited by William J. Dominik and Jon Hall, 163–80. Blackwell Companions to the Ancient World. Malden, MA: Blackwell, 2007.
Gaston, L. "Anti-Judaism in the Passion Narrative in Luke and Acts." In *Anti-Judaism in Early Christianity. Vol. 1, Paul and the Gospels,* edited by Peter Richardson and David M. Granskou, 127–54. Studies in Christianity and Judaism 2. Waterloo, Ontario: Wilfrid Laurier University Press, 1986.
Gathercole, Simon J. *The Composition of the Gospel of Thomas: Original Language and Influences.* Society for New Testament Studies Monograph Series 151. Cambridge: Cambridge University Press, 2012.
Geddert, Timothy J. *Watchwords: Mark 13 in Markan Eschatology.* Journal for the Study of the New Testament: Supplement Series 26. Sheffield: JSOT, 1989.
George, Augustin. "Israël dans l'oeuvre de Luc." *Revue biblique* 75 (1968) 481–525.
Giblin, Charles Homer. *The Destruction of Jerusalem according to Luke's Gospel: A Historical-Typological Moral.* Analecta biblica 107. Rome: Biblical Institute, 1985.
Gibson, Craig A. "Learning Greek History in the Ancient Classroom: The Evidence of the Treatises on Progymnasmata." *Classical Philology* 99 (2004) 103–29.
———, trans. *Libanius's Progymnasmata: Model Exercises in Greek Prose Composition and Rhetoric.* Writings from the Greco-Roman World 27. Atlanta: Society of Biblical Literature, 2008.
Goodacre, Mark S. *Goulder and the Gospels: An Examination of a New Paradigm.* Journal for the Study of the New Testament: Supplement Series 133. Sheffield: Sheffield Academic, 1996.
———. *Thomas and the Gospels: The Case for Thomas's Familiarity with the Synoptics.* Grand Rapids: Eerdmans, 2012.

Gorman, Heather M. "Crank or Creative Genius? How Ancient Rhetoric Makes Sense of Luke's Order." In *Marcan Priority without Q: Explorations in the Farrer Hypothesis*, edited by Jack Poirier and Jeffrey Peterson, 62-81. Library of New Testament Studies. London: T. & T. Clark, 2015.

Goulder, M. D. *Luke: A New Paradigm*. 2 vols. Journal for the Study of the New Testament: Supplement Series 20. Sheffield: JSOT, 1989.

———. *Type and History in Acts*. London: SPCK, 1964.

Grant, F. C. *The Growth of the Gospels*. New York: Abingdon, 1933.

Green, Joel B. *The Death of Jesus: Tradition and Interpretation in the Passion Narrative*. Wissenschaftliche Untersuchungen zum Neuen Testament 2/33. Tübingen: J. C. B. Mohr, 1988.

———. "The Demise of the Temple as 'Culture Center' in Luke-Acts: An Exploration of the Rending of the Temple Veil (Luke 23:44-49)." *Revue biblique* 101 (1994) 495-515.

Grundmann, Walter. *Das Evangelium nach Lukas*. Theologischer Handkommentar zum Neuen Testament 3. Berlin: Evangelische Verlagsanstalt, 1966.

Haenchen, Ernst. *The Acts of the Apostles: A Commentary*. Translated by Bernard Noble and Gerald Shinn. Oxford: Blackwell, 1971.

———. *Der Weg Jesu: Eine Erklärung des Markus-Evangeliums und der kanonischen Parallelen*. Berlin: Töpelmann, 1966.

Harrington, Jay M. *The Lukan Passion Narrative: The Markan Material in Luke 22,54—23,25: A Historical Survey, 1891-1997*. New Testament Tools and Studies 30. Leiden: Brill, 2000.

Harrington, Wilfrid J. *The Gospel according to St. Luke*. New York: Newman, 1967.

Heath, Malcolm. "Theon and the History of the Progymnasmata." *Greek, Roman, and Byzantine Studies* 43 (2002) 129-60.

Heusler, Erika. *Kapitalprozesse im lukanischen Doppelwerk: Die Verfahren gegen Jesus und Paulus in exegetischer und rechtshistorischer Analyse*. Neutestamentliche Abhandlungen 38. Münster: Aschendorff, 2000.

Hirsch, Emanuel. *Frühgeschichte des Evangeliums: Die Borlagen des Lukas und das Sondergut des Matthäus*. Tübingen: J. C. B. Mohr, 1941.

Hock, Ronald F., and Edward N. O'Neil, eds. *The Chreia in Ancient Rhetoric: The Progymnasmata*. Society of Biblical Literature Texts and Translations 27. Atlanta: Scholars, 1986.

Hoehner, Harold W. *Herod Antipas*. Grand Rapids: Zondervan, 1980.

Hogan, Derek K. "Forensic Speeches in Acts 22-26 in their Literary Environment: A Rhetorical Study." PhD diss., Baylor University, 2006.

Hoover, Roy W. "Selected Special Lukan Material in the Passion Narrative: Luke 23:33-43, 47b-49." *Forum* 1 (1998) 119-27.

Horn, Friedrich W. "Die Haltung des Lukas zum römischen Staat im Evangelium und in der Apostelgeschichte." In *The Unity of Luke-Acts*, edited by Jozef Verheyden, 203-24. Bibliotheca ephemeridum theologicarum lovaniensium 142. Leuven: Leuven University Press, 1999.

Hughes, Frank W. "The Parable of the Rich Man and Lazarus (Luke 16:19-31) and Graeco-Roman Rhetoric." In *Rhetoric and the New Testament: Essays from the 1992 Heidelberg Conference*, edited by Thomas H. Olbricht and Stanley E. Porter, 29-41. Journal for the Study of the New Testament: Supplement Series 90. Sheffield: JSOT, 1993.

Jeffrey, David L. *Luke*. Brazos Theological Commentary on the Bible. Grand Rapids: Brazos, 2012.
Jeremias, Joachim. *The Eucharistic Words of Jesus*. Translated by N. Perrin. London: SCM, 1966.
———. "Perikopen-Umstellungen bei Lukas?" *New Testament Studies* 4 (1958) 115–19.
———. *Rediscovering the Parables*. Translated by Frank Clarke. New York: Scribner, 1966.
———. *Die Sprache des Lukasevangeliums: Redaktion und Tradition im Nicht-Markusstoff des dritten Evangeliums*. Göttingen: Vandenhoeck und Ruprecht, 1980.
Johnson, Earl S. "Is Mark 15:39 the Key to Mark's Christology." *Journal for the Study of the New Testament* 31 (1987) 3–22.
Johnson, Luke Timothy. *The Gospel of Luke*. Sacra Pagina. Collegeville, MN: Liturgical, 1991.
Karris, Robert J. "Luke 23:47 and the Lucan View of Jesus' Death." *Journal of Biblical Literature* 105 (1986) 65–74.
———. *Luke, Artist and Theologian: Luke's Passion Account as Literature*. New York: Paulist, 1985.
Kennedy, George A. *The Art of Rhetoric in the Roman World, 300 BC–AD 300*. Princeton: Princeton University Press, 1972.
———. *Classical Rhetoric and Its Christian and Secular Tradition from Ancient to Modern Times*. Chapel Hill: University of North Carolina Press, 1980.
———. *Greek Rhetoric under Christian Emperors*. Princeton: Princeton University Press, 1983.
———. "Historical Survey of Rhetoric." In *Handbook of Classical Rhetoric in the Hellenistic Period, 330 BC–AD 400*, edited by Stanley E. Porter, 3–41. Leiden: Brill, 1997.
———. *New Testament Interpretation through Rhetorical Criticism*. Chapel Hill: University of North Carolina Press, 1984.
———, trans. *Progymnasmata: Greek Textbooks of Prose Composition and Rhetoric*. Writings from the Greco-Roman World 10. Atlanta: Society of Biblical Literature, 2003.
Kilpatrick, G. D. "A Theme of the Lucan Passion Story and Luke xxiii. 47." *Journal of Theological Studies* 43 (1942) 34–36.
Kloppenborg, John S. "*Exitus Clari Viri*: The Death of Jesus in Luke." *Toronto Journal of Theology* 8 (1992) 106–20.
———. *The Formation of Q: Trajectories in Ancient Wisdom Collections*. Studies in Antiquity and Christianity. Harrisburg, PA: Trinity International, 2000.
Kodell, Jerome. "Luke's Use of *laos*, 'People,' Especially in the Jerusalem Narrative: Lk 19,28—24,53." *Catholic Biblical Quarterly* 31 (1969) 327–43.
Koester, Helmut. *Introduction to the New Testament, Vol. 2: History and Literature of Early Christianity*. 2nd ed. New York: Walter de Gruyter, 1995.
Kurz, William S. "Hellenistic Rhetoric in the Christological Proof of Luke-Acts." *Catholic Biblical Quarterly* 42 (1980) 171–95.
Lana, Italo. *I "progimnasmi" di Elio Teone*. Turin: Giappichelli, 1959.
Lausberg, Heinrich. *Handbook of Literary Rhetoric: A Foundation for Literary Study*. Edited by David. E. Orton and R. Dean Anderson. Translated by R. Dean Bliss, Annemiek Jansen, and David E. Orton. Leiden: Brill, 1998.

Linnemann, Eta. *Studien zur Passionsgeschichte*. Forschungen zur Religion und Literatur des Alten und Neuen Testaments 102. Göttingen: Vandenhoeck & Ruprecht, 1970.
Loisy, Alfred. *L'Évangile selon Luc*. Paris: Emile Nourry, 1924.
Maddox, Robert. *The Purpose of Luke-Acts*. Studies of the New Testament and Its World. Edinburgh: T. & T. Clark, 1982.
Marcus, Joel. *Mark 8–16: A New Translation with Introduction and Commentary*. Anchor Bible 27A. New Haven, CT: Yale University Press, 2009.
Marguerat, Daniel. *The First Christian Historian: Writing the "Acts of the Apostles."* Translated by Ken McKinney, Gregory J. Laughery, and Richard Bauckham. Society for New Testament Studies Monograph Series 121. Cambridge: Cambridge University Press, 2002.
Marrou, Henri I. *Histoire de l'education dans l'antiquité*. Paris: Le Seuil, 1948.
———. *A History of Education in Antiquity*. Translated by George Lamb. New York: The New American Library, 1964.
Marshall, I. Howard. *The Gospel of Luke: A Commentary on the Greek Text*. New International Greek Testament Commentary. Grand Rapids: Eerdmans, 1978.
Martin, Josef. *Antike Rhetorik: Technik und Methode*. Handbuch der Altertumswissenschaft 2.3. München: Beck, 1974.
Martin, Michael W. "Philo's Use of Syncrisis: An Examination of Philonic Composition in the Light of the Progymnasmata." *Perspectives in Religious Studies* 30 (2003) 271–97.
———. "Progymnasmatic Topic Lists: A Compositional Template for Luke and Other Bioi." *New Testament Studies* 58 (2004) 18–41.
Matera, Frank J. "The Death of Jesus according to Luke: A Question of Sources." *Catholic Biblical Quarterly* 47 (1985) 469–85.
———. "Luke 22,66–71: Jesus before the ΠΡΕΣΒΥΤΕΡΙΟΝ." *Ephemerides theologicae lovanienses* 65 (1989) 43–59.
———. "Luke 23,1–25: Jesus before Pilate, Herod, and Israel." In *L'Évangile de Luc: Problèmes littéraires et théologiques*, edited by F. Neirynck, 535–51. Rev. ed. Bibliotheca ephemeridum theologicarum lovaniensium 32. Leuven: Leuven University Press, 1989.
———. *Passion Narratives and Gospel Theologies: Interpreting the Synoptics through Their Passion Stories*. Theological Inquiries: Studies in Contemporary Biblical and Theological Problems. New York: Paulist, 1986.
Matson, Mark A. *In Dialogue with Another Gospel? The Influence of the Fourth Gospel on the Passion Narrative of the Gospel of Luke*. Society of Biblical Literature Dissertation Series 178. Atlanta: Society of Biblical Literature, 2001.
Mattill, Andrew Jacob. "Jesus-Paul Parallels and the Purpose of Luke-Acts: H. H. Evans Reconsidered." *Novum Testamentum* 17 (1975) 15–46.
McConnell Jr., James R. *The Topos of Divine Testimony in Luke-Acts*. Eugene, OR: Pickwick, 2014.
Meijering, Roos. *Literary and Rhetorical Theories in Greek Scholia*. Groningen: Forsten, 1987.
Metzger, Bruce M. *A Textual Commentary on the Greek New Testament*. 2nd ed. London: United Bible Society, 1994.
Meynet, Roland. *L'Évangile selon Saint Luc: Analyse rhétorique*. 2 vols. Paris: Cerf, 1988.
Mitchell, Margaret M. "Rhetorical Handbooks in Service of Biblical Exegesis: Eustathius of Antioch Takes Origen Back to School." In *The New Testament and*

Early Christian Literature in Greco-Roman Context: Studies in Honor of David. E. Aune, edited by John Fotopoulos, 349–67. Supplements to Novum Testamentum 122. Leiden: Brill, 2006.

Moessner, David P. "The Appeal and Power of Poetics (Luke 1:1–4) Luke's Superior Credentials (παρηκολουθηκότι), Narrative Sequence (καθεξῆς), and Firmness of Understanding (ἡ ἀσφάλεια) for the Reader." In *Jesus and the Heritage of Israel*, edited by David P. Moessner, 84–123. Harrisburg, PA: Trinity International, 1999.

———. "'The Christ Must Suffer': New Light on the Jesus, Peter, Stephen, Paul Parallels in Luke-Acts." *Novum Testamentum* 28 (1986) 220–56.

———. "The Meaning of καθεξῆς in the Lukan Prologue as a Key to the Distinctive Contribution of Luke's Narrative Among the 'Many.'" In *Four Gospels, 1992: Festschrift Frans Neirynck*, edited by F. Van Segbroeck, 1513–28. 3 vols. Bibliotheca ephemeridum theologicarum lovaniensium 100. Louvain: Peeters, 1992.

Morgan, Teresa. *Literate Education in the Hellenistic and Roman Worlds*. Cambridge Classical Studies. Cambridge: Cambridge University Press, 1998.

Morgenthaler, Robert. *Lukas und Quintilian: Rhetorik als Erzählkunst*. Zürich: Gotthelf, 1993.

Müller, Karlheinz. "Jesus vor Herodes: Eine redaktionsgeschichtliche Untersuchung zu Lk 23, 6–12." In *Zur Geschichte des Urchristentums*, edited by Gerhard Dautzenber, Helmut Merklein, and Karlheinz Müller, 111–41. Freiburg: Verlag Herder, 1979.

Murphy, James J. "Roman Writing Instruction as Described by Quintilian." In *A Short History of Writing Instruction from Ancient Greece to Twentieth-Century America*, edited by James J. Murphy, 19–76. Davis, CA: Hermagoras, 1990.

Murphy, James J., and Prentice Meador. "Quintilian's Educational and Rhetorical Theory, with a Synopsis of His *Institutio oratoria*." In *A Synoptic History of Classical Rhetoric*, edited by James J. Murphy and Richard A. Katula, 177–203. 2nd ed. Davis, CA: Hermagoras, 1995.

Myers, Ched. *Binding the Strong Man: A Political Reading of Mark's Story of Jesus*. 20th Anniversary ed. Maryknoll, NY: Orbis, 2008.

Neagoe, Alexandru. *The Trial of the Gospel: An Apologetic Reading of Luke's Trial Narratives*. Society for New Testament Studies Monograph Series 116. Cambridge: Cambridge University Press, 2002.

Neirynck, Frans. *Jean et les synoptiques: Examen critique de l'exégèse de M.-E. Boismard*. Bibliotheca ephemeridum theologicarum lovaniensium 49. Leuven: Leuven University Press, 1979.

———. "La matière marcienne dans l'évangile de Luc." In *L'Évangile de Luc: Problèmes littéraires et théologiques*, edited by F. Neirynck, 157–201. Bibliotheca ephemeridum theologicarum lovaniensium 32. Gembloux: J. Duculot, 1973.

Neyrey, Jerome H. "Jesus' Address to the Women of Jerusalem (Lk 23:27–31)—A Prophetic Judgment Oracle." *New Testament Studies* 29 (1983) 74–86.

———. *The Passion according to Luke: A Redaction Study of Luke's Soteriology*. Theological Inquiries. New York: Paulist, 1985.

Nolland, John. *Luke 18:35—24:53*. Word Biblical Commentary 35C. Dallas, TX: Word, 1993.

Omanson, Roger L. *A Textual Guide to the Greek New Testament: An Adaptation of Bruce M. Metzger's Textual Commentary for the Needs of Translators*. Stuttgart, Germany: Deutsche Bibelgesellschaft, 2006.

Padilla, Osvaldo. "Hellenistic παιδεία and Luke's Education: A Critique of Recent Approaches." *New Testament Studies* 55 (2009) 416–37.
Paffenroth, Kim. *The Story of Jesus according to L.* Journal for the Study of the New Testament: Supplement Series 147. Sheffield: Sheffield Academic, 1997.
Parsons, Mikeal C. *Acts.* Paideia. Grand Rapids: Baker Academic, 2008.
———. *Body and Character in Luke and Acts: The Subversion of Physiognomy in Early Christianity.* Grand Rapids: Baker Academic, 2006.
———. "Luke and the *Progymnasmata*: A Preliminary Investigation into the Preliminary Exercises." In *Contextualizing Acts: Lukan Narrative and Greco-Roman Discourse,* edited by Todd C. Penner and Caroline Vander Stichele, 43–63. Society of Biblical Literature Symposium Series 20. Atlanta: Society of Biblical Literature, 2003.
———. *Luke: Storyteller, Interpreter, Evangelist.* Peabody, Mass: Hendrickson, 2007.
Parsons, Mikeal C., and Richard I. Pervo. *Rethinking the Unity of Luke and Acts.* Minneapolis: Fortress, 1993.
Parsons, P. J. "A School-Book from the Sayce Collection." *Zeitschrift für Papyrologie und Epigraphik* 6 (1970) 133–49.
Patillon, Michel, and Giancarlo Bolognesi, eds. *Aelius Théon: Progymnasmata.* Paris: Les Belles Lettres, 1997.
Patterson, Stephen J. *The Gospel of Thomas and Jesus.* Foundations and Facets. Santa Rosa, CA: Polebridge, 1993.
Perry, Alfred Morris. *The Sources of Luke's Passion Narrative.* Chicago: University of Chicago Press, 1920.
Pitre, Brant James. "Blessing the Barren and Warning the Fecund: Jesus' Message for Women Concerning Pregnancy and Childbirth." *Journal for the Study of the New Testament* 81 (2001) 59–80.
Pliny. *Epistulae.* Translated by Betty Radice. 2 vols. Loeb Classical Library. Cambridge: Harvard University Press, 1969.
Plutarch. *Aemilius Paullus.* Translated by Bernadotte Perrin. Loeb Classical Library. Cambridge: Harvard University Press, 1918.
———. *Demosthenes.* Translated by Bernadotte Perrin. Loeb Classical Library. Cambridge: Harvard University Press, 1919.
———. *Mullerum Virtutes.* Translated by Frank Cole Babbit. Loeb Classical Library. Cambridge: Harvard University Press, 1931.
———. *Pericles.* Translated by Bernadotte Perrin. Loeb Classical Library. Cambridge: Harvard University Press, 1916.
Popkes, Enno Edzard. *Das Menschenbild des Thomasevangeliums: Untersuchungen zu seiner religionsgeschichtlichen und chronologischen Einordnung.* Wissenschaftliche Untersuchungen zum Neuen Testament 206. Tübingen: Mohr Siebeck, 2007.
Praeder, S. M. "Jesus-Paul, Peter-Paul and Jesus-Peter Parallelisms in Luke-Acts: A History of Reader Research." In *SBL Seminar Papers, 1983,* edited by Kent H. Richards, 23–39. Society of Biblical Literature Seminar Papers 23. Chico, CA: Scholars, 1984.
Quintilian. *Institutio oratoria.* Translated by Donald A. Russell. 5 vols. Loeb Classical Library. Cambridge: Harvard University Press, 2001.
Radl, Walter. *Paulus und Jesus im lukanischen Doppelwerk: Untersuchungen zu Parallelmotiven im Lukasevangelium und in der Apostelgeschichte.* Europäische Hochschulschriften 23. Bern: Hebert Lang, 1975.

Rau, Gottfried. "Das Volk in der lukanischen Passionsgeschichte, Eine Konjektur zu Lk 23:13." *Zeitschrift für die neutestamentliche Wissenschaft und die Kunde der Älteren Kirche* 56 (1965) 41–51.

Rehkopf, Friedrich. *Die lukanische Sonderquelle: Ihr Umfang und Sprachgebrauch.* Wissenschaftliche Untersuchungen zum Neuen Testament 5. Tübingen: Mohr, 1959.

Reich, Keith A. *Figuring Jesus: The Power of Rhetorical Figures of Speech in the Gospel of Luke.* Biblical Interpretation Series 107. Leiden: Brill, 2011.

Robbins, Vernon. "Narrative in Ancient Rhetoric and Rhetoric in Ancient Narrative." In *SBL Seminar Papers, 1996*, edited by Kent H. Richards, 368–84. Society of Biblical Literature Seminar Papers 35. Atlanta: Scholars, 1996.

Roberts, Michael John. *Biblical Epic and Rhetorical Paraphrase in Late Antiquity.* ARCA Classical and Medieval Texts, Papers, and Monographs 16. Liverpool: Francis Cairns, 1985.

Rothschild, Clare K. *Luke-Acts and the Rhetoric of History: An Investigation of Early Christian Historiography.* Wissenschaftliche Untersuchungen zum Neuen Testament 2/175. Tübingen: Mohr Siebeck, 2004.

Rowe, C. Kavin. *World Upside Down: Reading Acts in the Graeco-Roman Age.* Oxford: Oxford University Press, 2009.

Rowe, Galen O. "Style." In *Handbook of Classical Rhetoric in the Hellenistic Period, 330 BC–AD 400*, edited by Stanley E. Porter, 121–57. Leiden: Brill, 1997.

Ruppert, Lothar. *Jesus als der leidende Gerechte? Der Weg Jesu im lichte eines alt- und zwischentestamentlichen Motivs.* Stuttgarter Bibelstudien 59. Stuttgart: Katholisches Bibelwerk, 1972.

Sanders, E. P. *The Tendencies of the Synoptic Tradition.* Society for New Testament Studies Monograph Series 9. London: Cambridge University Press, 1969.

Sanders, Jack T. *The Jews in Luke-Acts.* Philadelphia: Fortress, 1987.

Scaer, Peter J. *The Lukan Passion and the Praiseworthy Death.* New Testament Monographs 10. Sheffield: Sheffield Phoenix, 2005.

Schmid, Josef. *Das Evangelium nach Lukas.* 4th ed. Regensburg: Pustet, 1960.

Schmidt, Daryl. "Luke's 'Innocent' Jesus: A Scriptural Apologetic." In *Political Issues in Luke-Acts*, edited by Richard J. Cassidy and Philip J. Scharper, 111–21. Maryknoll, NY: Orbis, 1983.

Schouler, Bernard. *La tradition hellénique chez Libanios.* 2 vols. Collection d'études anciennes. Lille: Atelier national reproduction des thèses, Université Lille III, 1984.

Schramm, Tim. *Der Markus-Stoff bei Lukas: Eine literarkritische und redaktionsgeschichtliche Untersuchung.* Society for New Testament Studies Monograph Series 14. Cambridge: Cambridge University Press, 1971.

Schweizer, Eduard. *The Good News according to Luke.* Translated by David E. Green. Atlanta: John Knox, 1984.

Sherwin-White, Adrian Nicholas. *Roman Society and Roman Law in the New Testament.* Oxford: Clarendon, 1963.

Shiner, Whitney. "The Ambiguous Pronouncement of the Centurion and the Shrouding of Meaning in Mark." *Journal for the Study of the New Testament* 78 (2000) 3–22.

Soards, Marion L. "A Literary Analysis of the Origin and Purpose of Luke's Account of the Mockery of Jesus." In *New Views on Luke and Acts*, edited by Earl Richard, 86–93. Collegeville, MN: Liturgical, 1990.

———. *The Passion according to Luke: The Special Material of Luke 22*. Sheffield: JSOT, 1987.

———. "Tradition, Composition, and Theology in Jesus' Speech to the 'Daughters of Jerusalem' (Luke 23:26–32)." *Biblica* 68 (1987) 221–44.

———. "Tradition, Composition, and Theology in Luke's Account of Jesus before Herod Antipas." *Biblica* 66 (1985) 344–64.

Spengel, Leonhard von, ed. *Rhetores Graeci*. Vol. 2. Teubner. Leipzig: Teubner, 1853.

Stamps, D. L. "Rhetoric." In *Dictionary of New Testament Background*, edited by Craig Evans and Stanley E. Porter, 953–59. Downers Grove, IL: InterVarsity, 2000.

Stanton, Vincent Henry. *The Gospels as Historical Documents*. 3 vols. Cambridge: Cambridge University Press, 1903.

Stegemann, W. "Nikolaos." In *Paulys Realencyclopädie der classischen Altertumswissenschaft*. Edited by G. Wissowa. New edition. Vol. 17. Munich: A. Druckenmüller, 1980.

———. "Theon." In *Paulys Realencyclopädie der classischen Altertumswissenschaft*. Edited by G. Wissowa. New edition. Vol. 5A. Munich: A. Druckenmüller, 1980.

Stenschke, Christoph W. *Luke's Portrait of Gentiles prior to Their Coming to Faith*. Wissenschaftliche Untersuchungen zum Neuen Testament 2/108. Tübingen: Mohr Siebeck, 1999.

Sterling, Gregory E. "*Mors Philosophi*: The Death of Jesus in Luke." *Harvard Theological Review* 94 (2001) 383–402.

Strauss, Mark L. *The Davidic Messiah in Luke-Acts: The Promise and Its Fulfillment in Lukan Christology*. Journal for the Study of the New Testament: Supplement Series 110. Sheffield: Sheffield Academic, 1995.

Streeter, B. H. *The Four Gospels: A Study of Origins, Treating of the Manuscript Tradition, Sources, Authorship, and Dates*. London: Macmillan, 1924.

Suetonius. *De grammaticis*. Translated by J. C. Rolfe. Loeb Classical Library. Cambridge: Harvard University Press, 1914.

Sylva, Dennis D. "The Temple Curtain and Jesus' Death in the Gospel of Luke." *Journal of Biblical Literature* 105 (1986) 239–50.

Talbert, Charles H. *Literary Patterns, Theological Themes, and the Genre of Luke-Acts*. Society of Biblical Literature Monograph Series 20. Cambridge: Society of Biblical Literature, 1975.

———. "Martyrdom in Luke-Acts and the Lukan Social Ethic." In *Political Issues in Luke-Acts*, edited by Richard J. Cassidy and Philip J. Scharper, 99–110. Maryknoll, NY: Orbis, 1983.

———. *Reading Acts: A Literary and Theological Commentary on the Acts of the Apostles*. Rev. ed. Reading the New Testament. Macon, GA: Smyth & Helwys, 2005.

———. *Reading Luke: A Literary and Theological Commentary on the Third Gospel*. Reading the New Testament. New York: Crossroad, 1982.

Tannehill, Robert C. *The Narrative Unity of Luke-Acts: A Literary Interpretation*. 2 vols. Philadelphia: Fortress, 1986.

Taylor, Vincent. *Behind the Third Gospel: A Study of the Proto-Luke Hypothesis*. Oxford: Clarendon, 1926.

———. *The Passion Narrative of St. Luke: A Critical and Historical Investigation*. Society for New Testament Studies Monograph Series 19. Cambridge: Cambridge University Press, 1972.

———. "Rehkopf's List of Words and Phrases Illustrative of Pre-Lukan Speech Usage." *Journal of Theological Studies* 15 (1964) 59–62.

———. "The Value of the Proto-Luke Hypothesis." *Expository Times* 36 (1924) 476–77.

Tolppanen, Kari Pekka. "A Source Critical Reassessment of the Gospel of Luke: Was Canonical Mark Really Luke's Source?" PhD diss., University of St. Michael's College, 2009.

Trocmé, Etienne. *The Passion as Liturgy: A Study in the Origin of the Passion Narratives in the Four Gospels*. London: SCM, 1983.

Tuckett, Christopher M. "Thomas and the Synoptics." *Novum Testamentum* 30 (1988) 132–57.

Tyson, Joseph B. *The Death of Jesus in Luke-Acts*. Columbia, SC: University of South Carolina Press, 1986.

———. "Jesus and Herod Antipas." *Journal of Biblical Literature* 79 (1960) 239–46.

———. "The Lukan Version of the Trial of Jesus." *Novum Testamentum* 3 (1959) 249–58.

———. "Source Criticism of the Gospel of Luke." In *Perspectives on Luke-Acts*, edited by Charles H. Talbert, 24–39. Danville, VA: Association of Baptist Professors of Religion, 1978.

Untergassmair, Franz Georg. *Kreuzweg und Kreuzigung Jesu: Ein Beitrag zur lukanischen Redaktionsgeschichte und zur Frage nach der lukanischen "Kreuzestheologie."* Paderborner theologische Studien 10. Paderborn: Schöningh, 1980.

———. "Zur Problematik der lukanischen Passionsgeschichte." In *Schrift und Tradition*, edited by Knut Backhaus and Franz Georg Untergassmair, 273–92. Paderborn: Schöningh, 1996.

Walaskay, Paul W. *"And So We Came to Rome": The Political Perspective of St. Luke*. Society for New Testament Studies Monograph Series 49. Cambridge: Cambridge University Press, 1983.

———. "The Trial and Death of Jesus in the Gospel of Luke." *Journal of Biblical Literature* 94 (1975) 81–93.

Walton, Steve. "The State They Were In: Luke's View of the Roman Empire." In *Rome in the Bible and the Early Church*, edited by Peter Oakes, 1–41. Society for New Testament Studies Monograph Series 116. Grand Rapids: Baker Academic, 2002.

Wardman, Alan. *Plutarch's Lives*. Berkeley: University of California Press, 1974.

Watson, Duane F., and Alan J. Hauser. *Rhetorical Criticism of the Bible: A Comprehensive Bibliography with Notes on History and Method*. Biblical Interpretation Series 4. Leiden: Brill, 1994.

Weatherly, Jon A. *Jewish Responsibility for the Death of Jesus in Luke-Acts*. Journal for the Study of the New Testament: Supplement Series 106. Sheffield: Sheffield Academic, 1994.

Webb, Ruth. "The *Progymnasmata* as Practice." In *Education in Greek and Roman Antiquity*, edited by Yun Lee Too, 289–316. Leiden: Brill, 2001.

Wolter, Michael. *Das Lukasevangelium*. Handbuch zum Neuen Testament 5. Tübingen: Mohr Siebeck, 2008.

Zöckler, Thomas. *Jesu Lehren im Thomasevangelium*. Nag Hammadi and Manichaean Studies 47. Leiden: Brill, 1999.

Index

alliteration, 98n75
anecdote, 43
antithesis, 117–18, 120, 165
antonomasia, 86, 164
Aphthonius, 33, 35n29, 36, 38–42, 44, 49, 50n73, 56–61, 161, 168, 170
apostrophe, 55–56
Aristotle, 33n17, 35n28, 45–46, 51n78, 52–53, 55, 58, 163, 168
arrangement, 22, 35, 45–46
assonance, 98, 117–18, 165
asyndeton, 54n92

Barabbas, 94n68, 98, 112–14, 137n78, 140, 143, 157
brevity. *See* conciseness.

centurion, 5n13, 9n34, 10–13, 28, 75, 81, 117, 138, 152–60, 167, 169, 177–78, 182
Chosen One, 130–31, 135, 162
chreia, 22, 34, 38–41, 49n70, 54, 71
Cicero, 33, 35n28, 44n56, 45–46, 48n69, 49n71, 51–53, 54n91, 55n94, 58, 60–61, 65, 68–69, 95n70, 101, 131, 145n105, 162–63, 168n8
circumlocution, 86n37
clarity, 61–63, 82, 95, 97, 132, 139, 150, 152, 160, 172–74, 177
common-place. *See* topics/*topos*.
comparison. *See* synkrisis.
conciseness, 61–63, 82, 97, 105n96, 139, 148, 160, 172–74, 177
confirmation, 23–24, 27–28, 37–39, 41, 43, 46–54, 71–78, 91, 97, 99–100,

112–14, 116, 120, 129–39, 150, 154, 160–64, 173, 176, 179, 181
consistency, 82n17, 88n44, 89, 91, 125, 130, 152, 162, 173–74
contradiction, 37–38, 40, 42
criminals, 11, 20, 28, 75, 81, 98n78, 122, 130, 132, 136, 137n75, 140–45, 152n141, 160, 162–63, 164n1, 166–67, 169, 178
crown of thorns, 103–5, 174

darkness, 75, 81, 152n141, 159n165, 167, 173–74
daughters of Jerusalem, 87n40, 98n78, 117–29, 165
delivery, 22, 35, 45–46, 55
description. *See* ecphrasis.
δίκαιος, 1, 9n34, 10–13, 27–28, 76n3, 152–54, 178–79, 181
δικαίως, 11, 161
Dionysius of Halicarnassus, 33n14, 36, 45, 62
Dionysius Thrax, 30n1

ecphrasis, 33n17, 38–39, 41–43
education, advanced, 21–24, 31, 35, 64, 72
education, general, 21–24, 27, 29–36, 40–42, 72
education, intermediate, 21–22, 30–31, 35, 49, 54n92, 64, 77
education, primary, 21, 29–30, 31n6, 40–41, 44
elaboration, 37–38, 40, 42

elementary education. *See* education, primary.
encomion, 33n17, 38–39, 41–43, 51, 57, 72
epanaphora, 85, 164
ethopoeia, 34n23, 39–40, 42, 72
exemplum, 118
exordium, 45

fable, 22, 30n3, 33n17, 34, 38–39, 41, 43, 49n70
Farrer Hypothesis, 2n1, 24–26
figures of speech. *See* rhetorical figures.

Gospel of Peter, 141n90
Gospel of Thomas, 123n33, 126–28
Griesbach Hypothesis, 2n1

Hermogenes. *See*. Ps.-Hermogenes
Herod Agrippa, 102–3, 116
Herod Antipas, 11, 28, 75, 80, 91, 96, 100–14, 116, 119n13, 123, 125, 138, 145, 162–63, 167, 176, 178
hypophora, 84n25

infancy narrative, 5
innocence, 10–13, 27, 73–75, 82, 85, 87, 90, 97–99, 101–2, 105–7, 109, 111–15, 118, 121–22, 128–30, 138, 140, 144, 146, 152–60, 163, 165–71, 176–80, 182
invective, 39, 41–43, 51, 57, 72
invention, 22, 32, 35, 45–46, 51, 72
irony, 82, 86, 130, 132, 162, 166
isocolon, 118, 164–65

James, 16n65, 17, 103n93
Jewish council, 27, 80, 82–91, 96, 98n78, 103, 163–64, 172, 174
Jewish leaders, 74n1, 75, 82, 84–91, 101, 103, 112, 115–16, 119n13, 121, 122n28, 135, 156, 161–62, 166, 168–69
John the Baptist, 83n21, 84n25, 88n45, 101, 102n91, 108, 163
John, Gospel of, 1, 3, 4n10, 9, 26, 116n136, 142n95, 177, 182

L, 6–7, 25n104, 109, 124n36, 143
Last Supper, 12, 79
law, 38–39, 42–43, 49n70, 51, 54
Libanius, 33, 35n29, 36, 38–39, 42–43, 49–50
Lord, 84, 108, 131–32, 147, 168

martyrdom, Jesus' death as, 10, 12, 16, 18, 98n79, 129n58, 139n82, 154, 169, 178
Matthew, 1–3, 4n10, 7n22, 16n66, 24–26, 96n72, 107n103, 125, 127, 150n131, 171n14, 177n23, 182
maxim, 33n17, 39–41, 43
memory, 22, 35, 45–46, 55
Messiah, 10, 18, 80, 84, 88–89, 91–94, 130–31, 135–36, 158n165, 162, 166
metaphor, 101

narration/narrative, 22, 24, 27–28, 33n17, 37–39, 41, 43, 46, 49n70, 50–51, 60–63, 72–74, 77–78, 116, 160, 172–74, 177–78, 181
narrative virtues, 60–63, 160, 172
Nicolaus, 33, 35n29, 36, 38–42, 44, 49–50, 56, 57–58, 60–61, 99, 161–62, 168

oral presentation, 37–38, 40, 42

parallels, 1, 12–19, 27–28, 73, 76–77, 93–95, 102, 111, 116, 145, 147, 154–155, 160, 166–72, 176–77, 179–82
paraphrase, 22, 24, 27–28, 34, 37–38, 40, 42, 44, 46–47, 63–74, 77–78, 110, 116, 139n87, 157n162, 160, 175–77, 181
paronomasia, 98n77, 115n134, 118, 165
partition, 46
Passion Narrative Source, 2, 4, 6, 7n24, 8–9, 25–26, 77, 78n11, 81, 88n44, 107, 109, 110n117, 123–26, 128, 136n72, 141–44, 152, 157–59, 176–77, 181–82
Passover, 83
Paul, 1, 12–19, 27, 73, 76n3, 93–95, 102, 111, 116, 145–46, 149, 155, 166–72, 176, 179–82

INDEX

peroration, 46
Peter, 14, 16n65, 19, 24, 79–80, 82–84, 103n93, 116n135, 145n104, 151n132, 171–72
Pilate, 11, 28, 74–75, 80, 87, 91–117, 119n13, 137n78, 140n88, 145, 156, 161–65, 167–68, 178
plausibility, 61, 63, 82–83, 160, 172–74, 177
pleonasm, 117, 165
Pliny, 47, 65n121, 69, 70n134, 71, 175
Plutarch, 17, 30n1, 47, 58–60, 71n135, 77n4, 146n109, 170–71, 179–180
polyptoton, 114, 115n134, 165
progymnasmata, 21–24, 27, 29, 31–44, 47–54, 56–65, 67, 69, 71–72
proof, artificial, 52–53
proof, inartificial, 45, 52–53
prosopopoeia, 22, 39–43
Proto-Luke, 7, 8n28, 79
proverb, 165
Ps.-Hermogenes, 35n29, 36, 38–42, 44, 49–50, 56–57, 60, 161, 168

Q, 1, 7, 24, 109n114, 124n36, 125, 127
Quintilian, 19n88, 20n90, 23, 30n1, 31, 33–37, 44, 45n58, 46–48, 50–57, 60–65, 68–72, 84n27, 86n35, 97, 99–101, 112, 117n3, 118n4, 130, 132, 139n85, 140, 143n96, 148, 150, 162–63, 166, 168n8, 172–75

reading aloud, 37–38, 40, 42
refutation, 23–24, 27–28, 37–39, 41, 43, 46–54, 71–78, 91, 100–12, 114–16, 120, 129n61, 130n62, 137, 140–60, 144–50, 152–64, 173, 176, 179, 181
rending of the veil, 75, 79, 81, 144–50, 159n165, 167, 173
repeated negation, 84, 164
repetition, 112, 165
Rhetorica ad Alexandrum, 33, 61
Rhetorica ad Herennium, 33n18, 35n28, 46, 52, 54, 55n94, 56, 58, 60–61, 84n27, 85, 86n35, 101, 115n134, 117n3, 118n4, 162, 168n8
rhetorical criticism, 19–28

rhetorical figures, 20, 22, 24, 27–28, 36, 47, 48n66, 54–56, 72, 74, 76–78, 84–88, 90–91, 101, 116–19, 128, 129n58, 160, 164–66, 170n13, 175–76, 179, 181
rhetorical handbooks, 22–24, 27, 29, 31, 44–49, 51–58, 60–65, 68–73, 98n75
rhetorical question, 87, 118, 121, 140, 164–65, 166
righteous, 10–13, 153–54, 158, 178, 182

Savior, 130–131, 140, 166
secondary education. *See* education, intermediate.
silence, 88, 91, 96–98, 103, 172, 174
Simon, 80, 117, 119, 123
soldiers, 28, 75, 79–80, 101, 103–4, 106, 117, 130, 135, 138–40, 162–63, 164n1, 166, 174
Son of God, 10–11, 80, 84, 86–89, 93, 157–59
Son of Man, 85–86, 88, 132n68
Special Passion Source. *See* Passion Narrative Source.
speech-in-character, 38, 43
statistical method, 6n20, 8, 10n36, 110–11, 124, 139n87, 142n92, 177
Stephen, 1, 13–14, 16n65, 17–19, 27, 73, 76n3, 93n66, 147, 152, 168–72, 176, 179–82
style, 22, 35, 45–46, 54
Suetonius, 31n6, 34, 47, 65n122
Suffering Servant, 10–11, 131n65, 159
synecdoche, 117, 165
synkrisis, 24, 27–28, 38–39, 41–43, 47, 56–60, 72, 74, 76n3, 77–78, 160, 166–72, 180–81
Synoptic Problem, 2n1, 24, 77n6

temple, 76n3, 79, 84n25, 90, 93n67, 120, 134, 138, 145n104, 148–50, 152, 159n165, 167, 173
tertiary education. *See* education, advanced.
testimony/witness, 46, 52–54, 74n1, 87–91, 130–31, 140, 144–46, 149, 154, 163, 165, 166, 170, 173

Theon, 22, 32–33, 35–44, 49–51, 53–72, 77n4, 78, 82, 97n72, 99, 104, 105n96, 110, 132, 139n85, 148, 150, 161–62, 168–69, 172–75

thesis, 33n17, 38–39, 42–43, 49n70, 50–51, 54

topics/*topos*, 20n89, 23, 27, 33n14, 38–39, 41, 43, 46, 49–51, 52n81, 54, 57–58, 60, 72, 75, 97, 114, 117, 130, 140, 160–63, 168, 176, 179, 180n27

tradition(s), 1–5, 7n22, 9, 24–26, 116n136, 128, 136n72, 141n90, 144, 148n119

transfiguration, 5n13, 130

Two-Source Hypothesis, 2n1

wailing women. *See* daughters of Jerusalem.

witness. *See* testimony/witness.

www.ingramcontent.com/pod-product-compliance
Lightning Source LLC
Chambersburg PA
CBHW070328230426
43663CB00011B/2249